For the Love of Skiing

WHAT THE PROFESSIONALS ARE SAYING ABOUT *For the Love of Skiing:*

"Alan Engen's book fills a gaping void in the history of skiing in America. Until now, there has been a dearth of published information about early skiing in Utah and thereabouts, and particularly of those like the legendary Alf Engen who early on built the bridges from Nordic to Alpine skiing via four-event competitions. This account is an easy educational read."
— ALLEN H. ADLER
    Chairman, USSA National Historical Committee

"Alan Engen's monograph For the Love of Skiing *lives up to the fullest of the promise of its title. It is . . . a prodigious compendium of the history of skiing—Nordic, Alpine with its variants, snowboarding, and ski jumping. . . . I predict that it will be a treat for ski buffs to read about and a treasure trove of information."*
— OTTO LANG
    Filmmaker and Ski Pioneer
    Author, A Bird of Passage
    Honored Member, National Ski Hall of Fame

"History is best written by those who have lived it, and having lived it to the hilt, Alan packs every page with marvelously descriptive, frequently funny anecdotes about his father and other major figures of skiing that bring them very much alive.
    *"*For the Love of Skiing *is a superb read and a major contribution to the literature of skiing."*
— W. MASON BEEKLEY
    President, International Skiing History Association

"History dull and boring? Not Alan Engen's meticulous and lovingly written book about his legendary father, Alf Engen, and uncles, Sverre and Corey, who came to our Intermountain area to join other daring young men in the air and on the snow to start a ski sport we all love and benefit from. A fascinating read from start to finish."
— SUZY HARRIS RYTTING
    U.S. Olympic Ski Team, 1948–52
    Honored Member, National Ski Hall of Fame

"Ski jumping in the 1930s showcased superstar athletes, courageous physical feats and big crowds watching every move. It was American showmanship and daring at its best and the Engen brothers were some of the biggest stars. The insights and anecdotes into this time and the people that Alan Engen shares in For the Love of Skiing *are superb."*
— GLENN PARKINSON
    President, New England Ski Museum

*"*For the Love of Skiing *brings back so many old memories.... It's a great book, and a real collection of Utah skiing history and the people who made it happen."*
— JIMMIE R. NUNN
    President, Arizona Ski Museum

"A great nostalgic joyride with amazing historical significance."
— PAT MILLER
    Director of Skiing, University of Utah

"I find this book compelling in at least two ways. First, it paints an informative and humorous portrait of one of skiing's most beloved and respected pioneers, Alf Engen, and second, it pulls together events and anecdotes on the development of skiing in the Intermountain West as no other work on the sport has to date."
— JOHN F. BOWER
    Ski Jump/Operations Director, Utah Winter Sports Park
    U.S. Olympic Ski Team, 1962–68
    Honored Member, National Ski Hall of Fame

"A most remarkable and loving book about one of our all-time heroes. Alf Engen was a great skier, a great teacher, and a great human being. The book gives us a wonderful treasure and record of his career."
— BILL LEVITT
    Mayor, Town of Alta

"Alan has completed a great job of collecting information relating to the history of skiing [in] the U.S. and Utah. It is excellent and a real tribute to his father and Alan's efforts."
— JUNIOR BOUNOUS
    Director of Skiing, Snowbird
    National Gelande/Cross-Country Ski Champion, 1970
    Honored Member, National Ski Hall of Fame

"Alan Engen's For the Love of Skiing *is a tribute to Alf Engen, his Nordic background and their contribution to the history of skiing. It is well done and must reading."*
— BILL LASH
    Author, Outline of Ski-Teaching Methods
    Founder, Professional Ski Instructors of America
    Honored Member, National Ski Hall of Fame

"I found the treatment of ski history in the United States and the West very enjoyable. . . . After twenty-six years of working with Alf every day, I believe he was the greatest skier of this or any other era. Alf's story is the story of skiing's history."
— MAX O. LUNDBERG
    Vice President, International Ski Instructors Association
    Int'l Rep., Professional Ski Instructors of America

"I was surprised to learn so much about the great Engen brothers and Utah ski history. Alan Engen has demonstrated a remarkable ability to tie historical events into an enjoyable and captivating story."
— JIM GADDIS
    NCAA All-American, 1960–62
    Honored Member, Utah Sports Hall of Fame

FOR THE LOVE OF SKIING:
A Visual History

Alan K. Engen

GIBBS·SMITH
P
PUBLISHER

SALT LAKE CITY

First Edition
02 01 00 99 98   5 4 3 2 1

Published by
Gibbs Smith, Publisher
P.O. Box 667
Layton, Utah 84041

Orders: (1-800) 748-5439
Web site: www.gibbs-smith.com

Cover design by Design One
Book design and production by Lisa Critchfield,
    Black Sheep Design, Salt Lake City, Utah

Cover photograph of Alf Engen (circa late 1950s)
    by Fred Lindholm, Sun Valley, Idaho.
End paper illustrations by Roger Junak, Ishpeming, Michigan.
    Commissioned by and used with permission courtesy the
    U.S. National Ski Hall of Fame and Ski Museum, Ishpeming, Michigan.
Photographs and illustrations courtesy the Engen family,
    unless otherwise noted.

Printed and bound in Hong Kong by Toppan Printing

Library of Congress Cataloging-in-Publication Data

Engen, Alan K.
For the love of skiing : a visual history / Alan K. Engen.
p.   cm.
Includes bibliographical references and index.
ISBN 0-87905-867-6
1. Skis and skiing—United States—History.
2. Skis and skiing—Utah—History. I. Title.
    GV854.4.E54   1998
    796.93'09—DC21   98-19366
                                CIP

Contents

Acknowledgments

As I began preparing this book, it quickly became apparent that an undertaking such as this, particularly one with a definite historical perspective, required a strong support group of fellow skiers, historians, writers, and friends. I am not a writer by profession, so *For the Love of Skiing*, in many ways, is the end result of a dedicated team, devoting many hours and much effort to telling the story of ski history in the Intermountain West.

While it is not possible to list all of the individuals who contributed to this book, the following deserve a special thanks and are those whom I would especially like to acknowledge for their assistance, encouragement, and support.

- I doubt I would have ever considered undertaking such a project as this without the strong backing and counsel of my late father, Alf Engen, and my two uncles, Sverre and Corey Engen. They have been with me from the start, and I truly appreciate their sharing personal stories of their "swashbuckling" days with me.

- Dr. Gregory Thompson and Dr. Joe Arave of the University of Utah J. Willard Marriott Library, Utah Ski Archives, researched and authenticated much of the data in this book and provided invaluable assistance with the publishing arrangements.

- Mike Korologos wrote the foreword for this book and never failed to share his extensive knowledge of ski history as well as his expertise as a writer.

- Award-winning authors Shelley Hunt and François Camoin provided preliminary photographic layouts and helped to integrate the book's myriad topics into a cohesive format.

- For reviewing the manuscript and providing invaluable information and a national ski history perspective, special acknowledgment is given to Allen Adler, chairman of the USSA National Historical Committee; Morten Lund, editor of *Skiing Heritage;* Bill Lash and Otto Lang, ski pioneers and authors; Glenn Parkinson, president of the New England Ski Museum; Jimmie Nunn, president of the Arizona Ski Museum; and Mason Beekley, president of the International Skiing History Association.

- The staff members of Gibbs Smith, Publisher, have envisioned the book's potential and have been extremely supportive throughout the entire publishing process. Special thanks go to Gibbs Smith, president, and Madge Baird, editorial vice president, for bringing *For the Love of Skiing* to print.

- Finally, I express deep gratitude to my wife, Barbara; to Linda Nimori of Gibbs Smith, Publisher; and to Dr. Sid Jenson—master skier, author, professor, and current consultant for Franklin Covey Consulting Group—for devoting untold hours to editing and reediting the book's manuscript.

For the Love of Skiing reflects not only the passion for skiing of those highlighted in the book but also the passion shown by all of those who worked on the book to tell skiing's story.

Alan K. Engen

❋ All sales proceeds from this book will be used to support the Alf Engen Ski Museum—located at the Utah Winter Sports Park at Bear Hollow near Park City, Utah—site of the ski-jumping, luge, and bobsled venues of the 2002 Olympic Winter Games.

Foreword *by Mike Korologos*

The feeling was surrealistic. The thought always inspired me to ski better than I thought possible. I kept telling myself, "You're skiing on the heels of a legend . . . you're right in his tracks . . . graceful, smooth, effortless." I focused my eyes on the back of his boots and hoped somehow his easy, flowing motions would magically enter my boots and skis just once, if only for a few sweeping turns.

Skiing with Alf Engen was an experience you never forget. It not only hyped your physical senses, it filled your thoughts with his exploits that you'd read, heard, and written about—exploits that shaped the history of skiing in the United States.

Just as rewarding as the skiing experience was the ride up the mountain seated in a chairlift, ski-to-ski with this gentle giant. His voice would soften, his eyes brighten as he related stories of old Alta, of his barnstorming days, of his world records. The words were offered shyly, almost apologetically, but always sincerely, never boastfully. It was an honor to be on the receiving end of his anecdotes and nostalgia. As a ski writer, a longtime acquaintance of the Engen family, and a die-hard fan of Alta, where much of this history was nurtured, I sensed Alf knew his tales would be passed along.

Just as Alf and his brothers had a "love of skiing," the Engen story has a romance about it that should be preserved and repeated. It is, after all, a story that transcends skiing in the United States, the Intermountain West, and Utah. This story spans the sport—from its baggy-pants founding through the 2002 Olympic Winter Games, and beyond. Only through destiny—call it an uncanny mix of luck, foresight, and a collection of people with a penchant for preserving history—could a book such as *For the Love of Skiing* see the light of print.

Foremost among these people is Alan Engen, Alf's elder son and the author of this book. Alan had the insight to realize early the historical significance of what he was hearing, seeing, and reading. Like an archeologist who finds himself exploring a cavernous tomb or pyramid housing a treasure of historical data and artifacts, Alan was surrounded by the people and events that shaped the history of skiing in the United States. Though much of the book focuses on the saga of Alf and his two brothers, Sverre and Corey, there is in-depth information about how skiing came to the Intermountain region and portraits of many noteworthy pioneers and other ski champions who made valuable contributions to the sport.

The challenge Alan faced was how to weave an interesting story into a voluminous historical reference. This fusion has been achieved by augmenting the story with fascinating photographs, sidebars, and epigraphs. Because of Alan's intimate knowledge of skiing and its history, he is able to provide special insight into the evolution of the sport in America.

We also must credit Alan's grandmother, Martha Engen, who was a veritable museum curator when it came to preserving the incredible story of her sons, Alf, Sverre, and Corey, who immigrated to the United States from their humble beginnings in Norway. It was perhaps a mother's pride that inspired Martha to collect the memorabilia generated by her sons' new-world triumphs. With the zeal of a historian in pursuit of the Holy Grail, Martha compiled numerous scrapbooks of newspaper clippings, promotional flyers, event programs, and photographs. She supplemented that collection with medals, cloth patches, trophies, pins, ribbons, skis, boots, and other paraphernalia accumulated by her triumphant trio during their swashbuckling days.

The 1930s and '40s saw the Engens cut a swath across the United States that set world ski-jumping records, produce movies, explore and develop ski areas, establish ski schools, and organize ski patrols. In the case of Alf, those achievements included coaching the U.S. Olympic Ski Team, winning the national four-way title twice, getting inducted into several ski halls of fame, becoming known as the father of today's powder-skiing technique, and being named America's skier of the twentieth century. And through almost all of it—surely since the late 1930s—Alf's wife, Evelyn, kept a quiet and sturdy hand at the helm at home and in the business.

Another valued and unassuming contributor to this book is the Alta Ski Lifts Company, operating at one of America's premier ski areas. With his uncle, Sverre, and later his father directing the ski school at Alta, Alan grew up at the rustic mountain enclave where he is now the director of skiing. Since the age of two, when he learned to ski, Alta taught Alan to respect his forebears and the role this special place played—and continues to play—in the development

Long-time friends, Alta, Utah, circa 1994: (left to right, front) Alf Engen, Tom Korologos; (back) Alan Engen, Mike Korologos. Photo by Brenda Price.

of the dynamic sport of skiing.

From its raucous, gloves-off, silver-mining heyday of the 1870s and '80s to its determination to stay cozy and comfy during the heady megaresort days of the fledgling twenty-first century, Alta remains destiny's darling, always siding with tradition at the expense of trends. Nowhere is this more evident than in its adherence to a self-imposed, decades-old doctrine: To serve as a recreational paradise primarily for local skiers. This is the Alta gospel according to its founders and early leaders, people like the legendary "Mayor" George Watson, J. Laughlin, Joe Quinney, Fred Speyer, Chic Morton, the Engen brothers; it has been carried on by latter-day torchbearers—Alta mayor Bill Levitt and ski-lift company general manager Onno Wieringa.

With its roots deeply embedded in mining, the Alta Ski Lifts Company was meticulous in its record keeping. Those files fortuitously came under the guardianship of Alan, and in 1988, when the company observed its fiftieth anniversary, it bequeathed many historically significant materials to the University of Utah J. Willard Marriott Library's Special Collections. These items—supplemented by a generous financial

grant from the ski-lifts company—helped launch the library's thriving Ski Archives.

Together with the Alf Engen Ski Museum and the Utah Ski Archives, this exceptional book rightfully showcases the incredible story of skiing in the West for researchers, journalists, Olympic reporters, and others to enjoy, marvel at, ponder in amazement, and pass along to ensuing generations.

Alf Engen would have liked that. ❄

MIKE KOROLOGOS *is often called Utah's "Mr. Ski Writer." He is the former skiing editor for the* Salt Lake Tribune, *has written numerous articles on Utah since the 1960s for hundreds of national and international publications, and is a recognized ski historian, having authored a number of articles on ski history in the Intermountain West. In 1992 he was named "Ski Journalist of the Year" by the Utah Ski Association, and from 1995 through 1997 was the chief spokesman for the Salt Lake Organizing Committee for the 2002 Olympic Winter Games.*

Preface

Since the 1950s, I have attempted to capture and preserve the history of skiing in the Intermountain West (Utah, Idaho, Montana, and Wyoming). This area has a wonderful ski heritage, one of which I am proud, not only because my family is part of that history but also because much of what is taken for granted these days in skiing—the snow-safety procedures, sophisticated ski equipment, and professional ski-instruction methods—were to some degree pioneered here. This book is not intended to be a biography of my father, Alf Engen, but a story of many individuals who have contributed to the development of skiing in this area. However, in the Intermountain West, the name "Alf Engen" is synonymous with skiing, so it is impossible to separate the two.

My interest in this area's skiing history was fostered by the stories my father told of his early days in Norway and what happened after he immigrated to the United States in 1929 at the age of twenty. He was forced to leave his native land because of poor economic conditions. He felt he had left his jumping days far behind, but his future held much more for him—his destiny was to race and fly on skis into the annals of American sports history and folklore.

Though I have included several appendices containing selected skiing statistics, this book should not be considered the definitive work on the subject. Most of the information was gathered from my father's huge collection of photographs, books, and newspaper articles, as well as his memory. His mother, Martha, was one of his greatest fans, archiving newspaper clippings and photographs in myriad scrapbooks. Although she watched her famous son jump only once, she kept track of all his doings.

Alf's illustrious career began at an early age when he and his brother Sverre decided to take a shortcut to school. The Engen brothers lived at the top of a hill, approximately two kilometers from the small town of Mjøndalen. Alf and Sverre discovered that, by piling snow next to the neighbors' wooden fences, they could sail over the fences on skis and arrive in half the time. Unfortunately, returning home was not so easy, but climbing back up the hill honed their cross-country skiing skills.

From what I've been told, my grandfather Trond Engen was a winter Robin Hood. A blacksmith by trade, Trond procured food and other necessities of life through various means during the frigid winter months. He carried his loot miles into the backwoods on skis and left it for the poor. He was the most loved and feared man in the village and was regarded unquestionably as the strongest man and best athlete in that part of Norway. As a child, I pictured him as a man of Viking heritage who lived life to the fullest. But we never met; his life came to an abrupt end at the young age of thirty when he died in the Spanish flu epidemic of 1919.

Alf, the eldest of three sons, was only nine years old when his father died. Times were hard, so Alf dropped out of school and found work to help his mother keep the family together. However, because of his great love of skiing, he was frequently able to grab a pair of homemade skis and venture out with his brother Sverre to enter some type of ski tournament. Alf's youngest brother, Corey (christened Kaare; pronounced Kaw-ruh), provided cheering support and sometimes traveled several kilometers by himself to watch his two older brothers compete.

As I was growing up, I saw my father and uncles as living-day representatives of winter legends of Norse mythology. I imagined all of the Engen brothers, with their great physical strength, competitive drive, and love of winter, as evolving into skiing icons—and in truth they have.

Trond and Martha Engen with eldest son, Alf, in Norway, circa 1910.

Ullr and Skaade

Known for a long time as part Scandinavian historical fantasy was Ullr, the patron saint of skiing. According to E. John B. Allen, professor of history at Plymouth College, some of the earliest writings about Ullr came from the Eddas—Icelandic writings, circa A.D. 800–1200.

So told, the winter god Ullr was a bold figure, gliding along on his crude skis with long curved-up tips and a bow and arrows in his hands. His wife, Skaade, has been described as one of the "charmingly beautiful, violent, and passionate creatures of Norse mythology." Together they ruled as god and goddess of winter. According to legend, they would "spread their protective covering of heavy snow over the fertile Norse farmlands to shield them from the freezing blasts of winter winds." But with the coming of spring, they would return to the snow-covered mountain peaks and remain until the next fall season arrived.

Ullr and Skaade. Illustration by Larry Needle.
Courtesy Shawnee Peak, Maine.

Vikings—I grew up hearing firsthand accounts of the Old Country. Although Alf Engen is remembered as a champion skier and jumper in the United States, his career actually began in Norway. At age sixteen, he was invited to compete in a ski-jumping competition on his hometown's largest hill. At that time the hill was one of the larger ones in Norway and was reserved for jumpers eighteen years of age and older. To be invited to compete when younger was considered an honor.

"The hill looked very large to me, and steep!" Alf remembered. "On my first jump, I fell and split my pants wide open, all the way down my backside. I was extremely embarrassed and wanted to go home. However, the town brass band was playing nearby, and the bandleader came over to me and said, 'Alf, if you will go up and jump one more time, we will play for you when you jump.' So I did!

"My brother Sverre helped patch my pants with several old rusty safety pins. I then hiked up the hill for my second jump. I remember standing at the top of the hill just before I jumped and hearing the band playing, way down on the flat of the outrun. I thought to myself, 'Alf, you better not fall a second time. You might not have any pants left at all if you do.' I hit the takeoff right on the button and when I came to a stop, I heard a roar from the crowd. I had just broken the hill record."

Twenty-three years later, following Alf's coaching of the 1948 U.S. Olympic Team in St. Moritz, he and my mother, Evelyn, returned to Mjøndalen. When

Alf Engen, age 18, jumping at Holmenkollen, Norway, 1928.

he arrived, he heard that a tournament was being held on the same hill he had jumped on long before. Because my father had his jumping skis with him, he went out to the hill to see if he could jump. When he inquired, he was told a flat "No." With more than three hundred entrants, only those with special invitations could compete.

Then an older gentleman on the judges' stand spotted the discussion at the bottom of the hill and came down. He was the chief of the hill and immediately recognized my father. He questioned Alf, "You're Alf Engen, aren't you?" Dad nodded. The older man then pointed to a marker on the side of the hill that read, "Hill record set by Alf Engen—1925." After a bit more discussion, the officials agreed to let Alf compete—with the condition that he would jump first. In ski jumping the last are considered to have the advantage.

Alf's first jump didn't go well. "And then it came back to me," he said. "I remembered that the inrun had a small turn that you had to navigate just perfectly to get the speed needed for a long jump. So on my second jump, I changed my technique just slightly and hit the takeoff with full speed and power. When I came to a stop, I again heard the crowd roar. I had landed in the same spot as when I first broke the hill record many years earlier."

When the announcement was made that Alf Engen had jumped, the entire town went wild. A few days later, he and my mother were invited as special guests to Oslo, Norway. There he was presented with a special award by the Norwegian Parliament for being an outstanding ambassador for the sport of skiing.

Alf was considered good enough to be a candidate for the 1928 Norwegian Olympic ski-jumping team, and although he did not make the team, he defeated all its members right after the Olympics at Konnerud Kollen, a big hill near Mjøndalen. Alf also finished ninth in his class (eighteen and under) in the international championships at Holmenkollen in 1928. By this time Alf was recognized in Norway as a very promising ski-jumping star.

Alf Engen never competed in the Olympics, although he certainly possessed the athletic skills required for world-class competition. Age, World War II, and politics threw obstacles in his way. But though disappointed, he was never bitter about this omission in his career, choosing instead to take pleasure in participating in myriad ski-related endeavors and leaving a lasting legacy for future generations. My father did not compete in a vacuum, and by telling his story, I cannot help but tell many others, tracing skiing's history from the Old Country to its roots in American history and finally to the events leading to Utah being chosen as the site for the 2002 Olympic Winter Games.

With this background serving as a basic introduction, *For the Love of Skiing* has three broad objectives: first, to provide a nontechnical overview of skiing's origins and eventual beginnings in the U.S.; second, to devote a significant focus on skiing history in the Intermountain West and many of the players who have been a part of that history; and third, to enhance the reader's overall understanding and awareness with a rich assortment of vintage photographs and other illustrative materials.

Alan K. Engen

to the memory of
Martha M. Engen,
*whose strong but gentle spirit continues to
stir the hearts of the many whose lives she touched*

chapter one

MODERN SKIING:
ITS BIRTH AND DEVELOPMENT

The Vikings played an important role in Scandinavian history; they by no means were the first to venture out into the vast stretches of ice-covered land that included Norway, Sweden, Iceland, Finland, Denmark, parts of Russia, and much of the Germanic countryside. To understand how skiing evolved into the sport enjoyed by millions today, one must journey far back into the past when the world was ruled by ice, and the ability to migrate made the difference between life and death.

The American Indian has his snowshoe; the Eskimo his sled; and the Norseman his skis.

—Jakob Vaage
Norwegian ski historian

The last Ice Age ended about 10,000 B.C. In Europe the ice encompassed the Scandinavian Peninsula, Denmark, the Netherlands, northern Germany, the British Isles, and most of Russia and Poland. Huge glaciers reached out of the Alps, Caucasus, and Pyrenees mountains to smother extended regions of central Europe. The ice sheets expanded and contracted like an accordion, sometimes covering the Baltic Sea, which, in turn, provided short-cuts to the continent from Scandinavia. The Nordic nomads used these bridges to travel great distances in their search for food, and it is entirely possible they might have used some kind of primitive skis.

During the next several thousand years, the glacial ice cap retreated to the mountain ranges. Land and water were once more exposed. Reindeer herds, driven south by the extreme conditions, began a northward migration. Tribes of nomads followed, sometimes journeying as far as the upper reaches of Norway and into Russia; it is these regions that contain the earliest artifacts showing that skis were used for transportation.

No one knows for certain exactly where or when skis originated, but the study of petroglyphs indicates that their use dates back about seven thousand years.

Map depicting area buried by snow during the Ice Age.

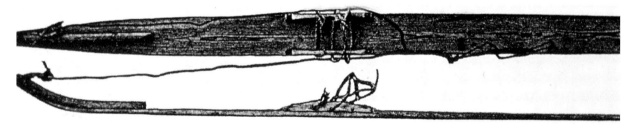

Old ski found in Hjørundfjord, Norway.

Far left:
The Rødøy
petroglyph.

Left:
The Zalavrouga
petroglyph.

The word *petroglyph* is composed of two parts: *petro* means "rock," and *glyph* means "symbol." Petroglyphs are carved or pecked into the stone and represent one of the earliest means of communication, providing a glimpse into the way people lived long ago. Ski historians believe a petroglyph located on an island in Rødøy, Norway, may well be one of the first representations of skiing. Archaeologists date these Stone Age petroglyphs between 2000 and 4000 B.C.

Another petroglyph, dated around 1500 B.C., was found at Zalavrouga, Russia, near the White Sea, and suggests that skis were used across a vast geographical range. The Zalavrouga petroglyph shows three skiers, each with a balancing/pushing stick. In the book *Nine Thousand Years of Skis,* author Ted Bays suggests skis evolved from sledge runners (sleds), which were used by nomadic Northmen to carry the kills of their hunters.

Although no actual authentication exists, J. C. Derks, Utah ski writer/historian in the 1930s, suggests that the word "ski" is an abbreviation of *suski,* a Finno-

Ugrian word meaning "snow-glide shoe." Derks writes that the nomadic Finno-Ugrian tribes wandered about not only in Europe but also throughout northern Asia.

Remains of what might have been skis have been located in the peat bogs of Norway, Sweden, and Finland. Some date back forty-five hundred years. The oldest artifact we can with certainty call a ski is the Hoting ski, dated about 2500 B.C., unearthed in northern Sweden in the 1930s and now residing in the Nerdiska Museum, Stockholm.

Unlike many of today's hard-core skiers who exist to ski, the earliest-known skiers skied to exist. Such knowledgeable ski historians as Jakob Vaage of Norway and Sir Arnold Lunn of Great Britain believe the Laplanders of Norway, Sweden, and Finland, and the inhabitants of the Ural Mountains in Russia first used skis because they depended on hunting. The Evenki people of Russia used two types of skis, both approximately two meters long and fifteen to eighteen centimeters wide. One ski had deer leather underneath the board. The other was a plain wooden ski for walk-

Woodcut: Swedish soldiers, wearing skis, on guard at Glebova, Russia, during peace negotiations between the two countries.

Birkenbeiner soldiers, Tor Stein Skeivla and Skjervald Skrukka, carrying the infant prince Hakon Hakonsson to safety at the time of the civil war in 1206. Illustration by Norwegian artist Knud Bergslien.

ing on icy surfaces (ice would damage the leather-lined skis). They used ski poles for balance and, with one end sharpened, hunting spears. Archaeologists named the Northmen who used these primitive skis Komsans and Fosnans after the Norwegian mountains and peninsula where their artifacts were unearthed.

One of the first written mentions of skiing occurs in Procopius (A.D. 526–550), who spoke of a race of *Skridfinnar,* meaning "gliding Finns." Later the Danish historian Saxo Grammaticus also gave an account of the Skridfinnar in his writings (about A.D. 1200).

Both Norway and Sweden equipped their troops with skis in the wars of 1452, 1590, and 1610. Since then, military skiing patrols have been part of their armed forces. Swedish woodcuts from about 1619 record skis being used in the military.

In 1206 King Sverre, fearing for the life of his infant son, Hakon Hakonsson, ordered two of his Birkenbeiner soldiers to carry the infant to safety from Gudbrandsdal to Lillehammer, a distance of fifty kilometers (approximately thirty miles). Birkenbeiners

were Norwegian soldiers who wrapped their legs in birch bark to protect them from snow. Because of this, they earned the nickname "Birchlegs." The U.S. National Ski Museum in Ishpeming, Michigan, has a central display featuring the Birkenbeiners.

The modern ski era can be said to begin in the nineteenth century. In his book *The Story of Ski-ing,* Sir Arnold Lunn divides the history of central European skiing into three distinct phases:

- **THE NORWEGIAN PERIOD,** during which the influence provided by Norwegians through personal example, books, and instruction led the way toward skiing's acceptance as a sport enjoyed by millions of people throughout the world.
- **THE ALPINE PERIOD,** during which the development of skiing was, in the main, influenced by skiers who were native to the Alps or spent their winters there. Mathias Zdarsky, Col. Georg Bilgeri, and Hannes Schneider of Austria; Hans Klopfenstein of Switzerland; and E. C. Richardson

and Vivian Caulfeild of Great Britain were the principal architects of Alpine skiing.

- **THE BRITISH PERIOD**, which overlaps with the second half of the Alpine Period. During this time, the British revolutionized competitive skiing by introducing the slalom and gaining recognition for downhill racing.

The Norwegian Contribution

In 1866 a Norwegian farmer, Sondre Norheim, born in 1825, revolutionized ski equipment when he developed the first good ski binding made from thin shoots of birch roots. Prior to Norheim, only a toe strap had been used, and this new heel binding dramatically improved ski maneuverability. It made getting airborne much easier for the early Norwegian jumpers and eliminated their fear of losing a ski while aloft.

In 1868 Norheim further impressed the ski world in Norway by demonstrating two new turns. The first involved a long-radius arc in which he pushed the outside ski much farther ahead of the inside one. This turn became known as the "telemark." The other turn used a shorter radius and demonstrated that Norheim could stop sharply from a running position. This turn became known as the "christiania," or christie. Norheim also developed a shorter ski with

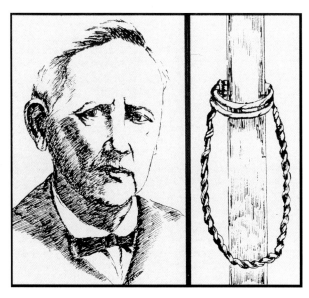

Sondre Norheim (1825–1895) and the Norheim binding.

slightly concave sides, which became the pattern for modern skis.

In the early to mid-nineteenth century, virtually every Norwegian valley developed its own type of ski and technique. But in the province of Telemark, where the Norwegians first organized skiing, the technique that became universally known as downhill was perfected. Mikkel Hemmestveit, one of the earliest Norwegian emigrants to America, spoke of

---

Sir Arnold Lunn

Sir Arnold Lunn is recognized internationally as the "father of modern ski racing." He was born in India in 1888 and skied many years in the Alps during the early 1900s. In the 1920s he invented the double-pole slalom and pioneered the Alpine combined, the first of which was the Arlberg-Kandahar in 1928. In 1952 Great Britain knighted him for his many contributions to the sport. As a pioneer of ski mountaineering, he wrote a number of books that have been translated into many languages. One of them, The Story of Ski-ing, published in 1952, is an excellent source for those who desire further information on early skiing history, particularly on Alpine downhill and slalom. His epitaph expresses his great love for the sport:

Levavi Oculos

Let me give thanks, dear Lord,
*   in the frailty of age,*
For the beloved mountains of
*   my youth,*
For the challenge of rock
*   and for the joy of skiing,*
For the friends with whom I climbed
*   and skied,*
*   and above all, dear Lord,*
For those moments of revelation
*   when the temporal beauty of the*
*   mountains reinforces my faith in*
*   the Eternal Beauty which is not*
*   subject to decay.*

Fridtjof Nansen, *Graphic Newspaper*, 1896.

his experiences with both downhill and slalom races.

Although one of the first organized ski competitions involved a cross-country race in Tromsoe, Norway, above the Arctic Circle in 1843, modern recreational and competitive skiing originated in Telemark during the 1850s.

The Norwegians also developed competitive ski jumping. A well-known American ski jumper, Roy Mikkelsen, along with John I. Johansen, published an article in the 1936 *American Ski Annual* recounting the first competitive ski-jumping tournament, held in 1845 in Troms, Norway. Although the Norwegians held many other jumping meets, one of the most important was a competition at Huseby Hill in 1879 on the outskirts of Christiania. The longest jump was approximately sixty feet. This tournament also marked the start of the ski club of Norway—Foreningen Til Ski-Idraettens Fremme.

In 1892 a new ski-jumping hill, Holmenkollen, was built not far away from the Huseby Hill. In 1903 the first Nordic Winter Festival took place there. Instead of a simple ski-jumping tournament, the festival involved an entire week of competition to celebrate winter sports. Included were ski jumping, cross-country, ski joring (skiers pulled by horses), ice skating, and sleighing.

The Holmenkollen tournament was originally limited to Norwegians, but starting in 1903, Norway invited competitors from the outside. The Holmenkollen Winter Festival has been an annual event ever since, interrupted only during the five-year Nazi occupation of Norway in World War II. In 1946 a record crowd of 120,000 spectators came to watch the first post–World War II tournament. Today the Holmenkollen competition is a highly regarded world-class championship.

The Alpine Contribution

Austrian Mathias Zdarsky (1874–1946) never saw skis until he was thirty-two years old, but he best personifies Lunn's Alpine Period. Most ski historians agree that Zdarsky had the greatest influence on transforming the sport from its emphasis on Nordic (cross-country and jumping) to Alpine (downhill) skiing. Zdarsky spent much time climbing mountains. He made three African expeditions and at an early age had climbed many of the highest peaks in the Alps.

Zdarsky purchased a pair of Norwegian skis in 1888 and taught himself to ski in Lilienfeld, Austria.

In 1889, as a young Austrian military officer, he read Fridtjof Nansen's book about his expedition across Greenland and realized the potential of skis for the Imperial Austrian Army. The mountainous terrain along the Austrian border had always been a difficult area to cover. For six years Zdarsky, using Nansen's information as a guide, developed a technique for safely skiing down steep slopes—an absolute necessity in the Alps.

Zdarsky's technique became known as "stem." It enabled the skier to make a controlled descent on steep terrain using a series of linked S turns. Zdarsky based his technique on much shorter skis than had been previously used—his five-foot-long, four-inch-wide skis made turning much easier—and he relied on one long pole for balance and braking, later changing to two poles.

In addition to the shorter skis, Zdarsky developed a new binding, the Lilienfeld, which enabled a skier to turn better in deep snow. The Lilienfeld was the world's first spring binding made primarily out of metal. All bindings before that time had been fabricated out of leather and hemp. The Lilienfeld clamped the boot firmly to the ski, allowing controlled turns.

Zdarsky's technique quickly became known around Europe. In 1896 he established the world's first organized ski school—the Lilienfeld Ski School—near Vienna, Austria, and published the first book on the theory of skiing, *Der Lilienfelder Ski-Lauf Technik*, in 1896. In this book Zdarsky volunteered to teach any

Mathias Zdarsky,
late 1800s–early 1900s.

one to ski in six days or less. The one distinguishing feature of Zdarsky's system was the use of a single stick as a brake. The skier assumed a low crouch position, and with the weight back on the skis, was able to navigate steep hills under control using the snowplow and stem christie turns. According to British ski pioneer

Zdarsky's Challenge

The new Zdarsky Technique enthralled skiers from many parts of Europe, but it infuriated Norwegians because Zdarsky publicly claimed that only he knew how to ski. For the Norwegians, this was close to blasphemy. Skiing had been a way of life in Norway for generations before Zdarsky was born. The controversy around Zdarsky's system continued to grow. In 1905 Zdarsky challenged the Norwegians to a contest to determine the best technique in the world. He proposed that they hold the tournament in Lilienfeld, Austria. The competition would consist of three slalom courses of approximately eighty-five gates, each course covering a distance of over one mile, with a sixteen-

hundred-foot total drop in elevation. The challenge was not accepted because Norwegians felt the event "was not a race but a virtuoso exercise."

Not long after, Zdarsky invited the Norwegians to a "day of skiing" rather than a contest. The Norwegians accepted and sent one of their top athletes, Hanse Horn, to Lilienfeld. According to Sir Arnold Lunn, Zdarsky and Horn, along with some of Zdarsky's star pupils, climbed to the top of a steep wooded slope. Zdarsky led off, his pupils following close behind. Horn started last. By the time they reached the bottom, however, Horn led the entire troop. Both Zdarsky and Horn developed a new respect for each other's skiing abilities and parted with no animosity.

Rickmers, one of Zdarsky's pupils, Zdarsky taught approximately twelve hundred people how to ski.

The British Contribution

Nansen's *The First Crossing of Greenland* also greatly influenced the British, who quickly saw new ways to enjoy the Alps. They obtained Norwegian skis and set off for various Swiss resorts to practice their new skills. In 1903 they created the Ski Club of Great Britain and introduced holiday skiing at various European resorts. The British also began downhill racing by organizing a club race called the Roberts of Kandahar Challenge Cup. The first club race took place in 1911 in Crans-Montana, Switzerland, on the Plaine Morte Glacier, an unmarked course with many natural obstacles and hazards.

Hannes Schneider introduced the Alburg Technique to teach beginners to ski.

Baron Pierre de Coubertin, founder of the modern Olympic games. Photo courtesy Stan Cohen.

The Modern Olympic Games

In 1896 the Olympic Games were revived after a fifteen-hundred-year lapse, largely due to the efforts of Pierre de Coubertin, a young French noble-man. Although Greece had tried to revive the games in the 1800s with little success, it was Baron de Coubertin's determination, along with his talent for organization, that was the catalyst for the modern Olympic movement. The first modern games were

Holmenkollen Hill, Oslo, Norway, circa 1960. The tower is 138 feet high.

held in Athens, Greece, honoring the memory of the ancient Olympians.

In 1924 the first Winter Olympics were held in Chamonix, France. The ski-jumping competition was dominated by Norway, as were the Olympic competitions that followed in 1928, 1932, and 1936. The 1924 games were limited to ski jumping and cross-country racing, called *langlauf*. Cross-country consisted of two events: the fifteen-kilometer and the fifty-kilometer races. Norwegian Thorleif Haug won both cross-country events hands down and finished third in jumping. Anders Haugen, a member of the first United States Winter Olympic Ski Team, placed fourth in the jumping competition, just behind the great Thorleif Haug. Many years passed before a

Norwegian, Thoralf Strømstad, discovered that the calculations made in 1924 for third place in ski jumping were incorrect. According to an article written by John Henry Auran in the first issue of *Skiing Heritage* (vol. 9, no. 1 [1997]). "With the discovery of the error in the official results, Jakob Vaage, the Norwegian ski historian; and the Norwegian Olympic Committee began making moves to set the record straight. Haugen was invited from his home in Yucaipa, California, and on September 12, 1974, at Holmenkollen, [Thorleif] Haug's daughter, Anne Marie Magnussen, presented the bronze medal to [Anders] Haugen." Haugen thus became the first American citizen to receive an Olympic medal for skiing—fifty years after the competition. ❄

Although no evidence exists, skiing in America may have started as early as A.D. 1000, when Leif Erickson, son of Eric the Red, beached his Viking ship on the shore of Vinland, now thought to have been somewhere between Massachusetts and Labrador. Another Viking, Thorfinn Karlsefni, visited what is now America shortly after Leif and founded a colony on the Atlantic coast. The early Vikings left Vinland and never returned; Karlsefni's colony was abandoned after three years. Not until the middle of the nineteenth century were skis ever actually authenticated in North America.

The first extensive use of skis in the United States occurred in the mountains of the West, the Lost Sierra, a high forested plateau northeast of Sacramento, California. The California gold seekers called their skis "snow-shoes"; thus, historians refer to the 1840s and '50s as the Snow-Shoe Era. Many of the miners were Scandinavian emigrants who, like Alf Engen, had come to America to escape poor economic conditions at home.

According to some historians, these first skiers may have been Scandinavian sailors who deserted

It was Norwegian emigrants who brought skiing to America and Canada. In many ways, as Jakob Vaage wrote in The World of Skiing, *"The sport of modern skiing was the gift of Norway to the world."*

—*Leif Hovelsen*
The Flying Norseman

their ships to join the rush for gold in 1849. Others claim that skiing began as a result of plain old "Yankee ingenuity," using very crude staves from flour barrels to get around in the snow. We know for certain that during the winter of 1853–54, gold miners used long skis they called Norwegian snow-shoes. Soon after, miners began using ten- to twelve-foot skis made from Douglas fir not only to get around but also to race down the hills.

Snowshoe Thompson

In 1837 fifty-two Norwegian emigrants sailed on a small vessel from Stavanger, Norway, to the United States. According to the Carson Valley Historical Society, one of the emigrants was a ten-year-old boy named Jon Tostenson (christened Jon Torsteinson-Rue). He went on to become the legendary Snowshoe Thompson who crossed the Sierra Nevada on skis, carrying mail between California and Nevada.

Thompson was born on April 30, 1827, on a small farm called Luraas-Rue Gard in Tinn, Telemark, Norway. When he came into this world, his father was

---

Emigrate? Immigrate?

Merriam Webster's Collegiate Dictionary, *Tenth Edition, defines the following words:*

emigrate: *to leave one's place of residence or country to live elsewhere.*

immigrate: *to come into a country of which one is not a native for permanent residence.*

Earliest Recorded U.S. Ski Trek

E. John B. Allen, in Skisport to Skiing, *traces the earliest recorded skiing in the United States to Gullik Laughen and a friend who skied from Rock Prairie to Beloit, Wisconsin, to purchase flour. Although it was not documented until 1841, the event is believed to have occurred in 1821.*

Statue of Snowshoe Thompson, Western America SkiSport Museum, Boreal, California.

sixty-eight years old, and died two years later in 1829, leaving his wife, Gro, and her children in a very difficult situation. When Gro was given the opportunity to immigrate to America, she gladly accepted. She and her son Jon left Norway on May 30, 1837, and arrived in New York three months later. The trip was long and difficult. Two of the immigrants died and were buried at sea.

Not long after arriving in the United States, Jon assumed the name "John Thompson" because he and his mother felt the Americanized version was similar to Jon's name and would be more easily understood. In 1846 Gro died in Iowa, and John went to live with one of his relatives, another immigrant. In 1851, at the age of twenty-four, Thompson crossed the midwestern plains to California to prospect for gold. After mining for a short while in Placerville, California, however, he decided that the life of a miner was not to his liking and that more gold could be made by providing services to the miners than panning for the yellow treasure.

The fifteen-foot snows in the Sierra Nevada made communication impossible between the eastern Nevada and western California sides of the mountains.

Some attempts had been made to carry mail by foot into these remote regions, but most often the result was death. In late 1856 this article appeared in the *Sacramento Union:*

People Lost to the World— Uncle Sam Needs Carrier

People living east of the Sierra Nevada Mountains and west of Salt Lake lose contact with the outside world as winter snows cut off all communications. The greatest cry from the people is for mail. Congress passed a bill August 18, 1856, providing for a post route from Placerville, California, to Genoa, Utah Territory. So far, no one has come to accept the mail-carrying job this year, according to Mr. A. M. Thatcher, postmaster of Placerville.

Thompson decided to give the job a try. He set off from the Sacramento Valley to Placerville. He knew he could get around better on skis, and that was how he proposed to carry mail to the miners. He crafted a pair of twelve-foot-long skis, three-and-one-half to four inches wide and approximately two inches thick in the center. His first skis were believed to have been made of oak or hickory and weighed about twenty-five pounds. Although they were heavy, they became lighter after the wood cured.

He practiced on the skis, using a long pole for balance, and became very proficient. After accepting the position as mail carrier, he sought people familiar with the rugged mountainous terrain to learn as much as possible about the challenges he could anticipate on his trip.

On January 3, 1856, Thompson traveled a total distance of ninety miles between Placerville, California, and Genoa, Nevada (near Carson City and part of Utah Territory at that time) and back again. The trek was difficult and he did it carrying a fifty-pound mailbag on his back. (Thompson was six feet tall, thin and wiry, and weighed about 160 pounds.) He returned to Placerville on January 18 and gained instant fame for his accomplishment.

Thompson continued to carry mail on skis for a number of years, but the trips became more infrequent in the middle 1860s because he spent much of his time running a freight service. His rounds became known around Lake Tahoe as the Snow-Shoe Express and were as popular as the Pony Express in other parts of the country.

Miners Take to Skiing

As in the Old World, skiing in the United States began as a necessity, but it wasn't long before it became a sport. The gold miners in the Sierra Nevada suffered cabin fever in the long winter months. Little work could be done; drinking and fighting were commonplace. Word of Snowshoe Thompson's use of Norwegian "snow-skates" got around; perhaps Thompson visited the camps on some of his trips. The miners began to amuse themselves by learning how to ski. In the mid-1850s, one of the miners came

Snowshoe Thompson's grave, Genoa, Nevada.

Misspelled Tombstone

Snowshoe Thompson died on May 15, 1876, at the age of forty-nine, probably of appendicitis with complications of pneumonia. Eight years after Thompson's death, his wife, Agnes, had a white marble stone erected on his grave. A pair of crossed skis and the words "Gone but not forgotten" are engraved on the tombstone—but his name is misspelled.

Robert Oliver. Photo courtesy Western America SkiSport Museum.

America's First Ski Champion

A number of knowledgeable ski enthusiasts (mostly from California) make a strong argument that Bob Oliver was America's first national ski champion and the world's first speed-skiing champion. The records of these California events provide evidence that competitive skiing there took place several years before the telemarkers in Christiania, Norway, gave their famous skiing exhibitions and fifteen years before the first European ski tournament.

up with the idea of holding speed-skiing races. At first informal, these races soon developed into highly competitive events. By the late 1850s ski races were very popular among the miners and involved wagering as to who would be the fastest coming down the hill. Cash and bragging rights were awarded to the victors.

The skis the miners used for racing were called "longboard snow-shoes" and were ten-and-a-half to thirteen-and-a-half feet long, varying in weight from thirteen to seventeen pounds per pair. The racers reached speeds exceeding eighty miles per hour by going straight down the mountain. The longboards had a square tip and toe straps made of leather into which the daring riders put their feet. A small block was placed crosswise to prevent the foot from slipping out of the toe strap if the heel was raised.

The mining camp at La Porte, California (settled in 1850), became the center for these competitions.

Longboard speed skiers, La Porte, California, circa 1860s. Note the man on the left with the gong, which was used to officially start the racers. Photo courtesy Western Skisport Museum.

During the late 1850s and through the 1860s, frequent tournaments were held. Races were organized for women and children as well as men. By 1867 racing had become so popular that La Porte skiers organized America's first ski club, the Alturas Snowshoe Club. Creed Haymond, its first president, formalized the racing rules. On February 1, 1868, La Porte held what is said to be the first organized ski tournament featuring multiple competitions; the tournament lasted one week and had a purse of three thousand dollars for the overall winner.

The first La Porte races had a nominal entry fee but offered cash prizes ranging from twenty-five to seventy-five dollars per event. The men's championship was held on the final day of competition. Two men, John Pollard and Robert "Cornish Bob" Oliver, tied for the fastest time of fourteen seconds to travel the 1,230-foot course on the first run. They raced again, and Oliver won the tournament on his second run, beating his competitor by four feet. The race officials calculated the time and distance traveled and determined that Oliver had exceeded sixty miles per hour in his descent.

Unfortunately, Bob Oliver's fame as a ski champion was short-lived. Not long after his record-breaking race, Oliver was shot and killed by a fellow skier in a saloon brawl. But the La Porte races continued into the early 1900s, ending in 1911. By then the gold rush days were over, the mining towns were fading away, and downhill ski contests were coming to an end. Regardless, a strong argument can be made that the world's Alpine downhill ski championships started in this California mining town many years before modern-day racing began.

La Porte, California, late 1800s, center of the first organized ski tournaments featuring multiple competitions. Photo courtesy Western America SkiSport Museum.

Poorman's Creek, Home of the Sierra Schussboomers

An unknown writer in California, who lived high in the Sierra Nevada at a place called Poorman's Creek, wrote an account of early snowshoeing in an article dated March 26, 1859. The article since has become known as the Poorman's Creek Letter that was published in the Quincy Plumas Argus *newspaper:*

"This has been the hardest winter within the knowledge of the oldest inhabitant in Poorman's. It is estimated that about twenty-five or thirty feet of snow has fallen, at different times this winter. The snow now lies from eight to ten feet deep, but it is not thought much of, for at Onion Valley, two miles from here, it is twelve or fifteen feet deep. It may be a matter of wonder to some how people can get about where there is so much snow, but it is the easiest thing in the mountains. Nearly all have Norwegian snow shoes, about nine feet long, four and one half inches wide, shaved thin and turned up in front like a sled runner, and by fastening them to the feet about the middle of the shoe and with a pole in the hands for a balance, a person can run over the light and new fallen snow at railroad speed."

Norwegian Jumpers Immigrate

In the late 1800s, some of Norway's finest jumpers came to the United States. Most of them had to sell the sterling silver trophies won in European competitions to pay for the trip to America; however, they soon found ways to communicate with each other and started ski-jumping clubs and built jumps on hills throughout the Midwest.

Two Norwegian boys, Torjus and Mikkel Hemmestveit, from Red Wing, Minnesota, are credited with starting the sport of ski jumping in the late 1880s. The brothers were part of the early Norwegian emigration to the United States. The first-known ski-jumping tournament in the U.S. was held at Red Wing, Minnesota, on February 8, 1887. The tournament was sponsored by the Aurora Ski Club, which had been organized in 1886. Mikkel Hemmestveit made a powerful leap of thirty-seven feet to establish the first American distance record. Interest in ski jumping spread to other regions, partially because of the Hemmestveit brothers' exhibitions.

Frank Steward (third from right), "doping" master, circa 1860s. Photo courtesy Western SkiSport Museum.

In 1887 it is written that a bottle of rum helped create one of the first ski clubs in America—the Norden Ski Club of Ishpeming, Michigan. One weekend a Norwegian emigrant, Ole Surdlie, along with several other men of Nordic descent, spent an afternoon enjoying skiing, as they had done in Norway. On that particular weekend, they met two saloon keepers who had a bottle of rum at the bottom of one of the hills. Every time they got to the bottom of the hill, they took a swig of rum. After an unspecified number of trips spiced by the rum, they decided they should form a ski club.

The Norden Ski Club held its first formal tournament on February 25, 1888. Ole Surdlie won with a leap of thirty-five feet. In 1891 the Norden Ski Club was renamed the Ishpeming Ski Club.

By 1891 ski clubs had been formed in several places in Michigan, Minnesota, and Wisconsin—Ishpeming, Minneapolis, St. Paul, Albert Lea, Winona, La Crosse, St. Croix, Eau Claire, and Red Wing. Eventually a number of these clubs formed a national group devoted to skiing. Harold A. Grinden, in the

1945 *American Ski Annual,* writes that the National Ski Association was founded by a group headed by Carl Tellefsen on February 21, 1904. The National Ski Association did not, however, come into full being until the following year on February 21, 1905, which became the official date.

Tellefsen was born in Trondheim, Norway, and immigrated to Ishpeming in 1887. At the first meeting, all of the members supported the idea of having a national organization and elected Carl Tellefsen its president. Many years later, the National Ski Hall of Fame and Ski Museum was founded in Ishpeming because of its rich skiing history.

Conrad Thompson of Ishpeming won the unofficial first National Ski-Jumping Championship, held on Suicide Hill in Ishpeming on February 22, 1904, the day after the National Ski Association was first discussed as an organization. On February 21, 1904, it had been decided by Tellefsen and his newly elected officers to call the 1904 ski tourney the first National Ski-Jumping Championship in order to advertise the event for the following year. However, the first officially recognized national ski-jumping gold medal was awarded to Ole Westgaard on February 22, 1905, at Ishpeming. According to ski historian Allen Adler, current records also reflect the official start of the National Ski Association as 1905 rather than 1904.

Right after the turn of the century, sports books began to include skiing as a viable recreation. *Ski-Running,* written by E. C. Richardson and published in England in 1904, was the first book in English that examined and promoted skiing as a sport. Richardson gained his knowledge of skiing in Norway. *The Winter*

Theodore Johnsen's vision of the typical woman skier of 1905. This illustration comes from *The Winter Sport of Skeeing* with the subcaption, "It Is Indeed an Ideal Outdoor Winter Pastime."

Suicide Hill in Ishpeming, Michigan. *Ishpeming* is an Indian word
meaning "heaven," likely given because of the natural beauty
surrounding this area at the eastern end of the Michigan highlands.

Sport of Skeeing, written and published in 1905 by Theodore A. Johnsen of Portland, Maine, was the second book published in English about skiing. Johnsen was a tradesman and a ski maker by avocation.

At the same time, Phineas T. Barnum and James A. Bailey jumped on the bandwagon. The Barnum and Bailey Circus, in addition to word-of-mouth advertising, put ski jumping into the minds of Americans by incorporating it into the circus. Ski jumping was billed as "The Perilous Scandinavian Winter Sport in All Its Wild and Wondrous Daring." As part of "The Greatest Show on Earth," the first circus ski jump took place in 1907 when Carl Howelsen jumped in Madison Square Garden in New York City. Howelsen earned the nickname "The Flying Norseman" for his jumping feats. Howelsen was referred to as "Captain" Carl Howelsen, a title given to him by the promoters. The world-famous Howelsen Hill in Steamboat Springs, Colorado, is named after him.

The Engens Come to America

The day Alf Engen left Norway in June 1929, the entire town, including a brass band, came to the pier to send him off. He was a jumping champion in Norway and considered a local hero. He was happy, looking forward to his new life in America. But within minutes after leaving port that June day, all the good feelings and confidence evaporated. He was only twenty years old, very much alone, and could not speak a word of English.

Alf's ship sailed into New York Harbor during the huge Independence Day celebration on July 4 with fireworks and rockets bursting overhead. He had no idea what was going on but appreciated the show nonetheless. He thought America was indeed one heck of a place.

Henry Hall being carried off after breaking the 200-foot barrier. Photo courtesy Caryl Hall Bergdahl.

Jumping hill typical of the one that Alf Engen first jumped on in the United States. Photo courtesy U.S. National Ski Museum.

The Barnum and Bailey poster showing Carl Howelsen sailing over mountains in a death-defying leap.

His impression was underscored by the stressful experience of processing through Ellis Island with hundreds of other immigrants. He often said that he felt very lucky to have made it through the intensive process as others who were on his ship were not so lucky and were detained for further questioning.

He found a job in Chicago, feeding radio panels to a drill press at Westinghouse, and worked the first week for no pay because no one told him to punch the time clock. It was hard dreary work, but he soon made friends with a couple of older men who assured him they would tell him everything he needed to know to do well in America. "If you really like something," they told him, "say 'goddamn.' It'll make a good impression."

So Alf did. One day he was invited to his boss's home for dinner. The boss introduced him to his wife, a fine cook. As soon as they started to eat, Alf decided to show off his mastery of his new language. "Pass the

goddamn potatoes, please," he said, and then went on to punctuate every sentence he could with his newly acquired phrase. When he was about to leave, the boss's wife took him aside.

"Alf, you are such a nice young man—why do you have to use such terrible language?" she whispered. Alf was horrified when he realized that he had been duped. After this humiliating experience, Alf rarely, if ever, used profanity of any type again.

Sverre, only eighteen, joined his brother in the United States in October of the same year, 1929, and had his own initiation to life in Chicago, a city more populous than his entire homeland. He was late getting home from his first day at his new job—stacking cement in a warehouse—because he spent four hours riding from one end of the streetcar line to the other. He couldn't remember which stop was his.

Both Alf and Sverre quickly applied for U.S. citizenship and began to study English by listening to

First U.S. Olympic Ski-Jumping Team (1924): (left to right) Anders Haugen, LeMoine Batson, Harry Lein, Sigurd Overby, and John Carleton. Not pictured: Ragnar Omtvedt. Photo courtesy Stan Cohen.

phonograph records, going to movies, and reading comic strips in the newspapers. They played soccer in the local leagues, worked hard, and tried not to think of giving up. But during those first months, it would not have taken much for them to exchange "the land of opportunity" for one whiff of pine smoke from their little town of Mjøndalen.

Leaving Norway was especially difficult for Alf because he was so close to his family and felt he was leaving his beloved rolling pine forests, fjords, mountains, and snow behind forever. All Alf knew of America came from the sensationalized press, which was preoccupied with the Wild West, cowboys, and the lone prairie. Alf arrived in America believing it was flat and snowless. Imagine his delight when he discovered that his new home was blessed with beautiful mountains and some of the best snow on Earth.

Shortly after arriving in the United States, Alf became involved with professional ski jumping. The early professionals jumped because they could fly, if

only for a few seconds. But in the late 1920s, Anders Haugen and several other jumpers discovered they could make money ski jumping and organized the first professional ski-jumping group. To their joy and relief, their love of jumping became more than just a hard-earned pastime; it was a way to make a living.

In 1922, the National Ski Association ruled at its national convention in Chicago that "there shall be but one class of skiers participating in tournaments held under the auspices of the National Ski Association of America; this class to be amateur skiers. . . . No skier who participates as a professional after December 21, 1922, shall be permitted to take part in any tournament held by a club belonging to the National Ski Association of America."

The decision was not popular with everyone. Jumpers were forced to choose between jumping in sanctioned events as amateurs, with the hope of qualifying for the national or forthcoming Olympic teams, or making money by doing what they loved. Lars Haugen, who in 1929 became part of the first professional jumping group, lobbied hard against the proposal but lost. The controversy over the division of skiing into amateur and professional categories still persists.

In 1929 the original U.S. professional jumping team was formed and included Anders Haugen, Alf Engen, Sverre Engen, Steffen Trøgstad, Sigurd Ulland, Lars Haugen, Halvar Hvalstad, Einar Fredbo, Alf Matisen, Olaf Thompson, Carl Hall, C. C. Torgersen, Halvor Bjørngaard, Ted Rex, Oliver Karldal, Gustav Lindbo, and Burt Wilchock. The pro jumpers were guaranteed a fixed amount of prize money by the promoters. All of the jumpers shared half of the guaranteed amount—even if someone was injured and could not jump (because of the hazards involved, all the professional jumpers rarely performed at the same time; someone was always out with an injury). The winners of the tournament shared the other half of the purse. Occasionally, as an incentive, the promoters put up a bonus, usually five hundred dollars, conditional on one of the jumpers setting a new professional-distance world record.

Alf came to be a member of the professional ski jumpers through a happy accident. About six months after he immigrated to America, he was taken by Norwegian acquaintances to watch a ski-jumping meet in Milwaukee. Expecting to be a spectator, Alf wore street shoes, a wrinkled sport coat with bow tie, and a beret. But when he saw the jumping hill, he surprised his friends by asking an elderly man standing near the outrun if he could borrow his skis.

The gentleman looked at Alf and then at his shoes and said, "Young man, apparently you don't know anything about ski jumping. You're not even dressed right. Besides, you couldn't use the skis because you don't have the proper boots to fit the bindings."

"I can tie my feet onto the skis with leather thongs," Alf said. The man conceded and lent Alf his skis.

At the Milwaukee meet, no one knew of Alf Engen's status as a ski-jumping hero in his native Norway. When he climbed to the top of the jumping hill, the competitors watched and quietly snickered at the sight of this inappropriately dressed kid; snide remarks and whispers were rampant. He certainly didn't look like a ski jumper. But all that changed once he jumped.

On his first try he flew to the bottom of the hill, well past the landings of the other jumpers. When Alf attempted to return the skis to the old man, the awestruck gentleman said, "Mister, I don't know who you are or where you came from, but as far as I'm concerned, you can jump on my skis all afternoon." Alf proceeded to do just that.

About mid-afternoon several jumpers approached Alf and said they knew some very fine jumpers in the area who were starting a professional ski-jumping group. Not long after, he was contacted by Anders Haugen and taken to meet the rest of the group. Some knew of Alf's achievements in Norway, and they quickly accepted this twenty-year-old as a member of the group. Alf Engen was back doing what he loved—and he was getting paid for it.

Of the fourteen members of the original professional jumping group, twelve were born in Norway and two in the United States (Ted Rex and Burt Wilchock). Sverre, after winning the Central Ski Association ski-jumping championship, resigned his amateur status and joined the pros for their western tour. According to Sverre, Ted Rex taught several of the Norwegians to speak English.

The professional tour started in Detroit, Michigan, in December 1929 and traveled to Glenwood and Westby, Wisconsin. From there, under sponsorship of

Carl Hall ski jumping at Banff, British Columbia, circa 1925. Photo courtesy Caryl Hall Bergdahl.

the Union Pacific Railroad, the jumpers started a tour that took them first to Omaha, Nebraska, where jumping conditions were not quite state-of-the-art.

"We arrived in Omaha in January 1930, and the promoters took a few of us to see the site of the jumping hill," Sverre remembers. "It was warm and snow was very sparse. Straw was mixed with soap to make the running surface slicker, causing less drag for the jumpers. The takeoff was set on a hill overlooking tracks used by streetcars. In all our jumping experiences, this was one of the most difficult tournaments we ever put on."

Sverre and the others jumped over the streetcars and could see sparks and flashes of electricity underneath as they flew overhead. Stopping was the hardest challenge of all. The outrun was very short, and the jumpers had to throw themselves into a large bale of hay. "I broke my toe trying to stop," Sverre said, "and that toe still hurts on occasion, more than sixty-five years later."

When Alf's turn to jump arrived, he dived head-first into the hay bale like everyone else, but a pitchfork accidentally left in the hay flew out. "He was lucky he was not killed," Sverre said, but by his tone of voice, one could tell he thought the entire incident was very comical.

One of the most humorous things to happen, however, involved Halvar Hvalstad, one of the top jumpers on the tour, who fell into a pool of mud at the bottom of the hill. "What a sorry sight he was— nothing but mud with a few pieces of straw sticking out of his hair," Sverre said. "I wish we had taken a picture of that for posterity. It would have been a sure winner!"

Following Omaha, the next tournament on the pro tour was at Becker Hill in February 1930 near Ogden, Utah. Alf and Sverre were impressed by the beauty of the area. The high Wasatch Mountains reminded them of their beloved Norway, and they quickly developed new friendships with Utah sports enthusiasts where ski jumping had been popular for some time. Although they did return to Minneapolis after the first pro ski-jumping season, both Alf and Sverre came to Utah again the next season beginning in December 1930 as part of the pro tour; but this time, they ended up staying. The rest of the story as it pertains to the Engen brothers' many contributions to skiing is about ready to unfold. ❄

chapter three

SKIING and SKI JUMPING BEGIN: The Utah Experience

Without a doubt, ski jumping made its mark early in Utah's ski development, but it was not the first. Alta, one of the premier Alpine ski destinations in the world, was once a rowdy silver-mining town whose major distinction was its numerous bars and high homicide rate. Details regarding the earliest inhabitants are sketchy, but we know that Ulysses S. Grant signed the original deed for the Alta Basin in 1854. The government issued the deed to Amanda Brown, but no one knows what she did at Alta.

Miners Introduce Skiing to Utah

In 1862 approximately 750 men of the Third California Volunteers, under the command of Col. Patrick Edward Connor (1820–1891), arrived in the Salt Lake Valley to protect the Overland Mail from raids and keep an eye on the Mormon settlers. Some of the soldiers were volunteers from California and Nevada who had extensive prospecting experience and had probably used skis before coming to Utah.

Shortly after they arrived, Colonel Connor encouraged his men to search the nearby Oquirrh and Wasatch Mountains for gold and silver. In July 1864 silver-bearing ore was discovered near the top of Little Cottonwood Canyon. The following year the first verifiable mining claim was filed and staked on the Silas Braine fissure where the Alta Peruvian Lodge is located.

It is in skee jumping that the skill of the expert skidor [skier] can best be judged. Here is a sport which calls for courage, skill, and endurance, a cool head and a quick eye, and above all, a nice sense of balance, every one of which essentials, if not already the skidor's own, can be acquired through pluck and practice. Skee jumping means a jump out and down rather than a jump up, and the difficulty lies not so much in the length of the jump as in retaining an upright position on alighting. To make a jump of ten feet and stand is much more difficult than to jump a hundred feet and fall, provided the hill has a sufficient slope.

—Theodore A. Johnsen
The Winter Sport of Skeeing

By 1868 the first settlement was built, and by 1870 Alta's population was more than a thousand, mostly miners digging for silver, lead, zinc, and tungsten. A very small amount of gold was mined. To extract the ore, more than a hundred miles of tunnels were dug beneath the hillsides of the Alta Basin during the 1870s and '80s.

As it does today, Alta received, on average, more than five hundred inches of snow each winter, and the miners lived there year-round. In *My Summer in a Mormon Village* (1893), Florence A. Merriam described a visit to Alta and her conversations with one of the miners. She asked him what he did during the long winter months. He showed her "a pair of snow-shoes—skis— fourteen feet long and six inches wide" that he called "his winter walking boots—his only means of going abroad."

GEORGE WATSON

In the early 1900s, George H. Watson found his way to Alta from Michigan at the age of nineteen, intent on finding his fortune by mining. He planned to strike it rich at Alta but never succeeded. He did, however, become one of the most colorful characters ever to grace its slopes.

Watson started taking sightseers up and down Little Cottonwood Canyon on a buslike vehicle that

Alta City, circa 1870s. Photo courtesy Alta Historical Society.

Reenactment of an early miner in the 1800s skiing down a hill in Utah. Photo courtesy University of Utah J. Willard Marriott Library, Utah Ski Archives.

ran on rail tracks (he called it a "jitney"). In addition to running the jitney, he began buying old claims because he felt a mining boom was imminent. But Alta no longer flourished as a mining town and times were difficult. In an effort to secure some tax relief, he deeded the surface rights to more than eighteen hundred acres of his land to the U.S. Forest Service so that a ski area serving the local population of Salt Lake City could be built in Alta. Shortly after, he appointed himself mayor.

Mayor Watson was probably Alta's greatest promoter; he always referred to the area as "romantic Alta." He was the self-styled "king of the prospectors," and every year he sent out membership cards in the Great American Prospectors Association to selected notables throughout the U.S. The card read, "This card is a pearl without price . . . guard it as you would your flask. It entitles you to the sacred portals of the Great American Prospectors Association . . . flash it in distress, solemnly saying the mysterious password, 'There's No Alta-tude like Alta.' "

Mayor Watson loved to invite skiers to his small cabin and serve them a special drink, his "ski-ball."

George Watson, the Humorist

Watson, in addition to being one of Utah's greatest ski promoters, was a humorist. He occasionally got a glint of mischief in his steely gray eyes and kept his listeners guessing as to whether he was serious or merely having a little fun. One time he is said to have visited the Salt Lake Stock Exchange and dropped a report on the desk outlining his newest enterprise, Watson Imaginary Enterprises, Inc. In all seriousness, he announced the discovery of a vast vein of "confusilite" at Alta. Without cracking a smile, he continued, "the government in Washington is elated about getting an unlimited supply of confusilite, which is just what they need back there right now."

Mayor Watson also came up with the unique idea of selling "talking" tombstones with compartments for record players so that "visitors could hear the voices of their loved ones, long since gone away." Perhaps one of his most clever ideas was "private gutters." Watson felt that "if a fellow was to sink as low as the gutter, he should at least have the benefit of privacy."

George Watson, seated among his mining friends, early 1900s. Photo courtesy Alta Ski Lifts Company.

During winter months the snow piled up so high that entry to the mayor's cabin was through a special tunnel that included a climb down a fifteen-foot ladder. A sign at the entrance read, "This is the place but watch your first step." Watson kept the contents of the drink totally secret, but those who had one never forgot it. Sverre Engen remembers quite vividly the aftermath of Watson's parties.

"When many guests left Mayor Watson's cabin," he said, "they had to crawl out on their hands and knees because they could not stand up. Once they got to their feet, they would try to ride the rope tow up to the Alta Lodge. That was a sight to behold! The guests at the lodge came out on the porch to watch the spectacle—skiers falling all over the place, but they felt no pain, and all were in a state of pure euphoria."

Watson wrote an article for the *Salt Lake Tribune*, dated December 18, 1938, about the old mining days in Alta that demonstrates (in his unique way) how much the miners enjoyed skiing:

Shaft leading down to Mayor Watson's cabin when snow was deep. Photo courtesy Utah State Historical Society.

Old miner, circa 1880s. Photo courtesy University of Utah J. Willard Marriott Library, Utah Ski Archives, and Alta Historical Society.

Skiing at the turn of the century in Alta was much different than it is now. In those days, our "flipflops," now skis, were not quite so fast, but we could "yump." Ole Norby was our Alf Engen and Axel Jacobsen was good too. I will never forget the big ski championship day we had at Alta in '03. It was held on St. Patrick's Day, and a great day it was, not only for the Irish but the Norwegians as well. Our town hero, "Dub" O'Neil, started celebrating earlier than usual that day and by high noon he was challenging all comers and even challenged Ole Norby. He offered to bet his "Rough and Ready Mine" that he could do a better job coming down Emma Hill or even Rustler Mountain than Axel Jacobsen, and later on in the day, he said, "that goes for Ole Norby, too." To make a long story short, they were on their way past the old Savage Mine and some of them even up as high as the Makay and Revolution Mines. One of them was up on the Montezuma Mine dump, which is at least 250 feet above the Emma mine.

The first thing we knew, he was in the air, flipflops and all. Shortly after him came Ole Norby. What a picture to behold! He was going through the air like an eagle, and right after him came Axel Jacobsen, Swan Neilsen, Carl Larsen, and Paddy Daly. Well anyway, Dub was the last one of them to come down off Emma Hill, and it was a blessing that he lost his six-shooter in falling on the way down, for his time was the longest of any of them and he was very surly for the rest of the day. Well did we know the dangers when Dub was in a surly mood, for even at that early date, he had 13 notches on his six-shooter and the number totaled 17 before the Lord called him in '07.

The "flipflops" Watson referred to were broad boards with leather thongs attached for securing boots. Considering this equipment, Ole Norby, O'Neil, and the others did a great job just getting down the hill in one piece. Watson continued to live in Alta until he died in 1952 at the age of sixty-eight.

Early Utah Ski Clubs

WASATCH MOUNTAIN CLUB

The mountains of the Wasatch, with their high jagged peaks and almost endless trail possibilities, attracted hikers and climbers early in the nineteenth century. In 1912 Charles T. Stoney, a coach at Brigham Young University, founded the Wasatch Mountain Club. He and other outdoor enthusiasts made treks in the Wasatch Mountains near Park City, Brighton, and Alta. According to Utah ski historian Alexis Kelner, the group was "composed of artists, scientists and scholars, photographers and writers, teachers, doctors, and business people." They loved the outdoors and the adventure of hiking over a distant mountain pass. During the summer of 1917, the group assembled on Catherine's Pass, the divide between Brighton and Alta. Dr. W. H. Hopkins, one of the club's earliest members, suggested expanding activities to more than summer months. They decided to start experimenting with skis during the winter.

At first the club stayed mainly in the canyons nearest Salt Lake City. Emigration Canyon was a favorite place. Club members braved longer expeditions in the 1920s, going as far north as Ogden

Members of the Wasatch Mountain Club on one of their many ski outings.

Canyon and as far south as Provo Canyon. Ski trips from Park City to Brighton were especially popular. The outings usually lasted several days with only men involved. They boarded the Denver and Rio Grande train at the station in Sugarhouse, near the mouth of Parleys Canyon, and rode to Park City, a distance of twenty miles. From there, they put on skis and traveled to the Comstock Boarding House at the Comstock Mine in Thayne's Canyon. The following day, they crossed over the pass to Brighton and stayed the second night at a Salt Lake waterworks station. On the third day, they skied back to the Salt Lake Valley via Big Cottonwood Canyon. Some of the more adventurous continued from Brighton to the Alta Cardiff Mine and then to the bottom of Little Cottonwood Canyon. This trip normally involved an additional two days, if the weather cooperated.

Even with today's equipment, this itinerary requires skiing ability and physical endurance, and

Emblem of the Utah Ski Club.

the equipment the men of the Wasatch Mountain Club had was primitive. The skis were handmade with a leather toe strap to attach the boot; some of the members made heel straps from rubber inner tubes. At first the club members patterned their ski techniques after the miners, using a single long pole for stability. Because of the length of the skis, however, they went straight down the mountainside. Turning was not a consideration, but it wasn't long before the Wasatch Mountain Club acquired more sophisticated equipment and learned to turn and, thus, navigate.

The Wasatch Mountain Club had only a few hardy members. The general population of Salt Lake City and surroundings remained unaware of the club's ski touring; skiing, especially ski jumping, was a sport only for strong, slightly crazy men, according to public opinion.

UTAH SKI CLUB

Another early club that influenced the development of skiing in Utah was the Norwegian Young Folks Society, sometimes referred to as N.U.F. Sportslag. In 1915 several young Norwegians came to Utah to settle, including Martinius "Mark" A. Strand, Axel Andresen, Chris M. Christoffersen, Bernt Hovik, O. G. Jorgensen, and the brothers John and Carl Berntsen. This group started ski-jumping competitions in the Intermountain area. Once a year they held a tournament at Dry Canyon near Fort Douglas, now part of the upper campus of the University of Utah in Salt Lake City.

In 1920 the name of the Norwegian Young Folks Society was changed to the Norwegian-American Athletic Club. (The organization not only conducted ski-jumping events but managed the Vikings, a professional soccer team.) In 1928 Andresen moved to change the name of the club again, this time to the Utah Ski Club. The goal was to attract world-class jumpers to competitions in Utah.

Utah's Early Ski Promoters

Three men played a particularly important part in the development of skiing in the Intermountain West—Mark Strand, Pete Ecker, and Joe Quinney.

MARTINIUS "MARK" A. STRAND

Probably no other individual in the Intermountain region during the first half of the twentieth century had a greater influence on the promotion of skiing than Mark Strand. He would talk about the virtues of

Martinius "Mark" Strand, circa 1950.

skiing, particularly in Utah, to anyone who would listen: school officials, newspaper editors, the Salt Lake Chamber of Commerce, out-of-state ski officials, and even young children. He loved the sport, wanted everyone else to enjoy it, and if he could make a buck or two from it, so much the better. He was considered a promoter's promoter, known throughout Utah.

Strand emigrated from Drammen, Norway, in the early 1900s and settled in the Great Salt Lake Valley. Not long after arriving, he quickly recognized the skiing potential of the area: wonderful mountains, great snow conditions, and relatively mild temperatures when compared to the Old Country.

In 1914 he and a few other Norwegians held the first ski-jumping tournament in Utah at Dry Canyon. Being the good promoter he was, he was able to draw crowds of two hundred or more to come and watch the jumpers perform.

In 1929 Strand, more than anyone else, was responsible for bringing the professional ski jumpers to Utah and starting professional ski jumping throughout the western part of the United States. In the late 1930s he was also involved in constructing the nation's second chairlift at Alta.

PETER S. ECKER

A native of Norway, Pete Ecker came to the United States in 1917 and moved to Utah at the age of twelve. He established the Ecker Photo Studio and became well known as an expert photographer.

He also became very involved in early ski jumping and competed in one of the first tournaments at Dry

Peter Ecker,
early to
mid-1930s.

S. Joseph
Quinney,
circa 1960.

Canyon Hill in 1918. He was willing to work hard for the sport he loved and left his imprint on Utah jumping. Virtually every major ski-jumping event in the 1930s was secured and organized by either Ecker, Strand, or both. Ecker was president of the Utah Ski Club for many years and played a key role in bringing Utah its first amateur National Ski-Jumping Championship in 1937. Ecker Hill, which was named after him because he had contributed so much to the sport, became one of the most famous jumping hills in the world.

S. JOSEPH QUINNEY

S. Joseph Quinney was born in Logan, Utah, in 1892 and became well known as a skiing and ski-jumping promoter in the late 1920s and 1930s, when he began to associate with Strand, Ecker, the Engen brothers, and the rest of the Norwegian community of ski jumpers.

Quinney was a prominent attorney and civic leader. Elected to the Utah House of Representatives in 1921, he was well versed about state land laws, particularly as they applied to Forest Service holdings. This expertise became valuable to the ski industry later. Quinney served as judge for many of the tournaments held in the 1930s, and was one of the Utah Ski Club's strongest presidents, serving from 1935 to 1938.

In 1936 Felix Schaffgotsch, an Austrian count retained by Averell Harriman, came through Utah looking for a potential site for a future winter sports

Pete Ecker jumping on
Dry Canyon Hill, circa 1918.

Poster of one of the first Utah ski-jumping tournaments at Dry Canyon Hill.

Jumping in Utah

In January 1915, when Strand and a few other Norwegians held the first tournament at Dry Canyon, one of his friends claimed he could "promote a successful ski tournament with only a bucket of ice, two barrel staves, an ant hill, and a couple of fellow Norwegians!" The earliest documented ski-jumping event in Utah was held on Sunday, January 16, 1915, on a small hill near Dry Canyon. A newspaper article of the time credits Chris M. Christoffersen, chairman of the ski-jumping club, for establishing Utah's first tournament. Edvin Rosenberg won with a jump of fifty feet. Axel Andresen jumped seventy feet but fell and placed second. In 1918 Andresen won the Utah amateur jumping title with a seventy-eight-foot leap. This record stood until 1925, when Bill Hendricksen broke it by seven feet, jumping eighty-five feet. In 1927 Andresen again recaptured the Utah title with a leap of eighty-six feet. The public loved the daring and courage of these men: two hundred spectators showed up for the first tournament; by 1918 the number had grown to more than a thousand.

recreation area being planned by the Union Pacific Railroad. Quinney showed the count several local sites, but Sun Valley, Idaho, was ultimately chosen.

Disappointed but still determined to promote winter sports in Utah, Quinney and a few other enthusiasts formed the Salt Lake Winter Sports Association and designated Alta as a ski resort. Quinney organized the group, performed the legal work, and served as secretary-treasurer from 1939 to 1958 and president from 1958 until his death in 1983.

In recognition of his love for skiing and his contribution to the sport, Quinney was inducted into the National Ski Hall of Fame in 1975. In part, the citation reads, "His promotion of the sport has covered a span of more than 50 years, the period in which ski pioneers such as Joe Quinney successfully bridged the promotion gap between the old days of carrying long wooden skis up an endless mountain, to a complex of high-speed chair lifts carrying thousands daily to their favorite runs high on the mountains."

These three men (and many others) were crucial in furthering skiing as a sport. It was a sport still difficult for the average downhill skier, however. Although cross-country skiers are willing to climb slopes, and their equipment lends itself to the task, downhill skiers have to have a way to get up the mountain. Anyone who's had to climb even a few yards up a hill on skis—sidestepping like crazy—knows how difficult this can be, and ski boots are definitely not suited for walking. If the sport were to grow, some means had to be found to transport skiers.

Ski Jumping Expands in Utah

THE RASMUSSEN RANCH

In the summer of 1927 Strand, Ecker, and Andresen asked the Rasmussen brothers—Frank, James, and Lawrence—if they could establish a jumping facility at the Rasmussen ranch near Parleys Summit. Snow there was more predictable

Welcome Inn, which catered to early
Utah ski jumpers in the 1930s.

The Rasmussen brothers—
Frank, James, and Lawrence.

The Rasmussen jumping-hill scaffold, constructed back of
the Welcome Inn for children to learn to jump, circa 1929.

Three promising young jumpers standing
on the outrun of Ecker Hill, circa 1930.

Gus Becker, circa 1928.

than at Dry Canyon, and winter conditions lasted
longer, they reasoned. The Rasmussens operated the
Welcome Inn and encouraged the construction of
jumping hills on their property because of the business
and publicity the tournaments would bring.

The first ski-jumping hill at the Rasmussen ranch
was built by the Rasmussen brothers, who used a
wooden scaffold for the inrun. It was located in what
is now Pinebrook Estates. This small jumping
hill was used by children about six to fourteen years
of age. Construction began in mid-1928 on the
other jumping hill at the Rasmussen ranch in the
Snyder Basin area, not far from Park City, for more
experienced adult jumpers.

On February 22, 1929, the first ski-jumping
tournament was held. Two events were scheduled:
cross-country races started at 11:00 A.M. with jumping
beginning at 2:30 P.M. Everyone was invited to attend
and no advance formal applications were required to
compete. Gilbert Swensen set a new Utah amateur
record of ninety-two feet. According to records, the
jumping arena could accommodate a thousand cars.
Total attendance was often double that.

BECKER HILL

In 1929 Gus Becker, who operated a brewery in
Ogden—then a small community forty miles north
of Salt Lake City—was appointed by the Ogden
Chamber of Commerce to chair the Ogden Winter
Sports Committee. The committee's charter was to
put on an event in the Ogden area to promote and
stimulate business.

Becker and Strand had attended the annual
American Dog Day Festival in Ashton, Idaho, for
several years. Some of America's top dog-sled teams
competed for money and other prizes at the festival,
and the notoriety had put Ashton on the map. Becker
had a similar festival in mind for Ogden, and Strand
sold him on the idea of building a jumping hill and
bringing in some of the world's top ski jumpers.

A meeting was held at Pete Ecker's home to
discuss how to bring professionals from the Midwest
to Utah. Those present decided to bring the Utah Ski
Club into the America Ski Association so additional
money could be raised outside of Utah to help pay
for the professional jumpers' expenses. (The America
Ski Association had been formed in the late fall of

Several of the first professional ski jumpers of America, 1929: (left to right) Sigurd Ulland, Alf Engen, Halvar Hvalstad, Halvor Bjørngaard, Steffan Trøgstad, Anders Haugen.

1928 to conduct major ski-jumping events.)

The Utah Ski Club made arrangements for several of the professional jumpers from Minneapolis to come early to help construct the hill. Sverre Engen was one of the builders and remembers that he and fellow jumper Halvar Hvalstad made moonshine on the side. "There were days when not too much work was accomplished," Sverre remembers, chuckling. "Halvar was the *brew meister,* and there were two crocks which were kept in ice-cold water that flowed from one of the old mine shafts nearby. One was used in the brewing stage, and the other was for sipping and had a cup attached to it. Whenever we got a little thirsty, you can guess where we went. As the day progressed and became warmer, the trips to the crock became much more frequent. By afternoon our priorities had shifted from actually working on the hill to just discussing the next day's plan. As I think about it, it is remarkable

Becker Hill billboard: (left to right) Sverre Engen, Halvar Hvalstad, and Halvor Bjørngaard, circa 1930.

Becker Hill, 1930.

1930 Becker Hill Tournament Results

At that time the world's professional ski-jumping record was 229 feet, set by Henry Hall of Detroit, Michigan, in the 1920s at Revelstoke, Canada. A two-thousand-dollar bonus prize had been raised as an incentive for the jumpers to break Hall's record—a substantial sum in those days. Fourteen professional jumpers competed. Unfortunately, Hall's world record did not fall that day. The top five places were Sigurd Ulland (140 feet), Alf Engen (137 feet), Anders Haugen (125 feet), Lars Haugen (122 feet), and Sverre Engen (119 feet).

was held along with ski jumping. The festival lasted for three days.

On January 19, 1930, the new jumping hill in Ogden Canyon was dedicated. It was christened Becker Hill in honor of the man who had devoted considerable time and energy getting the hill built and the exhibition organized. At the time of the dedication, Becker Hill was touted as one of the largest in the world. It measured 489 feet from the takeoff to the transition in the jumping hill.

Another tournament held at Becker Hill on February 16, 1930, was a significant event because, through the efforts of Pete Ecker, Mark Strand, and a few others, the remainder of the original professional jumping team traveled from Westby, Wisconsin, to compete for prize money. They included Halvar Hvalstad, Alf Matisen, Anders Haugen, Steffen Trøgstad, Sigurd Ulland, Ted Rex, and Alf and Sverre Engen.

ECKER HILL

After the completion of Becker Hill, Sverre stayed in Utah to help build the second, larger hill at the

that we actually got the hill built that summer."

But the hill was finished, and the Ogden event was thought to be the "festival of festivals." It included a three-way partnership with Ogden; Ashton, Idaho; and Lake Tahoe/Truckee, California. A dog-sled race

Sverre Engen displaying his ski-jumping prowess at Becker Hill, 1930.

Rasmussen ranch. The hill was ready for competition in early 1929, but no tournaments were held until March 2, 1930, when two thousand spectators came to watch. Calmar Andreasen set a new amateur Utah jumping record of 114 feet. In the professional class, Halvar Hvalstad won the event with a 142-foot jump; Sigurd Ulland placed second, jumping 141 and 133 feet; and Steffen Trøgstad placed third with jumps of 135 and 136 feet. According to newspaper accounts, "Every one of the fans left the canyon site feeling that their time had been well spent."

Alf Engen, only twenty years old, made the longest jump of the day. He amazed the crowd with a 164-foot jump, the longest recorded so far on that hill. Unfortunately, he fell on landing and placed eighth in the competition.

At this tournament the Utah Ski Club named the jumping hill in honor of its new president, Pete Ecker. George H. Dern, then governor of Utah, delivered the dedication address prior to the competition; however, efforts began almost immediately to relocate the hill so jumpers could fly greater distances the next ski

Early Ecker Hill, 1930, now surrounded by Pinebrook Estates, located just past Parleys Summit.

season. Also during 1930 the jumpers dissolved the America Ski Association and created a new national organization—the Western America Winter Sports Association (WAWSA). President Ecker

Mel Fletcher at the Rasmussen ranch near the Welcome Inn, circa 1938–39. Photo courtesy Mel Fletcher.

applied for WAWSA membership in late December 1930 so that Utah could hold formal, sanctioned competitive events.

CREOLE HILL

In the early 1930s, the Park City miners decided to build a ski-jumping hill near the Creole Mine on a hillside overlooking Park City. Mel Fletcher, a noted Park City ski jumper from the late 1930s through the 1950s, remembers that the work involved in preparing the jumping hill was so difficult and sometimes the men got so tired that "they were physically unable to jump until another day. The jumpers were only able to go a maximum of approximately eighty feet on Creole Hill, but that was considered a long jump in those days."

MEL FLETCHER, PARK CITY SKI PIONEER

Fletcher was born in 1918 and became interested in skiing in 1924 when he watched, from his grandmother's front porch, some of the Park City miners skiing straight down the nearby hillside on long boards. For balance they held a seven- to eight-foot-long wooden pole.

Fletcher wanted to try it. One day he found an old

pair of skis belonging to a neighbor and strapped them on. The ten-foot-long skis had only leather toe straps for bindings. He had a very difficult time navigating, but eventually his father got him a new pair of six-foot skis, which he valued as one of his prized possessions.

Skiing continued to grow in Park City throughout the 1920s partly because a friendly carpenter in the town made skis for the townspeople, says Fletcher. "I remember how impressed I was with the way this man made the skis. I remember watching him saw the pieces from old logs and put the wooden slats into press molds to form them after they had been softened in boiling-hot water."

Fletcher learned to ski jump on Creole Hill. Occasionally, the Norwegians from nearby Ecker Hill—including Alf and Sverre Engen, Einar Fredbo, Lars Haugen, Halvar Hvalstad, and a few others—staged jumping exhibitions there. Fletcher "found it very interesting just listening to them communicate with each other in the Norwegian language and talk to the townspeople in broken English. But they were always very polite, and everyone who met them looked forward to their return each season to put on their show."

Fletcher soon had enough experience on Creole Hill and moved down the road a short distance to the Rasmussen ranch to try out the small jumping hill, the one that had a scaffold for an inrun. He remembers a harrowing experience he had. "I had just started down the scaffold inrun when I saw Frank Rasmussen cross the hill right in front of the takeoff," he said. "The tail of my skis actually hit his shoulders, and I took a terrible spill which completely knocked the air out of my lungs. The other jumpers came running over to see if I was still alive. I was, and I survived but gained a healthy appreciation for how easy it was to injure yourself.

"Those were truly fun days in the early 1930s," he remembers. "Our whole life in the wintertime centered around going to the Rasmussen ranch to ski jump and watch the big boys—the professional jumpers who were jumping on the big Ecker Hill not far away. I remember some of the young boys did not have any money but wanted to watch the ski-jumping tournaments on Ecker Hill, which required a fee. So they would hike way around the back of the hillside where the jumps were conducted and watch from a distance."

In 1997 Fletcher related his first jumping experience off the big takeoff on Ecker Hill. "I was president

John Spendlove standing on the Creole Hill takeoff at Park City,
circa early 1930s. Photo courtesy Park City Museum.

of the Snow Park Ski Club at the time, and a number of us had entered one of the big tournaments. Since there were so many competitors in the B Class, the tournament organizer, Mark Strand, told us that some of the jumpers were going to have to come off the big takeoff. So since I was president of the club, I said I would go and asked the other jumpers if any wanted to go with me. I talked John Spendlove, Cornell Diamond, Don Young, and Bill Bailey into going.

"Boy, what a thrill it was! All I can remember was when I took off in the air, it felt like I had a man pushing on my chest, and I could not get up over my skis and stay there because the pressure of the air was so much greater than anything I had ever experienced. I managed to stay on my feet, and I remember what a great sense of accomplishment I felt when I came to a stop at the bottom of the hill. Over the next several years, I went over the big takeoff a number of times, but I always had a feeling that what I was doing was something very special that only a relatively few courageous individuals would ever have the opportunity to experience."

Ski jumpers traveled from Salt Lake City to stage tournaments in Park City during the late 1920s and early 1930s. Alf, who was an established ski star by this time, remembers several trips to Park City during the early 1930s in which he put on jumping exhibitions at the base of Creole Hill. After an exhibition, he "would help the little kids who came to watch" by showing them how to s████. "I loved the kids, and I think they liked me, too. I always enjoyed helping them. They were so excited to see us when we came and always thanked us. One of the young Park City fellows, Mel Fletcher, later became a very good Utah ski jumper."

Fletcher has contributed to skiing history in many ways over the past seventy-plus years. He directed the ski school at Snow Park (now Deer Valley) from 1952 to 1964, and was ski-patrol director at the Park City ski resort from 1965 to 1977. In addition he was a key player in getting Ecker Hill on the Utah Historical Register in 1986. Today the Ecker Hill jumping era is only a memory, but Mel Fletcher remains one of the Park City pioneers who played a meaningful role in local skiing history.

THE NORWEGIAN INFLUENCE

Norwegian skiers were the standard of excellence for all competitions that involved ski jumping and

Alf Engen at Creole Hill in Park City with some of his favorite people—children, 1932.

cross-country skiing in the early 1920s. They were trendsetters and influenced the way competitions were conducted and scored in Europe and America. The Haugen brothers, for example, stood at the forefront in the United States in the early 1920s. Lars, the oldest, won virtually every national title. His brother, Anders, became a member of America's first Olympic winter team and eventually brought the United States its first Olympic ski-jumping medal.

All of this influenced ski jumping in the Intermountain West. When early Utah ski jumpers, such as Axel Andresen, Carl Berntsen, and Mark Strand, gathered at Dry Canyon, they had mental images of how the "big boys" were doing it and, according to Strand, said to themselves, "Someday soon, we'll have our own ski-jumping champions who can compete with the world's best, and Utah will also become recognized as a jumping mecca." Perhaps at the time this dream was wishful thinking; perhaps it was vision; but the rest, as they say, is history. ❄

chapter four

BARNSTORMING AND WORLD RECORDS:
Ski Jumping in the 1930s

Ski jumpers in the United States played an important role in gaining worldwide attention for the sport of skiing. Whether in the Midwest, the Far West, the Northeast, or the Intermountain region, the jumpers in the 1930s drew hundreds of thousands of spectators, creating excitement and interest in the sport. Whether professionals or amateurs, they were daredevils—charismatic showpeople who attracted crowds and gave the people what they wanted.

Those were the barnstormer days,
when men were men,
and most were
crazy as hell.

— *Jack Walker*
Cofounder, Mt. Olympus Ski Club

Fame came with a price. In spite of the tremendous skill and daring displayed by these jumpers in the 1930s, many sustained injuries that pained them for the rest of their lives. Two outstanding young men died. All were destined to fly and will be remembered not only for showcasing ski jumping to the world but also for the whistle of the wind against their bodies as they flew overhead.

World Records Established

On New Year's Day 1931 at Ecker Hill, a crowd of twenty-five hundred watched Alf Engen break the world's professional ski-jumping record—not once but twice. On his second official jump of the tournament, he went 231 feet, eclipsing the previous world record by two feet. Then, on his third and final jump, he shattered the world record again with a spectacular 247-foot leap, eighteen feet farther than the established record of 229 feet set eleven years earlier. Alf won the tournament; Halvor Bjørngaard was second; Halvar Hvalstad, third; Einar Fredbo, fourth; and Sverre Engen, fifth.

Ecker Hill had been remodeled the previous summer. It had an 800-foot inrun and a 20-foot-high takeoff. To clear the knoll, a jumper had to fly approximately 150 feet. The underhill (the landing area) was 300 feet long. The outrun was 300 to 350 feet. The designers set the incline of the underhill at thirty-six degrees.

The Utah Ski Club had applied for membership in the Western America Winter Sports Association (WAWSA) one week earlier, but the application had not yet been approved. Nevertheless, the club submitted a special petition to obtain formal recognition for Alf's record performance that day. Unfortunately, his jump was never accepted in the official record books; however, this would not be the only time he leaped farther than anyone else in the world.

On January 24–25, 1931, a two-day competition was held at Ogden's Becker Hill. On the first day, Einar Fredbo won the tournament and set a new hill record of 203 feet. This mark became the longest official jump ever made on that hill. Alf Engen was second with a 200-foot leap; Halvor Bjørngaard was third, jumping 180 feet; Sverre Engen was fourth, jumping 167 feet; Alf Matisen was fifth with a leap of 154 feet. On the second day, Alf Engen won the tournament with a 190-foot leap.

The next major ski-jumping tournament was held at Big Pines, California, on February 1, 1931. Alf Engen jumped 243 feet and again beat the official world jumping record. This time the tournament was officially sanctioned by the WAWSA, and his leap was immediately accepted as an official world record, eliminating the need for recognition of his earlier jump at Ecker Hill on New Year's Day.

Alf Engen jumping at Big Pines, California, 1931.

The *Los Angeles Examiner* ran an article by Maxwell Stiles the next day:

> Feb. 1 [1931]—Alf Engen, Viking son of Norway and representing Salt Lake City, Utah, today smashed all official competitive world records in the ski jump to thrill a throng of 25,000 people gathered from all parts of Southern California for the final day of the fifth annual Winter Sports Carnival at Big Pines.
>
> Gaining a speed of 90 miles an hour down a 700-foot runway, the daring and nimble-footed Engen shot out like a clay pigeon into the chill mountain air to land on a 39-degree hill 243 feet beyond the takeoff. Engen finished standing up far down the apron, 1,400 feet from the top of the runway while thousands cheered his gallant and record-smashing effort.

Shortly following his sterling performances at Ecker Hill, Becker Hill, and Big Pines, the WAWSA designated Alf Engen as the undisputed national professional ski champion. Behind Alf in the standings were Halvor Bjørngaard, second; Sverre Engen, third; Ted Rex, fourth; and Lars Haugen, fifth.

On February 12, 1931, the Utah Ski Club received word that the world body in Norway had officially credited Alf's 247-foot leap at Ecker Hill. The note went on to say, however, that the record had since been eclipsed by Birger Ruud, who had jumped 76.5 meters (251 feet, 7 inches) at Oddnes Hill, Norway, on January 19, 1931. World records were being set at an accelerated pace. The eyes of the world were now on Utah and Alf Engen as enthusiasts anxiously awaited another world-record attempt.

During the summer of 1931, Sverre Engen worked with Lars Haugen to again extensively remodel Ecker Hill and make it the hill most likely to produce new world records. In a newspaper interview, Haugen said, "We measure the quality of a ski hill by the results which it produces, and since this hill will probably lead to the best records, we can call it the best hill. There will be none finer, even in the Old Country."

Sometime between late November and early December 1931, Sigmund Ruud, Birger's brother, surpassed Birger's mark by unofficially leaping to a new world record of 265 feet while competing in

Einar Fredbo, Sverre Engen, and Lars Haugen rebuilding Ecker Hill, circa 1931.

Germany. The gauntlet was thrown down, and Alf never backed away from a challenge.

His first opportunity came on December 20, 1931, again at Ecker Hill. Although this competition was not a sanctioned event, Alf raised the ante by making the "world's longest known leap," as a *Salt Lake Tribune* headline boasted, not once but four times. The first time Alf jumped, he flew 253 feet, surpassing his previous best effort of 247 feet. His second jump of 256 feet broke the record he had just set. His fourth jump was an impressive 264 feet. Then, on his final attempt of the afternoon, he surpassed all known records, official or unofficial, with a 266-foot jump. The jump could not be formally recognized because the competition was unsanctioned, but it did stand as an official record for Ecker Hill. The *Salt Lake Tribune* carried the story: "Born with the heritage of his famed Norse forefathers, Alf Engen of Salt Lake City emblazoned his name across the modern pages of athletic endeavor Saturday with a 266-foot ski jump at Ecker Hill in Parleys Canyon that awakened memories of those courageous Norwegian pioneers of old."

The year 1931 proved to be a record-breaking and pivotal one for Utah. Perhaps jumper Axel Andresen, vice-president of the Utah Ski Club, summed things up best:

> Without one ounce of exaggeration, the skiing season at Ecker Hill during the past year was the greatest in the history of the Intermountain country and can rightfully be

called one of the greatest in the world for two reasons. First, the breaking of three globe records, and second, the establishment of an unofficial all-time record. Engen's record has resulted in a flood of inquiries from the United States and Europe concerning the conditions of the hill and interest in Utah.

The 1932 jumping season kicked off on January 2 and 3 with a tournament on Ecker Hill. By this time the locals in Salt Lake City and surrounding countryside were actively following each tournament, anticipating Alf's next professional world record. Advertising and notices appeared in papers, and flyers were hung all over town, whipping up public anticipation as well as offering advice.

On Saturday, January 2, Alf Engen won the tournament in the professional class with a jump of 239 feet. Sigurd Ulland was second; Halvar Hvalstad, third; Sverre Engen, fourth; and Ted Rex, fifth. On Sunday, January 3, Alf again won the professional class with two official leaps of 234 feet. No new records were set that day, but more than twenty-five hundred fans attended, the largest crowd ever gathered at Ecker Hill.

In late January the pro jumpers returned to Big Pines, California, for another ski spectacular. Many regarded that hill as the largest ski jump in the world. Whether that was an established fact is questionable, but it was certainly one of the largest ones around. Thousands of jumping fans came from Southern California, hoping to witness a new world record. They were not disappointed. The local newspaper carried the story:

> On Friday, January 30, 1932, Alf Engen again caused the crowd to roar its approval. He flew into the history books at Big Pines with a 257-foot leap. On February 4, 1932, A. F. Warden, Secretary of the Western America Winter Sports Association, made the announcement that the jump was being recognized as the world's professional record.

Canada's Nels Nelsen vs. America's Alf Engen

One of the most highly publicized events on Ecker Hill in 1932 involved a contest between Alf and Nels Nelsen, Canadian professional ski-jumping champion. The hoopla started when David Orr, secre-

tary of the Revelstoke Ski Club in British Columbia, sent a letter to the editor of the *Salt Lake Tribune* on behalf of Nelsen, challenging Alf to a jumping match. A couple of weeks later, Alf accepted. After reviewing the competition schedule, officials of the WAWSA and members of the Utah Ski Club decided that February 21, 1932, would be the day for this challenge jump.

Alf had just set the new American and professional ski-jumping record at Big Pines. Nelsen had set a world ski-jumping record in 1925 in his hometown of Revelstoke. He was thirty-six years old and five feet, six inches tall. He worked part of the year as a trainman for the Canadian Pacific Railroad, but during winter months he fully dedicated his time to his main love, flying high in the air on skis. He was considered a national hero in Canada, just as Alf was in the United States. The contest was viewed as an epic battle between two world-class champions.

The takeoff on Ecker Hill was raised five feet and moved back about twenty-five feet to prepare for the competition, a change that made three-hundred-foot jumps possible. The other pro jumpers could not resist a chance at such a feat, and many entered the tournament as well.

Nelsen arrived in Salt Lake two days before the tournament. He was friendly enough but gave the distinct air of having definitely come to set a new world record. He was asked by reporters why he had decided to challenge Alf Engen. In an article dated February 20, 1932, in the *Salt Lake Telegram,* written by sportswriter Max Goldberg, Nelsen replied,

> "I decided to challenge him for two reasons. I read about his marvelous jump in all the Canadian papers. And I also read about that big hill outside of Salt Lake City. I haven't had much competition in Revelstoke, winning all my meets there by a margin of 50 or 60 feet. And without much competition, a person doesn't do his best. I figured, with such competition as Alf can give, I can make some really outstanding jumps.
>
> "My aim is to jump 275 feet tomorrow, and I think I can do it. In the first place, I will have the advantage of the high altitude here which makes ski jumping easier. That should lengthen my jump 30 to 50 feet. And if the hill has been repaired, like I've heard it has to make jumps of 300 feet possible, I think I will

be able to do around 275 feet."

"How do you account for the altitude helping you?" he was asked.

"Well," he explained, "the air pressure is heavier back in Revelstoke. The altitude there is only 1,400 feet while [at] Ecker Hill it's around 4,000 feet. The lightness of the air here will make jumping much easier."

Nelson obviously had not realized the true difficulties of competing at a higher altitude: shortness of breath and reduction in stamina. Two days was not nearly enough time to acclimate.

The first day of the tournament was sunny, but strong crosswinds made jumping very hazardous. Consequently, the officials and jumpers decided not to use the large "A" takeoff but rather the "B" instead. This did not please spectators, who had hoped to see history made.

Halvar Hvalstad took the day with a 210-foot jump. Alf followed with a 200-foot leap, and Sverre Engen finished third at 192 feet. Nels Nelsen jumped 159 feet, finishing well back in the field. It was decided by the officials to have another tournament the following day but on the A takeoff, weather permitting.

Monday, February 22, dawned clear and calm. The jumpers prepared for their first chance at breaking 300 feet, but it was not to be. Halvar Hvalstad again won the tournament in the professional class, flying 248 feet with excellent form. Alf finished second, even though he had the longest jump of the two-day tournament, 252 feet. His overall form, however, was not as good as Hvalstad's and cost him the meet. Sverre finished third again with a 222-foot jump.

And what of Nels Nelsen? Well, he had his problems. Max Goldberg followed up his previous story in the *Salt Lake Telegram* with the comments "Nels Nelsen, Canadian champion, incurred an ankle injury on his first effort, which kept him out of competition for the remainder of the day. He spanned 215 feet when he fell."

Despite his high hopes, clearly the experience had not yielded the kind of results Nelsen had expected. He returned to Canada without the record he had come to set. But before leaving Salt Lake City, Nelsen was liberal with his praise of the entire group who performed on Ecker Hill, stating, "This group of skiers is the best in the world, and competition is of the highest type."

Johanna Kolstad, women's world ski-jumping champion in the mid-1930s.

Pro/Am Records Established

The year 1933 saw the establishment of new amateur and professional jumping records. On February 26, 1933, at Ecker Hill, Calmar Andreasen established himself as one of the finest amateur jumpers in Utah's history. He surprised even his most ardent supporters by jumping 174 feet, a jump much longer than the 144 feet he had previously set as Utah's amateur jumping record.

In that same year, Johanna Kolstad, a young Norwegian woman, stated her intention to jump the big hill at Ecker in a noncompetitive exhibition. She lived up to her promise, jumping 115 feet on her first try. She leaped 113 feet on her second try and flew an amazing 135 feet on her last jump. She turned twenty the same day.

Although Kolstad's accomplishment was extraordinary, the highlight of the day proved to be another world record-breaking jump by Alf Engen. A newspaper carried the story:

Engen Breaks World Mark

It was Engen's day. After opening the meet by a beautiful twin jump with Miss Johanna Kolstad of Norway, feminine world's champion, he took up the pursuit of a new record. With the giant takeoff moved back from its usual resting place, Engen jumped 245 feet for his first attempt. Again he leaped and 254 feet was the result. Once more, the crowd roared at the announcement that Engen had shattered his recognized mark with a distance of 261 feet. But this was not enough for Alf. Again he trudged up the steep incline, and again he broke additional ground for the runway. On every leap, Engen had been going a little higher for his takeoff, and this was to be his supreme effort. There was drama in this fourth jump of the great skier, and the crowd sensed it immediately. From far up the hill Engen came, speeding to the giant takeoff, and the excited spectators cheered while he was still in midair, for it was evident to anyone along the side that this leap was much farther than any preceding effort. With Alf's perfect landing, it hardly needed the confirmation of Victor Johansen and Nord Nordquist, who measured the distance [of 281 feet], to convince the assembled winter sports enthusiasts that they had seen the world's greatest ski jump.

Following Alf's historic jump, he was asked by the press to describe the life of a professional ski jumper. He responded by saying, "It's just plain work, mixed with thrills induced by the knowledge that you

Calmar Andreasen (foreground) with fellow ski jumpers, circa 1933.

might break your neck at any time. It's fun jumping even as far as 200 feet. But when you try to go any farther than that, the possibility of serious injury is so great that most of the joy is taken out of the sport. But still, when you get by the first two or three tournaments of a season, you become used to it—and, well, I guess I get a kick out of it anyway."

In March 1933, Alf and Sverre's mother, Martha Engen, and their younger brother, Corey, then only seventeen, immigrated to the United States and settled in Utah. The Utah Ski Team recruited Corey right away. He competed in all the major tournaments, winning many in his class.

The year 1934, as far as ski-jumping history in the Intermountain area is concerned, stands as the most memorable of all the barnstormer years. Although the Engen brothers were at the forefront, their impact on ski-jumping history went far beyond Utah.

On January 1, 1934, Corey began to make his presence known at Ecker Hill by beating Calmar Andreasen. It was the first time Andreasen had lost in many seasons. Alf and Sverre also gave sterling performances. In the professional class, Alf won the tournament. He was followed by Halvar Hvalstad, and Sverre came in third. In the amateur Class C, a

Alf Engen,
World Professional Champion

Corey Engen,
circa mid-1930s.

Johanna Kolstad (the only woman to jump Ecker Hill) and Alf Engen flying the "B" Hill at Ecker, 1933.

young fourteen-year-old skier by the name of David Quinney, son of the prominent Salt Lake City attorney and ski enthusiast S. Joseph Quinney, showed great potential by placing third behind Karl Chindgren and Jack Walker.

The Eastern Professional Ski-Jumping Tour

Alf and Sverre Engen agreed to participate in three ski-jumping extravaganzas in the eastern United States. Part of the agreement included making sure that the day's events would be spectacular, thereby guaranteeing that thousands would attend. The first event was held in Winsted, Connecticut, on January 14, 1934. The two elder Engen brothers traveled by train across the country from Salt Lake and arrived just a day before the tournament. They were both very tired, and neither had seen the new hill at Winsted, adding to the pressure. Shortly after they arrived, they met two of the top ski jumpers in the East, Anton Lekang and Strand Mikkelsen, who joined them on the three-event tour.

Lekang was born in 1908 in Melbo, Norway, and was a well-known ski flyer in Norway before coming to the United States in 1927. He won the New York State amateur ski-jumping championship his first year

and in 1932 won the national amateur title in Lake Tahoe, California. Mikkelsen, also a Norwegian, had established himself as one of his home nation's finest amateur jumpers. This competition in Connecticut marked his professional ski-jumping debut. Both Lekang and Mikkelsen played key roles in setting up the professional tour.

The tournament at Winsted went off very well, and the *Salt Lake Tribune* ran a story the following day:

> Winsted, Conn., Jan 14 (AP)—On a snow-banked mountainside called "the longest hill in the world," the first professional ski meet of the Winsted Ski Club was held yesterday, with Alf Engen of Salt Lake City winning first money. The only woman competitor, Miss Johanna Kolstad of Oslo, Norway, made a single exhibition jump which was not measured, to carry off the women's prize.
>
> The meet started under ideal conditions with 10,000 persons grouped in cars at the foot of the incline, but flakes were in the air at the halfway mark and competition was halted when three-quarters over by heavy snowfall. However, Engen, with a few other jumpers, decided to jump anyway and started from the

Advertisements for professional ski jumping at Brattleboro, Vermont, circa 1934.

top of the hill in Colebrook River, four miles from Winsted. His first jump carried him 192 feet and his second 163 for a total of 355 feet. Second place went to Strand Mikkelsen of Greenfield, [Massachusetts], with a total of 310 feet for his two jumps. Lekang was third with a two-jump total of 289 feet. The winner's brother, Sverre Engen, of Salt Lake City, was fourth with 286 feet.

On the following weekend, January 20–21, the second tournament on the Eastern Professional Ski Jumping Tour was held at Brattleboro, Vermont. This time the promoters raised the ante, publishing the following advertising: "Alf Engen, Sverre Engen, Anton Lekang and Strand Mikkelsen absolutely guarantee to beat the present record of the hill, 208 feet, now held by Strand Mikkelsen."

The spectators came out in droves. They knew something spectacular had to happen or they would get their money back. Either way they would come out on the winning end of the deal. From the jumpers' point of view, however, this meant they had to put their necks on the line. They would end up with nothing to show for the risk if one of them could not break the hill record. The admission fees would have to be refunded.

The day of the tournament was extremely cold, so cold the jumpers' skis stuck to the snow and would not glide easily. None of the jumpers could come close to setting the promised hill record in these conditions. A giant refund loomed.

Strand Mikkelsen came up with an idea. An old farmhouse stood not far from the jumping hill. He ran over and filled two buckets with water and brought them back to the hill. He and several other jumpers then proceeded to sprinkle water on the takeoff— all the way to the top of the inrun.

The team chose Alf to jump because he offered the best chance of breaking the hill record. Sverre and a couple of others went to the top of the jump scaffold with him. The cold air had frozen the water to ice almost immediately, but the slick ice still wasn't enough to ensure the jump they all needed. They took up positions right behind and in front of Alf. When he was ready, they gave him a giant push/pull, catapulting him down the inrun at a greatly accelerated speed. Sverre laughs when he recounts the story: "I knew Alf was going to go somewhere! I watched him leave the end of the takeoff, and he started to climb. I thought he was going to fly all the way to the old farmhouse a quarter of a mile away. I could not see him land, but I heard hundreds of car horns start to honk. I knew Alf had set a new hill record." Alf jumped 216 feet on that jump and did indeed break the hill record.

The final tournament of the three-week series was again at Winsted, Connecticut, on January 28. This time it wasn't snowing—it was raining and coming down hard. And, of course, the promoters had again promised a hill record or your money back to the crowd of five thousand who had come to watch.

The first jump of the day was made by Anton Lekang. It was only a trial jump, but he flew 195 feet, bettering by three feet the hill record set by Alf two weeks earlier. The crowd went wild! Next came Alf. After his jump, the announcer informed the crowd that he had just gone 200 feet, again setting a new hill record. Because the first two jumps were records, the expectations went up, and so did the spills. Alf fell on his second jump (207 feet), badly twisting his ankle. At the end of the tournament, Strand Mikkelsen came out on top with jumps of 160 and 184 feet.

But the climax of the day came after the tournament. The *Evening Citizen* in Winsted reported the

event in an article on January 29, 1934:

All eyes turned skyward, to the tower's top 1,138 feet up the steep side of Woodruff Hill. Alf Engen, suffering from a wrenched ankle received in his previous spill (said to have been his first in four years), stood silhouetted against the leaden sky on the very top of the tower. Everyone seemed to realize that Alf was about to make his supreme effort of the afternoon.

Alf justified the crowd's expectations, shooting down the slippery slide with the speed of an express train, leaving the take-off with a speed estimated about sixty miles an hour. Engen soared high above the crowd in a marvelous leap of 216 feet. This was, by far, the best of the day and a new hill record for the Winsted Ski Club hill. The spectators certainly received their money's worth, in both thrills and spills.

These jumps ended the year's Eastern Professional Ski Jumping Tour, with plans already made for the following year; however, Alf and Sverre could not stay for discussion. They had to head back to Utah to prepare for Salt Lake City's big jumping tournament, coming up in February at Ecker Hill.

Tragedy on Ecker Hill

Ski jumping is a spectacular but dangerous sport. Even the best and most experienced jumpers can fall prey to the unexpected. Tragedy struck at Ecker Hill during the February 22, 1934, tournament when Calmar Andreasen, the Utah amateur champion, was killed while making his second jump from the large takeoff used by the professional jumpers. On his first jump, he had no difficulty and leaped 161 feet. When he finished his jump, he elatedly told his fellow jumpers that it had been the greatest thrill of his life. On his second jump, something went wrong. Sverre Engen, in his book *Skiing a Way of Life,* described what happened: "I jumped just ahead of him. I was on my way back to the transition of the hill when I saw him come over the takeoff and land upside down on the knoll of the hill, a distance of about 125 feet. As he tumbled the rest of the way to the bottom, it was plain to see that he was badly hurt."

According to Alf Engen, no one knows exactly

Calmar Andreasen on his way to the final jump of his life. Photo by Ralph Johnston. Photo courtesy University of Utah J. Willard Marriott Library, Utah Ski Archives.

what caused the accident. It could have been any number of factors. The wind was blowing that day and could have affected his vision or balance. Mel Fletcher was standing near the big takeoff when Calmar jumped.

"Calmar had a red bandanna around his neck, which was his trademark," Fletcher said. "I saw him coming, but just before getting to the takeoff, part of the bandanna blew up in front of his face. When he left the end of the takeoff, he was still in a crouch position. He tried hard to regain position in the air, but it was too late. The air pressure or a wind gust pushed him backward, and he came down on the knoll upside down. I could not see what happened after that."

Calmar Andreasen died on the way to the hospital less than an hour after the fall. A marker currently stands at the old Ecker Hill outrun as a memorial to Andreasen and a tribute to the jumpers who participated in events there.

The *Salt Lake Telegram* ran the following tribute to Andreasen by sportswriter Frank K. Baker:

A Message to Valhalla

Valhalla's portals have closed on another fallen warrior, but the North Gods were happy today; another gallant warrior had joined their ranks. Released from his mortal abode in a flashing instant of lightning-like speed, this well-beloved son of the north country passed on in the true warrior's manner, buckled in his armor and fighting for victory in his favorite conflict. Calmar Andreasen did not die in the usual manner of mortals, while nestled on the couch of Mother Earth, but was snatched by the Gods in eagle-like flight, and wafted to his waiting place in the warriors' Valhalla on flashing wings. No touch of fear nor period of suffering marked the passage of this valiant soul, but only the indescribable thrill of rapid motion that always stirred the depths of this fearless young man. Mortals may grieve at the loss of their brother, but who can gainsay the will of the Gods.

Courageous sports will ever be the ken of courageous men. Work-a-day recreations pale in comparison with this bird-like gliding on man-made wings. Only those who live in the great outdoors, under the spell of the spreading skies, can know the satisfaction to the sportsman who achieves the ultimate goal of his chosen sport. This feeling came to Calmar in the last moments of his life, and he died imbued with the full glory of that knowledge.

Constructing/rebuilding Ecker Hill, 1934.

Advertising ski-jumping events at Ecker Hill, circa 1934.

Alf's Records on Ecker Hill

Until April 3, 1934, Alf Engen held the officially sanctioned world professional ski-jumping record of 257 feet, set at Big Pines, California. In late April, Mark Strand, then president of the Utah Ski Club, received word from Norway that Sigmund Ruud had exceeded the 300-foot mark. On April 4, 1934, Ruud had leaped 303.5 feet in an officially sanctioned international tournament in Rapece, Czechoslovakia.

In Utah the remaining jumpers immediately planned to remodel Ecker Hill a third time so Alf could have a chance to exceed the 300-foot mark and perhaps set another world record. The plan called for work during the off-season to have the hill ready for a world-record attempt on New Year's Day 1935. Sverre Engen, Lars Haugen, and Halvar Hvalstad worked on the hill that summer. Alf Engen remembered that "the takeoff was moved back approximately thirty feet, not quite as much as initially planned but, with a little luck, sufficient to possibly jump 300 feet." When they were finished, the inrun had also been moved farther up the hill to allow jumpers to gain more speed.

Sverre laughed when he recalled memories of working on the hill that summer: "We had an old Chevrolet truck that we used as an engine to help hoist material such as lumber up the steep landing hill. The engine worked fine, but the old truck had long since died, and we wondered what to do with it when the summer work had been completed. We thought of moving the truck, but that was not easy because of

Utah amateur jumpers, Ecker Hill, 1935: (left to right) Dave Quinney Sr., Vern Nichol, Rowland Walker, A. L. Hamlin, Jack Walker, Alf Engen, Charles Wanless, Bill Bailey, unknown skier. Photo courtesy Jack Walker.

its location. We then thought of disassembling the truck and carting it away piece by piece. No one liked that idea, either. They finally decided to fill the cab with dynamite. You can guess what happened next— we found pieces of the truck blown to the main highway two miles away. No more problem!"

In December 1934 the remodeled Ecker Hill was ready for test jumping in preparation for the New Year's Day world-record attempt. On Christmas Day Alf Engen climbed to the top of the inrun to attempt his first jump on the new slope. "When I got to the top and looked down the inrun, I just knew I was about to go farther than I had ever gone before," he remembered. "I really did not know what to expect because no one had yet tried the hill with the takeoff moved so far back. My biggest fear was not being able to judge the speed and possibly outjump the hill and land on the flat. If that happened, it could cause severe injury or loss of life."

Sverre said that when Alf started down the inrun, all the jumpers and hill markers held their breath. Alf took off and started his flight, landing well down the hill. The markers on the hill yelled to him that he had just gone 296 feet, setting a new record for Ecker Hill. Not until then did Alf feel that someone could actually fly over 300 feet on that hill. Unfortunately,

Professional Ski Jumpers Disband

At the end of the 1934 ski-jumping season, the professional jumpers disbanded. According to Sverre Engen, this was done not for lack of offers to perform but because so many of the jumpers had been hurt and were unable to participate. Sverre says, "This made it harder for the remaining few of us to put on a good tournament. After considering all the options, it was finally agreed that it simply was not possible to continue."

When professional jumping was discontinued, it meant that for those who wished to continue competition jumping, they had to do it as amateurs. In order to obtain amateur status, the professional athletes had to refrain from taking any type of compensation and stay out of sanctioned competition for a minimum of one year. After that, they could then apply for amateur status consideration. A number of professional jumpers did this, including Alf and Sverre Engen. Corey Engen, the youngest brother, never did compete as a professional and therefore was not affected.

no one ever exceeded 300 feet on Ecker in officially sanctioned competition. Bad weather hampered the world-record attempt on New Year's Day 1935. Only the regular tournament could be held. While practicing in early 1935, however, Alf flew 311 feet. No one ever did better on that hill.

Engen Hill Constructed

In late 1935 Mark Strand, then vice-president of the National Ski Association, announced that the association would construct a new jumping hill at the Spruces in Big Cottonwood Canyon. Alf had determined the site for the jumping hill. At the time, the U.S. Forest Service employed him during the summer months to find suitable locations in the Intermountain West for ski areas.

The initial vision for this hill was to build the "world's largest snow jump" and dedicate it in time to host the 1937 U.S. National Ski-Jumping Championship. The association projected leaps of up to 350 feet on this hill and envisioned that Alf would probably be the person making them; however, because of funding constraints caused in part by the Great Depression, the hill was built much smaller than originally planned. It ended up as a forty-meter hill with the longest recorded jump being only 139 feet.

When the hill was dedicated on January 3, 1937, it was named Engen Hill in appreciation of Alf's work on the project. As part of the dedication, Alf and Sverre performed an exhibition jump before the competition began. Whenever a new hill was dedicated in the 1930s and '40s, it was traditional for two or three jumpers to fly side by side and release roses while in the air to commemorate the occasion.

Martha Engen, Alf's mother, had never seen her sons jump. Even when the boys were growing up in Norway, it was more than she could handle. But on the day that Engen Hill was dedicated, Martha decided she had better attend. The next day, the *Salt Lake Tribune* ran a picture of Martha with Alf on one arm and Corey on the other. The newspaper said that Martha "got a real thrill out of watching her boys," and I suppose that thrill was enough. She never watched them jump again.

The Wheaties Trade-off

The year 1936 brought its share of competitive ups and downs to the Intermountain region. But nothing was more disappointing to Alf Engen than being told by Mark Strand that he had been picked to represent the United States on the 1936 Olympic jumping team, only to be informed a short time later that he had been disqualified because his picture had appeared in a Wheaties advertisement.

The ad first came out in late 1935. All those who ate Wheaties saw Alf's face on their cereal boxes. Avery Brundage, head of the United States Olympic Committee, felt that Alf profited substantially from the advertisement. Therefore, in accordance with Olympic protocol favoring a "purist" approach toward amateurism, Alf was not allowed to participate. He often joked about this. "I did not ever get any money for my picture on the Wheaties boxes, but I sure got a lot of Wheaties," he laughed. "Everyone in my family had plenty of Wheaties!"

No one knows how the 1936 Olympic ski-jumping tournament would have turned out had Alf competed. However, one thing can be said for certain: in 1936 Alf Engen was in his ski-jumping prime and considered by many to be the best jumper in the world.

The Wheaties advertisement that prevented Alf Engen from competing in the 1936 Olympics, circa 1935.

Alf Engen jumping on Ecker Hill, 1934.

The 1937 National Ski-Jumping Championship

The National Ski-Jumping Championship came to Ecker Hill in 1937. The Utah Ski Club and the Salt Lake Chamber of Commerce raised thirty-five hundred dollars as a performance guarantee. Extensive efforts were made to get the huge jumping hill ready, and space was cleared to accommodate three thousand cars. One hundred volunteers, mostly Civilian Conservation Corps (CCC) workers, spent weeks prior to the tournament boot-packing the underhill, building the takeoff to absolutely correct specifications, and performing myriad other tasks.

J. F. Griffin, secretary of the United States Ski Association, wrote an article in the 1938 *American Ski Annual* in which he described his feelings about the hill: "I got my glimpse of Ecker Hill for the 1937 championship. As a point of information, I have been jumping on hills in various parts of the United States for many years, but I am willing to admit that what I

saw in that first look gave me something to think about. Needless to say, the size of the hill just awed me, and I know now why Salt Lake City advertises Ecker Hill as one of the largest ski hills in the world."

The competing field consisted of the best jumpers in the world. The top entrant for the national event was Sigmund Ruud from Kongsberg, Norway. He was one of Europe's superstars, along with his brother Birger. In 1936 Sigmund had soared 324 feet unofficially at Plakenska Planina, Yugoslavia. This was the longest jump ever made up to that time. Sigmund had also been an Olympic silver medalist in 1928.

Ruud's primary competition came from Alf and Sverre Engen and Sigurd Ulland from Lake Tahoe, California. Alf and Sigmund had been friends and strong competitors while they were growing up in Norway. This was their first meeting since both had come to the forefront as two of the world's best ski jumpers.

The advance billing touted this to be the greatest ski-jumping tournament ever held in this country, if

Alf Engen in his prime, displaying form typical of the mid-1930s. Photo by Charles Wanless.

A typical view of the takeoff from Ecker Hill during the 1937 U.S. National Ski-Jumping Championships.

not the world. One newspaper writer stated, "The two-day spectacle is expected to be the greatest ever staged (in the true sense of the word) in America. Not even the field at the 1932 Olympic Games at Lake Placid rivals the collection of 25 Class A riders, headed by Sigmund Ruud, famous Norwegian whose presence lends international flavor to the competition."

The rhetoric of the day succeeded. According to newspaper accounts, between eight and nine thousand spectators attended the National Ski-Jumping Championship at Ecker Hill. On February 21 a prelim-

Alf Engen and Sigmund Ruud, friendly competitors, 1937 U.S. National Ski-Jumping Championships at Ecker Hill.

inary meet narrowed the field of jumpers for the official competition the next day. Sigmund Ruud won the competition the first day. The longest jump of the day, however, was made by Alf who flew 237 feet on his second jump. A bad snowstorm hampered visibility the first day, and a number of the competitors fell because they could not see. Alf flew 218 feet on his first jump, but he touched his hand on the landing. Even though this is not considered a fall, there is a significant point deduction, so Alf was out of the running for top honors that day.

The next day everything was ready to crown the new national amateur jumping champion. Alf and Sigmund were focused, just as they had been twenty years previously when they had met in fierce competition as lads in Norway. On the first jump, Sigmund outjumped Alf, going 181 to his 177 feet.

Sigmund's second leap was 232 feet, exceeding his first one by fifty-one feet. Alf watched Sigmund's jump and heard the roar of the crowd. He knew Sigmund must have had a sensational jump. Beating him would be tough. Alf realized that to win he would have to equal or better the existing national amateur record of 240 feet, held at that time by John Elvrum. He knew the hill—he had helped build it. He had set a number of professional world records on it already and knew exactly what he had to do.

With a well-timed powerful leap, Alf flew past the amateur record mark. The crowd again roared its approval. The official announced that Alf had jumped 245 feet. The first to congratulate Alf was Sigmund, saying that this was the finest tournament in which he had ever competed. Later, when the trophies and medals were presented, Sigmund Ruud was asked to speak. He thanked the officials for allowing him to compete and then said, "I have never jumped against such competition. I have never seen anything like it. It was the most real, fighting competition I have ever known. Alf Engen is the most powerful jumper I have ever seen. I really didn't expect to see him go 240, but instead he did that and more, beating my best jump by thirteen feet. I had heard a lot about Alf since he left Norway. I was eager to meet him again in competition. He is a greater competitor even than they say."

He then went on to talk about Ecker Hill: "It is one of the three biggest hills in the world. The other two are Plakenska Planina, Yugoslavia, and Garmisch-Partenkirchen, Germany. Jumps of 325 will be possible on your hill if it is built up in the middle. I would like to help design it."

The first two places were very close—less than two points separated Alf and Sigmund. At a special banquet held the following evening (February 22, 1937), Alf was named the United States national amateur ski-jumping champion and was credited with a new American amateur distance record. It was a very festive affair, and Alf and Sigmund renewed a close and lasting friendship.

The local media stated that the two sportsmen had "brought out the best there is in sport competition." Alf took Sigmund to his plane to say farewell following the dinner. As they said good-bye, Sigmund told his friend, "Alf, there has never been anyone more deserving of winning than you. It has been a lot of fun jumping against you, and I hope that we can compete together again. Good-bye and good luck."

That, however, is not the end of the story. Unknowingly, the judges had used scoring tables based on distances in feet. The international tables, which had been accepted before the national tournament, were based on meters. In March 1937, a month after the national tournament, a protest over the calculations was submitted.

After considerable review using recalculations based on the metric system and use of the FIS tables for distance and style points, the tournament officials determined that seven-tenths of one point separated Alf's and Sigmund's scores, and Sigmund had the edge. In July 1937 Roger Langley, president of the National Ski Association of America, notified Alf that the deci-

Alf and Evelyn Engen, Sun Valley, Idaho, 1937.

sion had been reversed and the national championship title would go to Sigmund. This was a real disappointment to Alf, but he accepted the decision without protest. Alf and Sigmund never had the opportunity to compete again. Sigmund never returned to Utah and passed away in 1994 at his home in Norway.

Significant Interlude

In 1935 a young woman named Evelyn Pack, who attended Davis High School in Kaysville, Utah, arranged for Pete Ecker to take photographs at her high-school junior prom. Ecker told her about a nice young man he knew, Alf Engen.

When Ecker showed up at the prom, he had Alf in tow and introduced him to Evelyn. Things had gone well, and the two began dating. Evelyn knew that Alf was a skier, but she had never been on skis and was in no hurry to learn. That summer Evelyn had headed to college and Alf worked for the Forest Service. They kept in touch but at the time were just friends. The next two years fell into a pattern of letters and visits, nothing too serious, but they also made sure they didn't lose track of each other. Alf spent his winters traveling and competing; Evelyn was attending the University of Utah.

During the summer of 1937, however, it became evident to both Alf and Evelyn that they were slated to be more than friends. One day Evelyn asked Alf if she could have a ride on the back of his skis. "If you marry me," Alf replied, "I'll take you for a ride that will last the rest of our lives." Evelyn said yes, and the two were married on December 23, 1937.

Reidar Andersen, Norwegian champion,
at Ecker Hill, circa 1939.

The 1939 National Combined Championship

In 1939 Ecker Hill was once again host to a national event, this time the Jumping and Cross-Country Combined Championship on February 20–23. The primary contestants included Norwegian champion Reidar Andersen, who had jumped 344 feet, unofficially the longest jump on record in Europe. He was a strong favorite to win, as was Olav Ulland, younger brother of Sigurd, who had jumped at Ecker Hill many times. Olav was one of the young ski-jumping stars in Europe and had bettered the 300-foot mark several times. Alf held more United States hill records than any other skier. Canada also sent its national champion, Tom Mobraaten.

On Monday, February 20, 1939, the cross-country competition was held near Ecker Hill. Skiers covered a distance of eighteen kilometers (11.2 miles). George Gustavson from Placerville, California, won with a time of one hour, thirty-nine minutes, and forty-five seconds. Alf placed second, five minutes behind. Fred Brown of Wilson, Wyoming, was third; Jack Yokel,

fourth; and Lester Wren, fifth. Salt Lake City had three other entrants who finished in the top ten: Dick Kimbell, sixth place; David Quinney, eighth; and Chet Dalgleish, ninth.

Wind was usually a problem at Ecker Hill, but the weather on Wednesday, February 22, 1939, was perfect—a cloudless, calm sky. The competition proved as good as the billing. Reidar Andersen, Norwegian ski-jumping champion, won the Class A jumping event. He jumped 196 and 219 feet in competition and, because of his form, had a total of 226.3 points. Olav Ulland placed second with 220.1 points, and Alf Engen was third with 219.9.

Alf Engen won the U.S. National Jumping and Cross-Country Championship title. He far out-distanced his competition for the two-day event with a total of 422.2 points. Second place went to Lester Wren with 356.8 points, and his brother Gordon placed third with 349.6 points.

Four thousand spectators came to see who would jump the farthest and who would take the competition's combined title. This was one of the largest single-day crowds ever to witness a jumping event at Ecker Hill.

Mt. Olympus Ski Club jumpers, Ecker Hill, 1934: (front row, left to right) Barr Quist, Sharf Sumner, W. W. "Bill" Riter, Tom Todd; (back row) Jimmy Howell, Hall Thompson, Chet Dalgleish, Jack Walker [president], Ed Gorder, Frank Williams, Bill Cowan. Photo courtesy Jack Walker.

Mt. Olympus Ski Club Encourages Young Fliers

Although the well-reported and hard-fought competitions of the 1930s in Utah drew the attention of newswriters, spectators, and fans, they influenced the sport in other and perhaps more far-reaching ways. Jack Walker, one of the early Salt Lake jumpers, speaks about how he got started. As kids, he and his best pal, Vern Nichol, played hooky from school. They left home at 3:30 A.M. and hiked with skis on their backs about five miles to the mouth of Parleys Canyon. From there they hitchhiked to Ecker Hill so they could watch the "big boys" practicing. They tried to emulate them on the smaller takeoffs. After a full day of jumping, they reversed the journey, which got them home around 10:00 P.M.

Walker recounts that once, when they were playing hooky at Ecker Hill, they noticed a couple of older men approaching in dark trench coats. Suspicious that they might be truant officers, the boys quickly went behind the jumping hill down to Rasmussens' Welcome Inn parking lot, where they confirmed their hunch. Parked next to the Welcome Inn was a big shiny sedan with Granite School District markings on both doors.

After a quick discussion, they felt they'd better give themselves up. But first they wanted to show the gentlemen what they could do. They returned to the hill to get in one last jump before being nabbed. To their amazement the truant officers were so impressed with their jumping that they did not turn them in. According to Walker, "The only thing that saved us was the fact that we put on a damn good show for them."

After several years of ski jumping, Walker and Nichol had introduced a number of other young men to the sport. Because of their common love for flying on a pair of wooden skis, in 1932 they decided to form a ski club, which they named the Mt. Olympus Ski Club. Their purpose, according to Walker, was "to offer a degree of support to the Utah Ski Club and the professional ski jumpers by participating in their tournaments as amateurs in the customary A, B, C, and D Classes."

The Utah Ski Club and the professional jumpers enthusiastically accepted this support. The professionals freely offered advice and encouragement to the younger jumpers, who were feeling their way in this new and potentially dangerous but terribly exciting sport. The professionals taught them many things, including secret waxing techniques, timing the leap at the takeoff, the telemark landing, and the difficult transition at the bottom of the jumping hill, assuming you were still on top of your skis when you got there.

WAWSA granted recognition to the Mt. Olympus Ski Club in 1934. This authorized the club to organize and hold its own amateur jumping tournaments. The Utah Ski Club generously offered the use of Ecker Hill. Two consecutive annual jumping tournaments were successfully conducted by the Mt. Olympus Ski Club in 1934 and 1935. Some of the amateur jumpers were permitted to make exhibition jumps off the large ninety-meter hill.

The club held its meetings in a small log cabin built by Walker and his father in 1925. According to Walker, remains of the old log clubhouse can still be seen behind the Cottonwood Mall in Holladay, Utah.

"Business and social meetings were held regularly on Friday nights during the winter months, planning mostly for the coming weekend ski activities, in which transportation to Ecker Hill was paramount," Walker remembers. "The main transportation was usually furnished by Jimmy Howell in his 1931 Model A Phaeton, which was equipped with new 'doughnut' wheels and tires. We lovingly referred to this car as 'the little gem.' I can vividly remember many a trip up and down Parleys Canyon's snow-covered road with both fender wells filled with wooden skis and bamboo poles, the passenger capacity overflowing with fellow jumpers, and the car performing christies on every turn through the expert manipulation of the steering wheel by the ski-imbued driver. Those were the days—days worth remembering. I am glad I was there.

"Vern and I continue to ski and compete together, and if I say so myself, we are still damn good competitors in the seventy-plus age group."

Tragedy Strikes in Minnesota

One other jumper who was a part of the glory years of the 1930s was Paul Bietla, a native of Ishpeming, Michigan. He was among the best United States-born ski jumpers in the 1930s, competing with the finest jumpers of his time and considered one of America's brightest young stars. Sadly, on February 5, 1939, he was fatally injured during a practice jump off a scaffold hill in St. Paul, Minnesota, when he crashed into an iron restraining post.

Alf and Evelyn Engen were there at the time. "It was a sad day for all of the jumpers," Alf recounted. "Paul had been jumping very well. In fact, at the time, he was probably considered the top man to beat in the competition. I don't know if anyone really knows exactly what went wrong other than he lost his balance, fell, and unfortunately slid into a pole or post at the side of the hill. It was more of a freak accident, totally unexpected!"

None of those present thought Bietla's injuries were fatal. "We knew at the time that he had been seriously injured in the fall but certainly did not expect he would die," Alf said. "As I remember, he passed

The Flight of Birds

Capturing the spirit of ski-jumping is a short narrative titled "The Ecstasy of Flight" by an unknown ski jumper from a 1945 issue of Esquire *magazine:*

I have heard aviators talk of the thrill of flight. I have heard them describe the ecstasy that fills man's soul when he leaves the earth and finds himself suddenly, miraculously, in the realm of clouds.

I have heard the young birdmen back from the war speak of that freedom of flight, and I've seen their eyes shine when they talk of it.

I have flown the aviator's way— and I have flown as the bird flies. I have flown in great machines, and I have soared from the earth on skis. And I have decided that the only time a man comes anywhere close to what a bird feels, sees, senses, is when he finds himself airborne on a pair of simple skis.

When does the spirit truly soar and the mind take wings? When is man really free? Only when he rises from the earth by himself, when his arms are his only wings. . . .

There are no walls to hem in the view, no knobs and buttons that must be tended. . . . You soar for a single moment and then it is over. . . . But that moment is infinitely better than any hour-long flight sustained by man-made wings. That moment— dangerous, glorious—is like the flight of birds.

away a couple of weeks later from complications related to the injuries he sustained in the fall. Paul was only twenty-one at the time of his untimely death. He was attending the University of Wisconsin and was the reigning national collegiate jumping champion at the time of his accident." ❄

chapter five

FROM SPECTATORS TO PARTICIPANTS:
Hitting the Slopes

Utah ski history would not be complete without including the contributions of the Salt Lake Junior Chamber of Commerce (SLJCC), particularly in the 1930s and '40s. Interest in SLJCC winter sports activities began in the early '30s before there was very much public interest in skiing. Granted there were the ski jumpers, primarily of Scandinavian descent, who were actively putting on major ski-jumping attractions during that time; however, no real attempt was being made to encourage public participation in winter sports except as spectators.

In 1932 the SLJCC organized a winter sports committee "for the purpose of encouraging development of some of the matchless natural ski terrain in the adjacent Wasatch Mountains." As recreational skiing began to grow in importance throughout the 1930s, the SLJCC, with support of the Forest Service and the Chamber of Commerce in Salt Lake, began undertaking projects that promoted the sport around the region. Specifically, the SLJCC focused on "supporting actual events—ski meets and tournaments, carnivals, snow trains, and excursions." Many significant early Alpine ski competitions at Alta were sponsored by the SLJCC, particularly the Alta Carnival in December 1940 and the Snow Cup races during the 1940s. The SLJCC achieved national expo-

Winter outdoor recreation is in full swing in the Salt Lake valley. . . .

It seems that all of a sudden we are becoming aware of the possible **fascinating thrills** *in the combination of human enthusiasm, skis, toboggans and* **mountains of clean snow.**

We are finding new values in our high, *rugged mountains made smooth and accessible by deeply drifting snows. . . .*

While ski jump contests afford thrilling entertainment for spectators, on the sidelines, old men, middle-aged women, school girls and small boys mingle together sliding, racing and falling— **all thrilled with steady progress in the mastery of skis—** *all enjoying the other fellows' spills.*

—W. E. Tangren
Deseret News, *February 9, 1937*

sure through principal newsreel companies when they sent photographers to record the first Snow Cup race held on December 15. Well-known ski excursions to Park City and what is currently Deer Valley were primarily conducted by the SLJCC in the late 1930s.

In December 1946 Olive Woolley Burt wrote an article in *Utah* magazine in which she said, "As a result of the cooperation of the Wasatch Forest Service, the Salt Lake Chamber of Commerce and Junior Chamber of Commerce, the Salt Lake County and the Utah State Road Commissions, the various organized mountain and ski clubs, and the general public, all working together over the past 10 years, today skiing rates tops in winter sports interest throughout the entire state." That single statement provides a good summary of the key groups who were most responsible for the development of recreational skiing in Utah during the 1930s and '40s.

The spectacle of fearless jumpers hurling themselves off ski hills in defiance of gravity caught the imagination of the American public in the 1930s; the skiers became popular celebrities as they soared through the air for greater and greater distances. And little by little, what had been only a spectator sport began to be an activity that ordinary people could share. No one except a few dreamers wanted to follow the heroes of air and snow down the narrow and

Ski fashions of the 1930s.
Photo courtesy Stan Cohen.

terribly steep runs of the jumping hills, but more and more ordinary folk began to feel the urge to strap on skis and test themselves on the more gentle mountain slopes open to the public.

Skiing became such a rage that the U.S. Forest Service began to search for sites to develop ski areas. The Forest Service hired Alf Engen to explore selected mountain areas and evaluate them as candidates for development. During the next forty years, he played a key role in laying out more than thirty ski areas, including Alta and Snowbasin in Utah; Bear Gulch, Bogus Basin, and Magic Mountain in Idaho; and Snow King at Jackson Hole, Wyoming. Felix C. "Kozy" Koziol, supervisor of the Wasatch-Cache National Forest, wrote in the 1940–41 edition of the *American Ski Annual,*

Five years ago, the Forest Service, recognizing the need for more knowledge, better planning, and expert opinion, employed well-known Alf Engen to help. Alf prospected, investigated, and studied proposed winter developments on scores of suggested places on the Intermountain National Forests. He recommended and planned several of the best, and so from a small beginning a number

Development of Alpine Ski Competition

Nordic ski jumping received high media exposure during the early to mid-1930s. Although Alpine competitive skiing had started to develop, it as yet had attracted little attention; however, a few excellent old ski movies captured downhill racing at Cannon Mountain and Tuckerman's Ravine in New Hampshire. The film Dr. Quackenbush Skis the Headwall *provides good insight into the level of Alpine skiing in New England in the 1930s, particularly the types of ski equipment, methods to transport skiers, and the look of the New England scenery in those early days of skiing in the U.S.*

The National Ski Association sanctioned the first National Downhill Championship in 1933. The competition was held on Mt. Moosilauke in Warren, New Hampshire. Henry S.

Woods, a student at Dartmouth College, won the event. The following year, J. J. Duncan Jr., from a field of thirty-two skiers, won the second National Downhill Championship at Estes Park, Colorado.

In 1935 slalom was included for the first time as part of the national Alpine events. This first National Downhill and Slalom Championship was held on Mt. Rainier, Washington, as part of the United States tryouts for the 1936 Olympics at Garmisch-Partenkirchen, Germany. Hannes Schroll of Austria won the downhill and slalom events. Dick Durrance, a student at Dartmouth College, finished second, the top American.

No U.S. Alpine Championship was held in 1936 because of the Olympics. In 1937 Dick Durrance won the National Downhill and Slalom Championships at Sun Valley, Idaho.

Ski Trails of Wasatch Charted for Salt Lakers

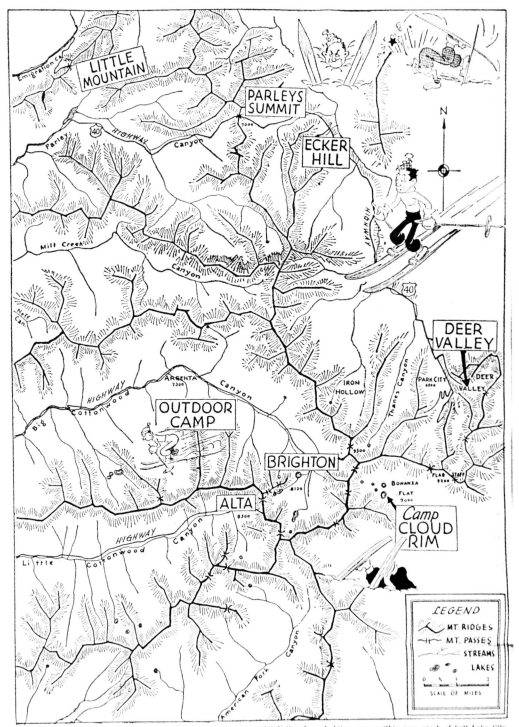

Plenty of places for Salt Lakers to ski...This map shows the multiplicity of good skiing areas within easy reach of Salt Lake City. Mountain passes, over which the skier may make his way from one canyon into another, or over a ridge and down into a valley are indicated. Take your choice of any of these ski spots for a winter morning's fun.

From the start, the Salt Lake Valley and canyons of
the Wasatch Mountains were popular with skiers.

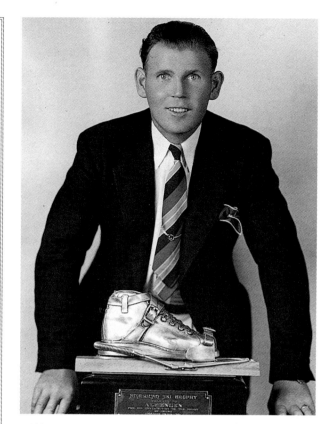

Alf Engen receiving America's highest recognition for skiing—the American Ski Trophy, 1940.

of centralized winter sports areas are now being developed by the Forest Service in cooperation with towns, ski clubs, and private individuals.

Uphill Ski Transportation

Hiking up hills back in the 1930s was not easy or enjoyable for individuals trying to learn to ski. If the sport were to grow, however, some means had to be found to transport the skiers up the hill.

There is no consensus among ski historians as to who first built a practical means for conveying skiers up the mountainside. Some say that a crude form of rope tow was used in Austria as early as 1905. Truckee, California, lays claim to the first such device in North America. Built in 1913 and powered by a steam engine, the Truckee tow consisted of two primitive toboggan-like sleds attached to a continuous loop cable. This lift, however, was developed to carry people and their sleds, not skiers. When one sled was going up the hill, the other was coming down. No other lifts are known to have existed in America until the 1930s.

First U.S. rope tow, Woodstock, Vermont. Photo courtesy Stan Cohen.

Europeans constructed ski lifts as early as the 1920s at Engelberg, Switzerland. About 1927 the first aerial tram for skiers was built at the same locale. During this same time period, some kind of lift device (the particular design is not clear) was installed at Chamonix, France.

The first method widely used in the United States was the rope tow, a relatively simple device that required the skier to grab a motor-driven rope and hold on for the ride. In 1932 the first modern rope tow in North America was built at Foster's Hill near Shawbridge, Canada. It consisted of an old Dodge chassis, a series of pulleys and wheels, and a continuous spliced rope approximately one inch in diameter. In 1934 the first rope tow in the United States went into operation on Gilbert's Hill on the outskirts of Woodstock, Vermont.

The rope tow was followed by two slightly more sophisticated modifications, the T-bar and the J-bar. Though all three methods made it easier to get up the mountain, they still required a fair degree of balance and athletic ability.

Prototype of America's first chairlift, designed by James Curran and constructed at the Union Pacific Railroad Shop, Omaha, Nebraska, circa 1935. Photo courtesy Stan Cohen.

The first chairlift in the United States began operating in December 1936 in Sun Valley, Idaho. It was underwritten by the Union Pacific Railroad, under the direction of Averell Harriman. Two years later a chairlift was constructed at Alta, Utah. Unlike the rope tow, J-bar, and T-bar, the chairlift required little skill on the part of the passenger, and any new skier could master the technique necessary to get up the mountain with a few minutes of instruction and a helping hand from the lift operator. Getting down with a measure of grace was, of course, a bit more challenging.

Skis, Boots, and Bindings

Although chairlifts helped popularize the sport, they also enabled people who were not trained athletes to plunge down mountain slopes at high speed, resulting in many injuries. A fall could turn the ski into a lever that wrenched ankle and knee joints and caused serious damage to the unlucky skier. A Norwegian emigrant named Hjalmar Hvam had an answer. In 1937 Hvam pioneered the invention of America's first safety binding. Hvam was born in Kongsberg, Norway, in 1902 and immigrated to America in 1927. He became very active in Nordic and Alpine competitive skiing and won the 1932 U.S. Nordic Combined Championship. As good a skier as he was, however, he broke his leg while skiing for recreation in 1937. While he was recuperating, Hvam developed the first release binding, which allowed the front of the ski boot to twist out and away from the ski, causing a revolution in ski-binding technology.

It comes as no surprise that Norway stood in the forefront of ski technology in the 1930s. Two Norwegian ski makers of note were Bjorn Ullevoldsaeter and Marius Eriksen. In 1935 they developed the Eriksen, a solid hickory ski with a new asset—steel edges. Eriksen, father of now-legendary Stein Eriksen, also invented the original bear-trap, iron-toe binding. The Eriksen was one of the most responsive skis of the mid-1930s. It was used by top racers such as Dick Durrance, who placed tenth in the 1936 Olympics.

Bjorn Ullevoldsaeter later developed the first laminated skis. They were stronger than the solid hickory skis and were called *Splitkein,* derived from the way the ski was constructed of thick layers of wood glued together in narrow strips called *cane.*

Thor Groswold, a Norwegian emigrant who settled in Denver, Colorado, started a ski-manufacturing com-

Earl A. Miller, circa 1960s.

pany. His laminated skis were state-of-the-art and remained so until the early 1950s when an American engineer named Howard Head developed a revolutionary new ski made of metal. Without ski inventors such as Hjalmar Hvam, Marius Eriksen, Bjorn Ullevoldsaeter, Howard Head, and Utah's Earl Miller and Mel Dalebout, the sport of skiing would not have enjoyed the kind of growth it has experienced over the last sixty years. These are by no means all of the ski innovators of that time period, but they are representative of some major accomplishments.

Utah Ski-Technology Innovators

EARL A. MILLER (bindings, skis, poles)

Earl A. Miller developed one of the first modern safety bindings. Miller's first ski experiences took place in the 1930s near Manti, Utah, where he was born and raised. Legend has it that he made his first skis from pickle-barrel staves. At sixteen he became so active in ski activities that he was elected first vice-president of the Intermountain Association. Then he quickly became head of several other Utah ski clubs. He won a number of tournaments, including the Intermountain

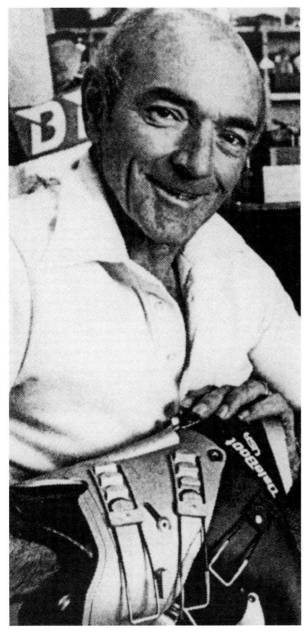

Mel Dalebout, circa 1970s.

Alta in which he offered a hundred dollars cash to anyone who could perform the same falls that he did without injury. He proceeded to stage, on an old mine dump under the Collins chairlift, some of the most horrendous falls imaginable (on camera, of course) to prove, without question, that his bindings would perform. The strategy worked well. Many ski racers used his bindings for years.

Miller also created his now-famous Miller Soft Skis in 1972. These deep-powder skis were years ahead of their time. The follow-up skis today are called Fatboys. Miller also invented a strapless platform-grip ski pole in the late 1960s that prevented skiers from wrenching their shoulder if a pole got snagged by a tree. For his many contributions to skiing over seventy-plus years, Earl Miller was inducted into the National Ski Hall of Fame at Ishpeming, Michigan, in 1995.

MEL DALEBOUT (boots)

The ski and the binding are two of the three essential components of the skier's tool kit. The third is the boot. Since the 1930s, there have been significant advances in boot technology. The early leather contraptions gradually gave way to today's high-tech plastic and metal boots. One of the innovators in ski-boot design is Mel Dalebout of Salt Lake City. In 1967 he designed and manufactured the DaleBoot. He made the initial DaleBoot from magnesium, which allowed him to achieve his goal of providing a "comfortable boot that would enhance the skier's performance." He went through some rough years at the start, but by the late 1980s, he had established himself in the market as a recognized American ski-boot manufacturer.

Dalebout did not start skiing until he attended the University of Utah, but he was a talented athlete and quickly became proficient. He did some local racing and eventually became a master course setter. He set courses for many local and national tournaments during the late 1950s, particularly the famous Snow Cup races at Alta.

ALF ENGEN (ski waxes)

If safety and comfort were important, speed also counted, particularly in competition. Since the days of the early "dopers," people had sought ways to lower the friction where the bottom of the ski met the snow. On January 2, 1935, the *Salt Lake Telegram* ran an article by Frank K. Baker titled "Waxing Skis Highly Important to Long Jumping":

Downhill Championship and the Utah Four-Way Championship, prior to the beginning of World War II.

In the early 1950s, Miller became one of the first to be certified as a ski instructor in the Intermountain Ski Instructors Association. He also became ski-school director at Timp Haven (now Sundance) in Provo Canyon.

Miller is best known, however, for his ski inventions; over the years he patented more than seventy. One of his best was a heel-and-toe release binding. To promote the Miller binding, he set up an event at

Alf Engen's line of ski waxes. Photo by Dobber Price.

Greasing skis is as much of an art as balancing a putter for an individual golfing style. Numerous kinds of ski wax are manufactured, but nearly every star has a special formula. Most of the pros protect their skis with a coat of shellac, which is carefully rubbed smooth. They usually then rub them with paraffin after each jump. Out of curiosity, a friend picked up one of ski jumper Einar Fredbo's skis at Ecker Hill and was surprised to note how irritated Einar was about the incident. "How could I hurt them just by handling them?" the friend asked. "I just waxed them," Einar said. "Your hand is warm. This causes the wax to become sticky and cuts down on the speed. If one ski is sticky and the other is fast, it's hard to keep your balance. This causes you to lose speed and distance."

Salt Lake ski jumper Jack Walker remembers getting information on waxing from Alf Engen. According to Walker, Alf was exceptionally knowledgeable when it came to waxing. "I remember Alf showing me how

to apply the shellac by pouring [it] into a rag containing a cotton ball," Walker told me. "The cotton was used as a filter to strain out any shellac impurities. The shellac was applied and allowed to dry, followed by using steel wool to smooth out any irregularities that may have resulted on the skis. This process was repeated several times until the underside of the jumping skis looked like glass. You could almost see your reflection, the skis were so shiny."

Alf went into the ski-wax business and had a complete line. Pine tar was used as a primary ingredient, which gave off an unmistakable, very strong odor similar to burning asphalt. Once, Evelyn Engen's mother, Valeria Pack, took the bus home after being in the wax lab for several hours. She had worn a fur coat that had totally absorbed the pine-tar odor. About halfway to her residence, the bus driver pulled over on the side of the highway, got out, and walked around, thinking the bus had developed a serious mechanical problem. Finding nothing wrong, he got back into the bus, sniffing the air, scratching his head, and mumbling to himself. He could not figure out what that strange smell was or where it was coming from. Mother Pack

Left: Alf Engen and Merrill Nielson with "Summer
         Snow," Mt. Baldy, California, circa 1956.

Above: Even the cows enjoyed watching the jumpers.
       Pontedilegno, Italy, circa 1959.

Germany and Italy Also Developing Plastic Snow

During the mid- to late-1950s West Germany and Italy also started experimenting with summer ski jumping on plastic hills. One such hill, reported in the October 1959 edition of Skiing News *magazine, was located at Neustadt, Germany. At this location, ski jumpers were reported flying as far as 160 feet on the plastic surface.*

kept a straight face and did not utter a word. When the bus arrived at her stop, she exited through the back door so as not to exacerbate the situation.

MERRILL NIELSON (artificial snow)

Skiing is, of course, a winter sport, and sometimes winter is not accommodating. Snow-making machines can help out where nature has not been sufficiently generous, but they can only operate in subfreezing temperatures. Nevertheless, in the mid-1950s, some visionaries decided that even if everyday skiing couldn't be done year-round, it might be possible to develop artificial snow that would make skiing or ski jumping possible.

One of the men who worked to develop artificial snow for jumpers was Merrill Nielson, a chemical engineer who was not a jumper but had a genuine interest in the sport. He experimented with a number of ideas

and finally developed a bluish-green granular substance he named Summer Snow. It reacted to skis like real snow and worked well as long as it did not get wet; then it turned into a very sticky mixture that could not be used until it thoroughly dried. The hill crew manually applied Summer Snow by carrying it up the hill in gunnysacks and spreading it with rakes.

Alf Engen was the first jumper to work with Merrill Nielson and his Summer Snow. Nielson had often watched Alf jump at Ecker Hill and wanted Alf to test his new product. Alf first jumped on Summer Snow in the backyard of Nielson's home, which was located in the foothills of Bountiful, Utah. The jump was very small, hand-built by Alf and Nielson. Although Alf only managed to jump about twenty feet, they decided that the material Nielson had developed was a practical substitute for the real thing.

Sverre Engen also became involved, and the three men formed a partnership. Through trial and error, Sverre, Alf, and Nielson made various modifications in batches of Summer Snow and finally created a substance that would allow the skis to slide easily and consistently. When most of the bugs had been worked out, they took Summer Snow on the road with ski-jumping exhibitions.

These Utah-based advances in ski technology, as well as others developed throughout the world, made skiing safer and more enjoyable for the growing number of ski enthusiasts. ❄

DESERET NEWS
Salt Lake Telegram

BUSINESS NEWS
FINANCE — INDUSTRY — OIL MARKETS — MINING

UTAH SNOW MAN—Merrill R. Nielsen, Bountiful, operates the machine which makes artificial snow for summer ski jumping.

ARTIFICIAL SNOW—The penny in the picture gives an idea of the size of the artificial snow flakes made by Utah men.

Artificial Snow Proves Success For Two Utahns

By GARY R. BLODGETT
Deseret News Staff Writer

BOUNTIFUL — Manufacturing of artificial snow may sound like a crazy idea to Utahns, but it has boomed into a "hot" business for a pair of Salt Lake area men.

The idea for use of artificial snow at ski jumping exhibitions came to Merrill Nielsen, 1330 S. 400 East, Bountiful, about 12 years ago when he resided in California.

Since then he, with his partner Alf Engen, many times national ski jumping champion and resident of Salt Lake City, have developed the idea into what looks like could be a real money-making business.

STAIRWAY TO HEAVEN—Workmen put the finishing touches on this 270-foot slope which reaches 130 feet into the sky. This is said to be the largest man-made ski jump using artificial snow. The jump was designed by Merrill Nielsen of Bountiful, and constructed under the direction of Alf Engen, noted Salt Lake City ski jumping champion.

1960 news about the success of Summer Snow.

chapter six

THE WAR AND BEYOND:
Skiing in the 1940s

During World War II, Alta played a role in the training of a company of paratroopers from Fort Benning, Georgia. The training started in January 1942 when Company B, consisting of 150 seasoned paratroopers of the 503rd Parachute Battalion, arrived in Utah. These men were mostly volunteers—men who, when war clouds gathered, stepped forward to serve their country in the dangerous area of parachute duty.

In the fall of 1941, Col. Jack Tappen of the War Department Plans and Operations division contacted Dick Durrance, who at that time was the ski-school director at Alta. Durrance was a noted Alpine racer and had established himself during the early 1940s as one of the all-time ski greats; he worked at Alta from 1940 to 1942. Tappen asked Durrance if he would train troops for winter warfare. Durrance agreed. For two months, military trucks transported the soldiers to Alta every day that they could travel up the canyon road. Lt. Col. Arthur F. Gorham (who was later killed in action in Sicily) commanded the troops.

Durrance and his cadre of instructors—including Walter Prager, Barney McLean, Gordon Wren, Art Johansen, Bill Redlin, Henry Simoneau, Hugh Bauer, Alex Baer, Bob Skinner, Sel Hannah, and Jimmy Durrance (Dick's brother)—divided the soldiers into ten classes, and over the course of six weeks proceeded

Troops arrived in Salt Lake City
with the specific objective of
learning to ski
as part of their preparation
for combat duty
in the mountains of Europe.
Very few had ever seen snow before.

The stated purpose of the exercise
was to determine
the feasibility of
training parachutists
to operate on skis,
with the implication that
an airborne winter warfare unit
was being considered.

—Brig. Gen. Edward H. Thomas, Retired,
in a letter to Alan Engen, 1996

to get them to a point where, according to Durrance, approximately one-third could ski quite proficiently and another one-third could "get by." The remaining third did not improve appreciably. Whether the objectives of the mission were met remains questionable. In the words of Brig. Gen. Edward H. Thomas: "While no conclusion was ever announced, we assumed that it was negative since no airborne infantry winter warfare unit was ever activated. To skate out on the thin ice of conjecture, I'd guess that at least one reason was the number of ski injuries we suffered. Contributing to these was the training drilled into paratroopers to tumble on landing as well as the basic 'devil may care' attitude of the airborne soldier."

Successful or not, one thing can be said with certainty—Alta, Utah, provided those daring young men with sufficient terrain to challenge the best of them. None of those involved ever forgot their Alta experience.

Although World War II dominated the first half of the 1940s, it could not diminish the many accomplishments made in skiing, particularly in the Intermountain West. A few competitions were held before the U.S. joined the battle in December 1941, but serious skiing did not resume until the end of the war in 1946. The 1940 and 1944 Olympics were canceled, and a generation of skiers who might have achieved fame in those games were denied their

Instructors who taught the ski troops at Alta in the early 1940s. On the left is Dick Durrance. Photo courtesy Brig. Gen. Edward H. Thomas, Retired.

Company B, 503rd Parachute Battalion, training at Alta, 1942. Photo courtesy Brig. Gen. Edward H. Thomas, Retired.

chance at immortality. Many people, including some who had been ski competitors, gave their lives.

Brothers in Flight— Tokle, Devlin, and Engen

TORGER TOKLE

Like Alf Engen, Torger Tokle immigrated to the United States from Norway in 1938. His fame as a ski jumper quickly spread throughout the nation. He was short and stocky, weighing about 160 pounds, but he possessed tremendous leg power. Newspaper articles described him as having the "power of a human howitzer," and he was frequently called the "Babe Ruth of skiing."

Tokle only jumped in the United States for four years (1939–43), but he compiled an amazing record that is matched perhaps only by his childhood role model, Alf Engen, ten years his senior. The record shows that Tokle competed in forty-four tournaments during this four-year period and won thirty-nine of them, establishing twenty-two new hill records.

Brothers in flight, Sun Valley, Idaho, circa 1941:
(left to right) Torger Tokle, Alf Engen, and Art Devlin.

On February 9, 1941, one of the greatest ski-jumping events in North American history took place when Alf Engen broke the American record on Pine Mountain in Iron Mountain, Michigan, with a jump of 267 feet, but he didn't keep the record very long. When Alf made this record leap, twenty-five thousand people were on hand. Alf bettered by ten feet the previous record set by Bob Roecker of Duluth in 1939. Two hours later, Torger Tokle broke Alf's record by jumping 273 feet in Leavenworth, Washington, several thousand miles to the west. Later that same year, Tokle won the National Ski-Jumping Championship at Snoqualmie Ski Bowl near Seattle, Washington, and set yet another American jumping record of 288 feet.

Tokle jumped last in Steamboat Springs on Howelsen Hill in March 1943. Alf and Torger were filmed together in Otto Lang's movie *Ski Gulls,* and few could tell the jumpers apart. They jumped with the same form, the same power, and landed in virtually the same spot on the hill. Immediately

following the jumping exhibition, Torger left for Camp Hale, Colorado, to join the Tenth Mountain Division. While serving in Italy in 1945, Torger was killed. His death was deeply felt by everyone in the country associated with ski jumping. Alf and Torger had been close personal friends as well as great competitors and champions. Fittingly, they were inducted at the same time into the National Ski Hall of Fame in 1959.

ARTHUR BRENDEN DEVLIN

Another skiing legend of the 1940s was Art Devlin, without question one of the best ski fliers America ever produced. Devlin was born in Lake Placid, New York, and started ski jumping at the age of five, using a cider barrel for a takeoff, barrel staves for skis, and rubber bands for bindings.

At the age of six, Devlin went off his first official jump, a twenty-meter hill on the grounds of the Lake Placid Club. By the age of sixteen, he had won the eastern jumping championship at Brattleboro, Vermont. Torger Tokle, four years older, was the only jumper able to beat Devlin with any consistency. The Tokle-Devlin rivalry during the late 1930s and early 1940s provided some of the most spectacular jumping events in the country. In 1942 Devlin, Tokle, and Alf Engen made a triple jump in an exhibition at Ruud Mountain in Sun Valley, Idaho. This was the only time the three ever jumped together, although they jumped against each other many times.

Merrill Barber, one of Devlin's closest rivals, said that Devlin was "like a block of ice" when he got to the top of a jumping hill. He was said to have very little sympathy for anyone and, according to Barber, "took the attitude that anyone who got hurt was a damn fool. But afterward, he was the first guy to show up at the hospital and the last to leave."

During World War II, Devlin flew as a bombardier on some fifty missions over Italy. He received a number of decorations plus nine pieces of flak in his leg and thigh. As soon as his war injuries healed, he reentered competition and made the 1948 Olympic ski-jumping team, which Alf Engen coached. Unfortunately, he took a bad spill in Davos, Switzerland, prior to the Olympic competition in St. Moritz and fractured the leg that had been wounded during the war. This kept him from competing. Nevertheless, Devlin went on to represent the United States in the 1952, 1956, and 1960 Olympics and became perhaps best known as a commentator on ABC's *Wide World of Sports.*

Filming *Ski Gulls:* (behind camera) Torger Tokle, (center, on skis)
film producer Otto Lang, (third from right) Alf Engen. Photo courtesy Otto Lang.

ALF ENGEN

An article by Oscar Cyr appeared in the January 9, 1942, edition of the *Ski Bulletin,* entitled "The All-American Skier," which singled out Alf Engen in highly complimentary terms:

Who is the best skier in this country? We are asked this question many, many times and, of course, we unhesitatingly say "Alf Engen. . . ." But then, some of our fine recreational skiers protest with the non-skiers and howl, "What about Durrance? What about Toni Matt?. . ."

The "best skier" would be the complete skier, the one who excels in all phases of the sport. Dick Durrance is our present national slalom champion. Toni Matt holds the downhill title. . . .

But none of the specialists were on

hand at the time of the national four-event championships. Here the excellence of [Alf] Engen was undisputed. He won first place in three events, downhill, slalom and jumping, and was third in the cross-country race—against the best skiers that America could gather together. Again the record book lists Alf Engen as the national four-event champion. . .

To be a winner in all four disciplines is to be truly an All-American skier and an All-American man.

Alf was recognized nationally by the Forest Service and many high-level military personnel not only as an outstanding athlete and competitor but also as a highly knowledgeable expert on ski technology and the role it could play in winter warfare. As a result, he was recruited to serve his country during the war in a civilian capacity rather than active military duty. During the years 1943 through 1945, he traveled extensively throughout the United States with top military leaders, conducting inspections of winter combat ski equipment and recommending its acceptance or rejection. Alf always considered it an honor to serve his country in any capacity where his skills could best be put to use.

Nevertheless, one of the most satisfying accomplishments in Alf's long career came after the war when he was thirty-seven. In those years, that was considered old, at least as far as competitors were concerned. Statistics at the time were filled with the exploits of younger men. But Alf never put much stock in statistics, relying instead on what his body told him was achievable. After much consideration, Alf decided to compete at the 1946 National Ski-Jumping Championship on Howelsen Hill in Steamboat Springs, Colorado. In February of 1947, the story of that tournament was recounted in *Collier's* magazine in a piece titled "Old Man of the Mountain" by Monty Atwater. Here are a few excerpts:

To Steamboat Springs came a few competitors who were laying for Alf. He had jumped the socks off them in meet after meet before the war. And here he was, undaunted by two trips to the hospital and the weight of his years, doing it again. There must be some way to get this old man of the mountain off their shoulders. They managed to convey to Alf's ears the thought that he would be doing a fine thing if he dropped out of Class A and competed only in the Veterans' Class. The old man, who had gone to Steamboat Springs undecided whether he would jump, was in doubt no longer. He said he'd rather come in last in Class A than win in any other division.

Next morning (the day before the championship tournament), Alf happened to be the last man to reach the hill. All the other jumpers were present but only the gliders were practicing. Even as he listened to the explanation, he saw that the gliders were getting much greater distances than before. He noted also that they were going dangerously high in the air and with narrowed eyes he gauged the angle of the take-off.

What Alf noticed was that during the night, changes had been made to the takeoff. The hill had been altered with what is called a kicker, which gives an added lift to the jumper. This action could put power jumpers such as himself in a very dangerous situation because they might outjump the hill. Atwater continued,

The other jumpers were for lodging a protest with the meet officials, but the old man plodded up the hill. He said he'd give it a try. They saw him studying the profile of the end run and the landing hill as he climbed; saw his shoulders dip as his muscles adjusted themselves to a set of new signals. The famous Engen leap forward and out would be suicide on the glider take-off. All in a few seconds, Alf had to rearrange the entire timing and pattern of his jump. . . . Alf gave himself to the hill, and every eye followed his crouching, accelerating figure.

Alf jumped the only way he ever had in his life, hard, but low and forward. Even then he rose to a fearsome height . . . the exaggerated lift of the glider take-off plus the drive of his own legs sent Alf on a distorted trajectory. When his forward momentum died, he was far above the ground and plummeted to earth in what amounted to a free fall. Every watcher felt his leg muscles knot as Alf's skis bit inches into the packed snow of the out-run, winced at the crack as the tortured wood slivered and split. Alf rode them out safely, but he would never jump again on those skis.

Instantly, a bitter wrangle flared around the take-off. Alf took no part, for he had broken his only pair of jumping skis and figured himself out of the competition. But the other jumpers flatly told the gliders that either the trick take-off came down or there wouldn't be any jumping meet. With Alf disposed of, the gliders were willing to compromise. The outcome of the argument was removal of half the chute. So ended the day before the tournament.

Alf had disappeared and little was heard of him until the contestants gathered again in the dressing room on the day of the championship. He had been busy most

Composite photos of Alta: (left) aftereffects of an avalanche on the old town of Alta with East Rustler hillside in the background, July 1885, photo by C. R. Savage; (right) same view showing Landes Hill location in the foreground, July 1995, photo by Alan Engen.

of the night waxing and refitting the bindings on a pair of old warped borrowed skis that had been loaned to him by a fellow jumper. No one present has cared to describe in detail that scene in the dressing room. But it is known that Alf told the gliders exactly what he thought of their fancy take-off, told them that he was still in the contest, and that if they beat him they'd have to do more than sail for it. . . .

The bugle rang out and the flag dropped. The lonely figure plummeted down the incline. He hit the take-off and launched himself into space as only Alf Engen can, like a projectile. Aching seconds passed while he drilled a straight line across the sky. Then gradually, his flying body began to curve towards earth, falling faster and faster. The crowd was so still that on the farthest rim they could hear the wind whine in the folds of his jacket. At the edge of the landing hill, directly under him, it was a rising screech ending in a crack like a rifle shot as his skis took the snow. His body contracted with the

shock, for he had flown high and far, farther than any jumper had ever flown before on that hill.

But it wasn't over yet. The heavy ten-foot slabs of hickory had driven inches into the snow. Would they hold together? Could Alf, at airplane landing speed, bring them to the surface and ride them out? His crouching body extended itself, the curved ski tips planed up and freed themselves. Only then did a long sigh rustle over the crowd as hundreds of throats released their pent-up breath. Alf had ridden his warped and untried borrowed skis over the gliders take-off to a new hill record and the National Jumping Championship.

The field that day included the best in the country. Most of the jumpers had been out of the armed forces only a few months, and this was their first big competition since the end of the war. A crowd of six thousand watched this reunion of former champions.

When all was said and done, the margin between Alf and Art Devlin, the second-place finisher, was only

0.09 of a point (229.55 points for Engen and 229.46 points for Devlin). Scoring increments do not get much closer! In the course of the day, five jumpers broke or equaled the hill record of 248 feet.

Exit—The Glory Days of Ski-Jumping

By the mid-1940s, use of the giant ski-jumping hills built during the 1920s and 1930s declined rapidly. The professional jumpers who provided the excitement of winter sports festivals had fallen victim to the increasing interest in Alpine skiing. But the jumpers did not disappear. Those who did not go into the military during World War II recognized the shift and quickly adapted their great skiing abilities to serve recreational skiing in the Intermountain West.

LANDES HILL, ALTA, UTAH

One of the significant attempts to resurrect ski jumping in Utah in the 1940s was the construction of Landes Hill at Alta. H. D. Landes, a well-known Salt Lake City businessman, donated ten thousand dollars to construct the hill and cover some operating expenses. Landes decided that a ski jump would be

FIRST ANNUAL

SKI JUMPS

at ALTA

Sunday, April 17
Landes Hill
1 P. M.

Whether you ski or not, you'll enjoy the rugged beauty of Alpine Mountains seen from Alta.

Lifts will be operating to the top of Peruvian Ridge, so you can plan to take that chair-lift ride you've been promising yourself. Enjoy a mountain top view of Salt Lake Valley from a ski-tow chair atop the ridge.

ALL ROADS LEADING TO ALTA ARE IN GOOD CONDITION

Poster promoting first annual ski-jumping tournament on Landes Hill, 1949.

the most appropriate memorial to his son, Ensign Robert J. Landes, who was killed at age twenty-two in action aboard a naval destroyer. Before entering the service, Landes had been an avid skier and had frequently enjoyed going to "romantic Alta." Construction of the hill was part of a seven-year plan to expand Alta as a winter sports center.

William J. O'Connor, Salt Lake Winter Sports Association president, organized a committee of local clubs to carry out the hill construction. Alf Engen served as construction advisor. Lee Irvine, Salt Lake Chamber of Commerce Winter Sports Committee chairman, stated that jumps on the hill would "fall somewhere between the A and B jumps at Ecker Hill."

Sverre and Corey Engen actively participated in the construction of Landes Hill. Both tell a story with a smile about one day when they were working on the hill with Alf. Apparently Alf was not pleased with the progress and had chided his brothers to work harder or he would take on both of them.

"Sverre and I winked at each other and said let's take him up on that," Corey remembers. They both grabbed Alf, and all three rolled head over heels all the way down the underhill. When they came to a stop, they were laughing, but Alf came out on the worst end. A small stick had gone through one of his ears and had to be removed. Alf said he would never again challenge his two brothers. He had learned his lesson.

The Landes Hill dedication was held on Sunday, November 28, 1948. The program featured two exhibition jumps. A spectacular side-by-side exhibition jump by the three famous Engen brothers—Alf, Sverre, and Corey—highlighted the activities. Alf Engen made the longest jumps of the day: 165, 168, and 181 feet. The 181-foot leap stood as the hill record until December 8, 1967, when Matz Jensen, a Norwegian who was the assistant ski coach of the University of Utah Nordic team, flew 200 feet in an officially sanctioned tournament.

The first officially sanctioned tournament on Landes Hill was held during January of 1949 as part of a combination cross-country and ski-jumping event. Junior Bounous won the four-and-a-half-mile cross-country race in twenty-seven minutes.

The Class D division was won by the author, Alan Engen, then nine years old: "It way my first competitive tournament. As the son of the famous Alf Engen, I was given a buildup in the local papers. I can still remember the pressure I felt of trying to live up to the

Professional ski jumpers Halvor Bjørngaard
and Steffen Trøgstad.

Championship and the Professional Gelande Ski-Jumping Competition. Jumpers came from all around the Intermountain area for these events because the competition carried prestige similar to that found at Ecker Hill tournaments.

Many fine jumpers competed at Landes; among them was Dick Simons, who came to Utah from the Pacific Northwest as one of that area's best jumpers. He was a true daredevil and would jump under the worst conditions. Simons once flew two hundred feet on Landes Hill but fell, so his jump did not count as a record. Simons was also a great parachutist and one of the very first sky divers to free-fall over Alta in the mid-1950s.

Frithjof "Bassie" Prydz from Norway was perhaps one of the greatest to jump Landes Hill. Prydz attended the University of Utah in the early to mid-1960s and three times won the National Collegiate Ski-Jumping Championship. He was an All-American and often trained on Landes Hill.

Landes Hill is no longer used for jumping. The hill takeoff is still visible, but the wooden judges' stand has been removed. Landes was supposed to be Utah's replacement for the once-famous Ecker Hill; however, that dream never materialized for two reasons. First, Alta receives too much snow. Often, after days of difficult hill preparation by athletes and officials, snow would fall, covering the hill with two or three feet of new powder. Second, the jump was not large enough to accommodate three-hundred-foot, world-class jumps. Regardless, Landes was a fine hill and a significant part of Utah's illustrious ski-jumping history.

BJØRNGAARD HILL, SNOWBASIN, UTAH

Another jumping hill built in the 1940s was Bjørngaard Hill at Snowbasin, named after professional ski jumper Halvor Bjørngaard, who had been killed in a 1934 motorcycle accident. The hill was dedicated on Sunday, February 16, 1941. According to the Ogden *Standard-Examiner,* "As the bugle call faded into echoes of the hill slopes, Alf and Sverre Engen, who were fast friends of Bjørngaard, soared off the trajectory in a graceful twin leap. Blood-red roses fell from their hands in mid-air onto the gleaming white of the hill in a dedicatory jump."

Sverre Engen says Bjørngaard "loved to play little harmless tricks on people." Once, in 1930, when the professional jumpers were staging a tournament at Lake Tahoe, California, Bjørngaard decided to have a

family name and worrying that I would bring discredit to my parents and uncles if I did not perform well. Before the tournament, I got myself into such a frame of mind that I was not able to do anything right. I fell on both of my practice jumps, and it seemed I was headed for a disastrous debut. Before the first official tournament jump, I remember going over to a tree and starting to cry.

"Dad came to me and asked what the problem was. I answered, 'The other kids don't have to win. I do!' Then my father put his arm around me and said, 'Alan, you don't have to please anyone but yourself. To be successful, you must want to compete, but, more importantly, you must have fun doing it. Forget what people think; just go have fun and mean business.' I never forgot this counsel during the many years that I competed."

Landes Hill continued as the site of many fine tournaments between 1949 and the late 1970s, including a number of Intermountain ski championships such as the National Junior Ski-Jumping

Alf and Sverre Engen making an exhibition jump at the dedication of Bjørngaard Hill, Snowbasin, February 16, 1941. Notice the customary release of roses as the skiers jump.

little fun at the Tavern Hotel. He and Sverre were hanging around the lobby after the tournament, and Bjørngaard pulled out a novelty item—a dark brown rubber blob that looked remarkably like dog poop—and put it in the middle of one of the couches. Then he crossed to the other side of the lobby and watched with "a twinkle in his eye and a big grin on his face."

Some women entered the lobby and went to sit down on the couch—you can imagine the horrified looks on their distinguished faces. It wasn't long before two lodge attendants picked up the couch and hauled it out of the room. As they passed by, Bjørngaard casually reached out, picked up the blob, and put it back in his pocket. "No one saw him do this besides me," Sverre says, "and we laughed about it for weeks afterward. I still giggle a little when I think about it."

ADDITIONAL JUMPING HILLS

Another sixty-meter jumping hill was opened at Snowbasin. On February 10, 1951, almost ten years after the dedication of Bjørngaard Hill, C. J. Olsen, regional forester, dedicated the hill, naming it Trond Engen Hill in honor of Alf's father. This hill continued

to be used until the late 1960s before being abandoned. Nothing remains to indicate that a jumping hill ever existed at the site.

Also in the early 1960s, Alan Engen designed and helped construct a forty-meter hill at Solitude ski area in Big Cottonwood Canyon, southeast of Salt Lake City. It was used for a number of years as a collegiate training facility and hosted several intercollegiate jumping events.

The 1948 Olympic Winter Games

On September 5, 1946, the first postwar congress of the International Olympic Committee selected St. Moritz as the site for the 1948 Olympic Winter Games.

Tryouts for the 1948 Olympics were conducted at Sun Valley, Idaho, for the Alpine events (downhill and slalom) and Lake Placid, New York, for the Nordic events (jumping, cross-country, and jumping/cross-country combined). The United States Winter Olympics Alpine Team was named at Sun Valley in the early spring of 1947. Several skiers from the Inter-mountain West qualified for the team—including Alf Engen, even though he was almost forty years old. Soon after, however, Alf was approached by the U.S.

1948 U.S. Olympic Ski Team—Nordic and Alpine.

Character illustration of U.S. Ski Team coaches Alf Engen and Walter Prager, Davos, Switzerland, 1948.

GRETCHEN FRASER

Among the team members was Gretchen Fraser, a young woman who had learned to ski in the Pacific Northwest under the tutelage of Otto Lang. The highlight of the 1948 Olympic winter competition for the United States was Fraser's gold medal in the women's slalom—the first Olympic gold medal for the United States.

Coach Engen was with Fraser on that historic day. "I can vividly remember when Gretchen won her gold medal in the 1948 Olympics," he said. "She had drawn number one in the Olympic women's slalom event that day. There was a lot going on before the race, and when she and I went to get on the lift to take us to the start, the crowd was so heavy that we were unable to make our way to the head of the line. Time was becoming critical because if we could not get on the lift soon, Gretchen would miss her designated start time and be disqualified.

"Luckily, several members of the St. Moritz Ski School happened to be near the lift and came to our rescue. They immediately got the crowd to open a path for us to get directly to the lift. To this day I say

Olympic Committee and asked to consider coaching the team, an offer he readily accepted. He considered it a great honor, a sign of respect for his experience. He was certainly well qualified to lead the team. He and Walter Prager tackled the job.

Gretchen Fraser, gold-medal winner in the women's slalom, 1948 Olympic Winter Games, St. Moritz, Switzerland.

a special thanks to them for their assistance. Without their help, the results for Gretchen would have been much different.

"When we arrived at the top of the slalom course, Gretchen had to go directly to the start. The starting official then put his arm on Gretchen and started the countdown. Five, four, three, two, one, HALT! Something was malfunctioning with the timing system, and the officials stopped Gretchen. The weather and snow conditions that day were such that standing around immediately caused the skis to ice up, meaning that ice formed on the bottom. As Gretchen was waiting to race, this was happening to her skis; I quickly had her put one ski up at a time so I could take the ice off with some Engen hard wax I had with me.

"Gretchen was then given the notice that the timing-equipment problem had been corrected, and the countdown began again. Five, four, three, two, one, HALT! For a second time, Gretchen was prevented from starting her run. You can only imagine what that was like for Gretchen. She was in the biggest

event of her life, had the adrenaline running in preparation for springing out of the starting gate, and then was stopped a second time. But I give Gretchen a lot of credit! She remained calm and did not get rattled one bit.

"The third time the officials started the countdown, she was allowed to go. She skied perfectly and did not make any mistakes on either of her two runs. Her skis had no ice on the bottoms of them, which gave her an added advantage over some of the other competitors who raced after her and encountered severe sticking problems. The results were that Gretchen finished, and, when the electronic timing board highlighted her time, it was clear that she had made history. She had won the first skiing gold medal for the United States."

DICK MOVITZ

One of the top male skiers from the Intermountain region who was a member of the Olympic Alpine team in 1948 was Dick Movitz. He was born and reared in the Salt Lake City area and started skiing near his home with his lifelong friend Dev Jennings.

"Every day after school, we would walk to the Bonneville Golf Course and start skiing," Movitz remembers. "Not long after, we moved our skiing up to the old Rasmussen ranch and started ski jumping on their small hill not far from the much larger Ecker Hill. My first ski race was at Brighton, and I raced in a downhill, Class D."

Movitz started taking ski racing seriously under the tutelage of Karl Fahrner, Alta's first ski-school director in 1938, one of his earliest racing teachers. Ski legend Dick Durrance, who took over the Alta Ski School in 1940, was another Movitz mentor.

"I remember one occasion when Dev Jennings and I were in high school," Movitz recalls. "We wanted to ski at Alta over spring break but the road was closed due to avalanches. So the two of us hiked into Alta from Brighton and spent four or five days with Dick Durrance, Gordy Wren, and Si Brand in glorious untracked powder snow. That was an experience I will never forget."

Over the years Movitz accumulated pointers from other ski legends such as Friedl Pfeifer (who became head of the ski school at Alta in 1942), Martin Fopp, and Sverre Engen. Most of the competitions were held in the Utah area or Sun Valley, Idaho.

"Jack Reddish and I went to Sun Valley during

Dick Movitz, circa mid-1940s.

Suzy Harris Rytting, circa mid-1940s.

the winter of 1941–42 and raced in the Harriman Cup," Movitz says. "As kids that was pretty tough! Then after World War II, I came home and went to the University of Utah. I decided then that I would dedicate my winters to skiing, so every winter I skied, for five winters. I went into competition in a serious way during those years, racing in Aspen, Sun Valley, and all over the country. I, along with Jack Reddish, Dev Jennings, and a number of other fellows, was part of the University of Utah's first ski team. Sverre Engen was our coach. We raced at Sun Valley as a team and won the first national collegiate championship we entered, beating other great teams such as Dartmouth and Middlebury Colleges, who were ranked as the best college ski teams in the country."

Although Movitz is known for his accomplishments as an Alpine racer, what is less known is that both he and his good friend Jack Reddish were accomplished ski jumpers. "We started ski jumping as very young kids at Rasmussen's ski jump but soon moved over to where the big boys like Alf Engen were jumping on Ecker Hill," he says. "We jumped in Class B for a number of years, as well as competed in the Alpine downhill and slalom."

In 1947 Movitz was selected to represent the United States as a member of the 1948 Olympic Ski Team. "When you look back on it, you realize how unknowledgeable everyone was. All the competitors, coaches, and managers really had no idea of what was involved when we went to Europe," Movitz recalls. "It was a totally new experience for all of us. The equipment we had was antiquated in comparison to

what the European competition was using. So we all had to learn, and learn very quickly. I think we did that, and we did better as the year progressed. We gained experience about what we were doing and how to do it in an international setting.

"The women did particularly well, especially Gretchen Fraser, who was sensational. That to me was perhaps the most exciting aspect of the '48 Olympics, watching Gretchen win her gold medal, and I was there, rubbing her back and neck just before she made her historic run. The Europeans were taken by surprise! How could this American, out of the clear blue, come in and beat them? I think they still feel that way! However, I think our team did well in other areas as well. Gordy Wren and Corey Engen performed very well in the Nordic events, and Jack Reddish was the best male skier on the team, finishing in the top ten in the slalom."

After the 1948 Olympics, Movitz became very active as an international ski official and played an important role through the 1960 Olympics at Squaw Valley. "At that point I decided to call it quits as far as high-level competition was concerned," he remembers. "What I found is that unless you are politically minded, you can only go on for so long. It is just a different ball game!" Movitz is an honored member of both the Utah Sports Hall of Fame and the National Ski Hall of Fame.

SUZY HARRIS RYTTING

One of the greatest "unsung heroines" of Olympic competition was Suzy Harris Rytting. She and her parents moved to Utah from Cleveland, Ohio, in January 1942. When she started skiing at the age of twelve on the Rasmussen ranch near the old Ecker Hill, her wooden skis had no edges, and she used her uncle's ski boots with only a leather toe strap for bindings.

"My first experience certainly was not what I call enjoyable," Rytting recalls, "and after falling down the hillside about every two feet and getting thoroughly wet and cold, I decided what I wanted to do was be an ice skater and immediately terminate any further experiences with the sport of skiing. The ski clothes in those days were all wool—woolen snow pants and jacket—and when I fell, I became a massive snowball. However, even though I was crying and wanted no more to do with skiing, my parents said it looked like a lot of fun and that the following year we were all going to learn how to ski. So we did! Eventually, with encouragement, my initial feelings about skiing did change, and it has become a part of my life ever since."

By age fourteen, Rytting had not only learned how to ski but had so impressed some of the ski patrol that they encouraged her to participate in ski races. "I remember my mother and I were sitting in the old Watson Shelter at Alta, and some of the ski patrolmen told my mother they felt I was doing really well and suggested she enter me in a race," Rytting remembers. "Because I had no knowledge of racing, the patrolmen took some Coke bottles, set them up on the table, and proceeded to show me what it would be like to go through gates. Shortly after, I entered my first race at Alta and placed dead last."

That quickly changed, however, and by the time Rytting was eighteen, she had established herself among the finest women skiers in the country. She won the prestigious Snow Cup race at Alta two consecutive years, 1947 and 1948, and became an alternate on the 1948 Olympic Alpine team. In 1949 she married Bill Rytting and continued to compete actively at the national level throughout the country. In early January 1951, she won the National Giant Slalom Championship at Alta.

"That race was the most exciting and memorable in my ski-competition years because it was on my home terrain at Alta, down Wildcat," Rytting says. "I was also working six days a week, running an elevator at a Salt Lake City department store, and had really had no time to train and prepare for this level of competition."

In 1952 Rytting was named a member of the U.S. Olympic Team that would represent the country in Oslo, Norway. The entire team went to Switzerland to train prior to Olympic competition. "My father traveled to New York with me on the plane, and, due to bad weather, we were grounded in Chicago over New Year's," she says. "I began getting a terrible cold. By the time I got to Europe, I was not feeling at all well and thought I had the flu. Finally, the cold started going away, but the flu symptoms did not. So I went to see a Swiss doctor and was told 'Madam, you are probably going to have a baby,' and that was indeed what happened."

When the U.S. Olympic officials found out about Rytting's pregnancy, they thought she had known about her condition when she made the team and, as a result, she was discharged and sent back to the United States. No official announcement was made concerning the decision. As a result, when Rytting arrived back in Salt Lake City just before the start of the Olympic competition, it caused a major stir around the country. One of the major sports commentators, Bill Stern, remarked, "It's the first time I've ever known you could be kicked off an Olympic team or be penalized in sports because of motherhood."

Other publications such as *Newsweek* and the *New York Post* printed similar comments in their editorials. Months later, when Suzy and Bill's baby girl was born, one of the nurses involved in the delivery asked, "Is this the little jinx that caused all the trouble?" The name stuck and to this day, their daughter, Jessica Jane, is known by the nickname "Jinx." According to Rytting, "Our second daughter, Robyn, is very relieved not to have a funny nickname!"

In 1988 Rytting was honored by being inducted into not one hall of fame but three: the Utah Sports Hall of Fame, the University of Utah Crimson Club Hall of Fame, and the National Ski Hall of Fame.

IT SHOULD ALSO BE MENTIONED . . .

Other members of the U.S. Olympic Team made respectable showings. Particularly worthy of mention is Gordon Wren, who finished fifth in the special jumping and second in the jumping portion of the Nordic combined. Corey Engen was close behind in the Nordic combined jumping with a third-place finish. In the Nordic combined, which includes jumping and cross-country, Corey Engen came in twenty-sixth and Wren was twenty-ninth. Other top-twenty finishes in the special jumping included

Corey Engen, 1948 Olympic Winter Games.

Sverre Fredheim, twelfth place, and Paul Perrault, fifteenth. These jumpers' successes directly affected skiing in the United States and particularly the Intermountain West.

The Last National Championship at Ecker Hill

When the 1948 Olympians arrived back on American soil, one of the last national championships was held on Ecker Hill in February 1949, an important but not well-remembered event. Some of the biggest names in ski jumping competed. In addition to Alf, Sverre, and Corey Engen, others included the 1948 Olympic champion, Petter Hugsted.

Hugsted, traveling by plane from the East, was delayed in Denver and did not make it in time to jump the first round. The tournament judges allowed him a first round bye, however, and he jumped just one time in the second round. According to a newspaper article, he arrived late with "sirens and a motorcycle escort." The rules specified that "a jumper who fails to show up on time must be disqualified," but because Hugsted was the reigning Olympic champion, this restriction was waived.

Hugsted's 262-foot jump and form were good enough to win the National Ski-Jumping Championship. Some jumpers felt that he should have been disqualified for not being present for the first round of jumping. The most vocal was Art Devlin, who registered a protest with the judges and demanded that Hugsted be ruled out. The judges, however, persisted and held to their original ruling. The record books still list Petter Hugsted as the 1949 national champion.

The 1949 National Ski-Jumping Championship was the last national event on Ecker Hill. Even though a number of Intermountain championships and tournaments took place there during the 1950s, the 1949 tournament marked the end of this hill's glory years.

The 1940s were at an end, and so, for quite some time, were the jumping heydays. Alpine skiing began to dominate the competitive scene. The Intermountain region jumping hills fell into disrepair because no one was using them. A strong new generation of jumpers failed to rise, and it appeared that ski jumping was headed toward being considered a thing of the past. But a renaissance was still to come.

SNOW SAFETY

Despite all the improvements in the technology of the sport, skiers can still fall, run into unyielding objects, or get caught in an avalanche. Skiers are subject to all the hazards of the high mountains in winter. When injuries occurred in the early days of skiing, there was little professional medical care available. The athletes and ski officials had to deal with problems themselves. When the general public started to ski and the number of participants increased, however, there was a new emphasis on the need for professionals on-site to deal with potential injuries.

The steep and beautiful terrain of Utah's canyons and mountain ranges receives vast amounts of snow each winter as the air that blows across the Great Basin is suddenly pushed upward and forced to yield its moisture. Snow falls on snow, layers of new snow pile on old, and avalanche danger is always present.

The Ski Patrols

THE NATIONAL SKI PATROL SYSTEM

As ski areas began to develop in the mid-1930s, the Forest Service and ski-area managers quickly realized that each area needed a ski patrol to assist injured skiers. The first ski patrols were composed of local citizen volunteers who loved skiing. The patrols worked as separate, independent units without benefit of a central organizational structure. They served primarily as volunteer guides and, when required, took care of injured skiers by getting them off the hill and administering first aid. Today, the ski patrols have become finely trained, superb professionals, whose essential skiing safety, first aid, avalanche control, and other services make possible day-to-day ski-area operations.

On March 6, 1938, at the end of the downhill and slalom championships held on Mt. Mansfield at Stowe, Vermont, Roger Langley, then president of the National Ski Association, asked Minot "Minnie" Dole to head

a committee to establish a national ski-patrol organization. For this national competition, the local ski patrol had organized a special patrol to care for any injured people. Langley was so impressed with how that special patrol functioned that he suggested patrols be organized on a national basis to give consistency to the procedures being employed throughout the United States.

Minnie Dole was from Greenwich, Connecticut, and a graduate of Yale University. He possessed a high intellect and a strong advocacy for improving the safety of skiers. He gained this interest because of a fractured ankle he incurred while skiing on one of New England's ski slopes. Unable to move without severe pain, he had to wait over one hour for assistance and another two-plus hours to reach proper medical attention. As a result of this experience and another in which a close friend lost his life because of ski injury, he became the primary spokesperson for establishing a ski-patrol assistance program.

The National Ski Patrol System was officially established in the summer of 1938. During the

Minot "Minnie" Dole, founder of the National Ski Patrol.

Above: Early Alta ski patrol, circa 1949: (left to right) Tom Foley, Harold Goodro, Gordon Allcott, and Dave Shelden. Photo courtesy Alta Ski Lifts Company.
Below: Key personalities involved in snow safety in the 1940s and 1950s: (left to right) Harold Goodro, Monty Atwater, Lee Steorts, and (center) Jim Shane. Photo courtesy Alta Ski Lifts Company.

first year, national membership consisted of only ninety-one individuals, who had to take a thirty-hour first-aid course administered by the American Red Cross and another course involving snow precautions in mountainous terrain. During the year 1938–39, the National Ski Patrol System continued to develop and was divided into seven divisions: Eastern, Pacific Northwest, Intermountain, Northern Rocky Mountain, Southern Rocky Mountain, Central, and California.

THE INTERMOUNTAIN SKI PATROL SYSTEM

The first ski patrollers were volunteers who loved skiing; they served as guides, took care of injured skiers, administered first aid, searched for lost skiers, and occasionally watched helplessly as avalanches unpredictably swept down the slopes.

Mike O'Neill, leader of the Salt Lake Metropolitan Ski Patrol, was instrumental in bringing the Inter- mountain patrols into the National Ski Patrol system in the late 1930s. He was also a strong advocate for ski development.

Jim Shane, a quiet, gentle giant of a man, is regarded by many as one of Utah's strongest men. He saved several lives single-handedly and is perhaps one of the Intermountain region's most unsung heroes. Shane played a key role in the ski patrol on a national level for many years and designed the Intermountain area's first toboggan using a rear brakeman. In more recent years, Jim and his wife, Elfriede, built and ran the Goldminer's Daughter Lodge at Alta. Jim passed away on March 28, 1998.

The best known of early Utah ski patrollers, however, is probably Harold Goodro. One of America's true mountain men and a legend in skiing and mountain climbing, Goodro began skiing about 1928 at the age of twelve when he made a pair of skis for himself out of pinewood. Those skis were the start of a ski career spanning more than seventy years.

In 1934, at age seventeen, Goodro left Utah and took a job as a mail carrier at a mining camp in the High Sierras, about seventy miles north of Reno, Nevada. The only thing he took with him besides clothing was a pair of eight-foot-long maple Strand skis.

Goodro was following in the footsteps of Snowshoe Thompson; however, he only delivered mail for one year because, as he put it, "everything went broke! The mines closed all over Northern California. I, along with two other men, had to ski out during a heavy snowstorm in May 1935. I remember we had to pull a very heavy sled, which had all our belongings on it. We made it to a small cabin and stayed overnight. Several days later we found out that some reporter had gotten wind of what we did and had written a story in the Sacramento newspaper about three young miners who lost their lives trying to escape a terrible mountain storm."

When Goodro returned to Salt Lake City, he joined the Works Projects Administration (WPA) and worked on the entrance to Big Cottonwood Canyon. Then, at age nineteen, he went to work for Utah Power and Light (UP&L) for eight years before enlisting in the navy, where he studied electronics. When he received his discharge, he returned to Utah to work for UP&L, where he designed and supervised the building of power lines to the ski resorts in Park City, Brighton, Alta, and Snowbird. According to Goodro, "They gave me the mountain territory because of my knowledge of the mountains." He worked for UP&L for the next

thirty-two years, retiring in 1975 with forty years of service. His retirement ended three weeks later when he accepted a position with the University of Utah as an outdoor-adventure instructor, which eventually led to his becoming head of the university ski programs. He spent twenty-plus years in that position until he retired for a second time in 1995.

During the years Goodro worked for UP&L, he was also a member of the ski patrol, beginning as a line patroller for the company and then moving into volunteer work with the Salt Lake Metropolitan Ski Patrol, headed by Mike O'Neil. "The early volunteer ski patrollers were mostly members of the Wasatch Mountain Club and skied primarily at Brighton because it had a small tow for recreational skiers and we could ski free," Goodro remembers. "However, for the privilege of free skiing, we furnished our own bandages and performed a number of rescues in the backcountry. On one occasion, we had to hike several miles to a woman who had broken her back. All we had to carry her out with was an old door we had taken off one of the cabins nearby. It was a tough trip for both her and us!"

Goodro assisted in the rescue of Jill Kinmont in 1955. Kinmont was one of America's most promising young women ski racers. A movie, *The Other Side of the Mountain* (1974), tells the story of Kinmont's skiing accident and her subsequent successful teaching career from a wheelchair. At the time of the accident, Kinmont was a participant in the Snow Cup race at Alta.

"We were spectators at the spot where Jill was injured. We saw her go up in the air, glance off a tree above us, come down not far away from where we were standing, and then hit a spectator," Goodro remembers. "At the time we thought the spectator was the most seriously injured. He had all his ribs caved in on one side and was having considerable difficulty breathing because of the severe blow he had received from Jill hitting him with her skis. However, once we got over to Jill, we knew we had to give her immediate assistance. We had to be extremely careful of how we moved her. One bit of luck was that there was a doctor there. He proceeded to show us how to put a traction hitch on her head, which elongated her neck and upper spine. This probably saved her life! Shortly after giving us the assistance, he left, and we never had a chance to thank him because we were very busy at the time. We elected to walk her down the mountain in a cage basket rather than try and move her in a

Sverre Engen, circa early to mid-1940s.

Lois Engen, Sverre's wife, taking snow measurements at Alta, 1941.

toboggan. When we got to the bottom, we realized we still had the injured spectator on the mountain and had to hurry back up and bring him down. Overall, it made for a very stressful day, and we were all extremely tired at the end."

Goodro continued to provide outstanding assistance on Alta's ski patrol for thirty-eight years, twenty-five of them as director. When he retired in 1975, he received a special National Ski Patrol award for his many years of service in the Intermountain West.

Avalanche Control

The U.S. Forest Service conducted the first organized scientific research into snow safety, particularly avalanche control. In the late 1930s, as interest in Utah skiing grew rapidly, the Forest Service realized that it had to protect skiers visiting the new resorts being developed under its supervision. Many local skiers were skiing Alta's steep, rugged terrain under very hazardous avalanche conditions. Alta and the road leading to it offered ideal conditions for monitoring avalanches and developing control techniques to minimize danger to skiers.

W. E. Tangren is credited by Sverre Engen as the first person assigned by the Forest Service to be a snow and avalanche observer. He was first stationed at Alta during the 1938–39 ski season, where he made observations and maintained a log. Tangren had some basic skiing skills that greatly helped him in his job.

During Tangren's first year, an avalanche hit Alta's Snowpine Lodge (originally built by the Forest Service as a public shelter) on February 18, 1939, and destroyed the partially completed second story. When the lodge was rebuilt, the owners redesigned it so that any subsequent avalanches would go over the top of the building.

Sverre Engen was America's first designated snow ranger. He was hired by James E. Gurr, supervisor of the Wasatch National Forest, at the end of the 1939–40 ski season. He worked with Tangren for the first year, performing various measurements and studies. The next season, 1940–41, Sverre assumed full responsibility for snow research at Alta.

The Forest Service defined Sverre's duties more specifically than Tangren's the previous year. Besides posting closure signs in areas designated as high avalanche risk and supervising ski-related safety, Sverre was asked to develop the first snow-safety plan for Alta. To help with that task, he and Tangren had acquired precipitation and wind-velocity gauges from the Salt Lake Weather Bureau. Using these instruments, Sverre and his wife, Lois, took measurements and recorded the data. Sverre writes about his experiences as a snow ranger in his book *Skiing a Way of Life*. He recounts that they read the gauges every day, and

> we dug deep pits into the snow so the different layers could be studied as to consistency, settling, creepage, and the effect the weather had on them. We soon learned that it was usually during a storm or soon after that an avalanche was most apt to come down. Any sudden change in temperature was dangerous as well. If the temperature stayed low, the new snow had a better chance of binding with the old snow. But if it warmed up, chances were good it would slide.

They discovered that the best way to deal with avalanches was to start them under controlled conditions. Sverre and Tangren planted dynamite charges in the fall before the snow came. They placed the charges in strategic spots on the mountainside where they knew avalanches frequently ran. When the snow built up during winter storms and the avalanche danger became high, they set off the charges. This system had limited benefits. They could bring down slides when they wanted, but once the dynamite had exploded, they had no way to repeat the process until the next ski season. Nevertheless, they knew they were moving in the right direction.

Felix Koziol replaced James Gurr as forest supervisor of the Wasatch-Cache National Forest in 1942. Koziol and Sverre discussed using a military cannon to shoot down avalanches. According to Sverre, Koziol negotiated for an old French artillery cannon from the Utah National Guard. The cannon was used only for ceremonies at the time, so the soldiers agreed to take it to Alta during the winter months. National Guard personnel fired the first shots. When no one was around, Sverre and a few others decided to shoot the gun. Their first shots missed the mountain entirely and landed in American Fork Canyon. No one was in that area at the time. They eventually learned to aim the shots more accurately, which reduced avalanche hazards significantly.

For a time after World War II, avalanche shooting was done with a very noisy 105mm howitzer. The

Felix C. "Kozy" Koziol, circa 1960s.

gun was effective, but it had to be fired with precision and could inflict serious damage if the shells missed their mark.

Montgomery "Monty" M. Atwater became a legend in snow safety because he invented the avalauncher, a recoilless rifle that uses compressed nitrogen to propel a projectile into avalanche-prone areas. The avalauncher makes very little noise compared to the howitzer. Atwater was a native of Baker City, Oregon, and graduated from the Massachusetts Institute of Technology. He joined the Tenth Mountain Division during World War II and learned how to use explosives. Following his military experiences, he came to Alta as a replacement for Sverre, who had accepted the position of Alta Ski School director in 1945. Atwater was a multitalented man who, along with triggering avalanches by skiing across the slopes—something still done on occasion!—made major advances in snow safety and authored a number of high-adventure books for children.

Edward R. LaChapelle was brought to Alta in the early 1950s by Atwater. He was a physicist, glaciologist, and expert mountaineer, having had advanced study in Switzerland. The two men worked closely for several years and pioneered a number of new instruments for gathering snow data. One of them was the snow settlement gauge, which measured the stresses on each layer of snowpack. LaChapelle eventually replaced Atwater as snow ranger.

Atwater left Alta in 1956 because of disagreements with Forest Service superiors in Washington, D.C., concerning avalanche research support. The U.S. Forest Service transferred him to Squaw Valley,

Alf Engen and a National Guard gunner
using a howitzer for avalanche control.

California, and he took over supervision of avalanche control for the 1960 Olympic Winter Games. Monty retired from the Forest Service in 1964 but continued to be involved as a consultant expert on snow-safety concerns throughout the country. In 1966 he became chief of avalanche control for the World Championships held at Portillo, Chile. He made monumental contributions to the science of snow safety, ending when he passed away June 14, 1976.

Alta's snow-safety personnel are some of the finest and best-trained professionals in the world today. Back in Alta's mining days, however, there was nothing to protect anyone against avalanches. Most of the timber had been cut to shore up the mine tunnels, leaving the mountainsides bare and extremely vulnerable to avalanche. History records that Alta was hit by avalanches several times. One occurred on December 26, 1872, burying several teams of horses, the Parlin and Thompson stage, and killing fifteen people. In 1874 a slide swept down Emma Hill, snuffing out the lives of sixty men in buildings on Main Street. Some reports stated the snow was forty feet deep. Fire added to the devastation. Noted artist Thomas Moran (1837–1926) was so impressed with the power generated by the avalanche that he portrayed the event on canvas in

Buried in an Avalanche

Alan Engen recounts a harrowing experience he lived through at Alta in early 1953 when he was about thirteen:

Alta had already accumulated ten feet when an unusual storm deposited an additional sixty inches of heavy, wet snow on the slopes. At about 3 A.M., a huge avalanche was triggered on both the Cardiff and Flagstaff ridges above and north of the Alta Lodge and the ranger station. The massive slide split, with half going down a gully, just missing the Alta Peruvian Lodge. The other half hit the Alta Lodge, knocking out the rope tow just west of the lodge and shearing off the thirty-year-old pine trees in front of the lodge as if they were matchsticks.

The effects of an avalanche are hard to forget. I was asleep on the lower floor of the lodge by the outer wall. I was sleeping on one side of the room with my parents on the other. The first thing I remember was hearing a loud roar, which was immediately followed by a crash as the avalanche hit the lodge. Then total silence. The snow filled my side from floor to ceiling. I thought that side of the building had collapsed. I couldn't move, and it was very difficult to breathe. Luckily, the drapery that hung in front of the window had blown over my head when the avalanche hit the room, preventing me from being severely cut by glass.

Then, I heard my mother yelling in panic, "Get him out, get him out!" Fortunately, the avalanche had only partially covered my parents. Dad freed himself and started digging for me. All the electric power to the lodge had been knocked out so there was no light. Dad knew generally where my head had been and dug down in the corner of the room where I lay, buried under several feet of snow. In his efforts to reach me, he was cut severely in several places by the glass hidden in the snow. If he hadn't

Thomas Moran painting of an 1878 Alta avalanche. Courtesy Thomas Nygard Gallery, Bozeman, Montana.

Ed LaChapelle (see circled area of photo) caught in an Alta avalanche off the Peruvian Ridge, circa1959. Complete photo story can be found in *Skiing News* magazine, vol. XIII, no. 1 (October 1960): pp. 12–17. Photo by Fred Lindholm.

gotten to me when he did, I wouldn't have survived much longer.

Chic Morton, manager of the Alta Lodge, was asleep in the next room when the slide hit. He came into our room shortly after Dad had dug me out. All he said when he shone his flashlight on the scene was "Holy cow!"

Miraculously, no one else had been buried by the avalanche, but cars parked in the lot above and north of the lodge were thrown all the way down the hillside close to where the Goldminer's Daughter Lodge currently stands. Ironically, the slide hit the Avalanche Study Center developed by Monty Atwater and Ed LaChapelle, destroying its bank of instruments. Considering the size of the avalanche, everyone was very lucky to escape further injury.

his 1895 oil painting *Avalanche in Cottonwood Canyon That Destroyed Alta in 1878.*

Today Alta's snow-safety program has pushed the science of avalanche control to a high level. Do avalanches still occur? Yes, of course. Is it possible for people to die in these massive slides? Absolutely. Even the experts can get caught, as evidenced in the avalanche photo above, where snow ranger Ed LaChapelle was caught in 1959 but luckily survived with no injuries. In early 1998 a "controlled" avalanche at Alta was a bit stronger than expected and slammed into one of the wings of the Alta Peruvian Lodge, knocking it partially off its foundation; however, the lodge wing had previously been evacuated—*just in case.*

The majority of people who lose their lives in avalanches use poor judgment—ignoring warning signs in avalanche-prone areas or being inadequately prepared or equipped for rapidly changing snow conditions. Most experienced skiers agree that the longer you spend in the mountains, the more you learn to respect the unpredictability of the slopes, thus taking more precautions. A few of those precautions include *always* skiing with a partner, *always* carrying an avalanche-rescue transceiver (PEEPS), and *always* checking with knowledgeable snow-safety professionals in the area before skiing untracked slopes. However, as Ed LaChapelle once said, "Use your head in deep snow but don't stay out of it—it's the greatest thrill in skiing." ❄

chapter seven

SKI RESORTS
in the Intermountain West

While ski jumping was at its peak in Utah, a new form of skiing was taking a strong hold in Vermont and New Hampshire under the guidance of Hannes Schneider. He promoted the Arlberg Technique and the use of skis shorter than seven feet. Downhill skiers could touch the tips of these new skis with the cup of the hand (these skis were one to two feet longer than skis today).

The Arlberg Technique and shorter skis also began to be used in the Intermountain region, and local skiers and promoters started to dream of ski resorts in the Wasatch Mountains. In late 1934 the Salt Lake Chamber of Commerce and leading local figures formed the Wasatch Outdoor Recreational Committee. This organization, headed by Gus P. Backman, secretary of the Chamber, proposed to "develop the natural recreational facilities until they become second to none in this country." The following week, December 14, 1934, the *Salt Lake Tribune* published an article titled "Winter Sports Drive Opens," touting steps necessary to make Salt Lake City and the surrounding territory into the "Winter Sports Center of America."

Other new technologies were being actively developed: ski poles; adjustable, tight-fitting bindings; sealskin climbers; a laboratory of ski waxes; light but windproof, snow-shedding clothing; goggles; and ointments to prevent windburn and sunburn. Some

Never before in the history of the state has there been such a keen interest in both major and minor winter sports. Civic groups and individuals seem to have become convinced that the natural facilities offered for recreational purposes in the nearby canyons equal those in other regions of the country, which are far more extensively advertised, and each season draws major events and thousands of fans and participants.

—Deseret News, *December 7, 1934*

merchants in Salt Lake City started carrying ski supplies. Members of the Wasatch Mountain Club began using the new equipment. Some of the ski jumpers and a few newer members of the club who had Alpine skiing experience gave the other members ski lessons. Interest in skiing as recreation, rather than as a spectator activity, grew rapidly.

In the late 1930s, the Utah Ski Club and the Wasatch Mountain Club announced that Utah was the "King of Winter Sports." The U.S. Department of Agriculture, the Forest Service, the Salt Lake Chamber of Commerce, and the Works Projects Administration (WPA) actively promoted skiing. The WPA built roads to ski areas and constructed public shelters such as the Snowpine Lodge at Alta in 1937–38.

The Development of Selected Intermountain Ski Areas

On the south end of the Salt Lake Valley lie Big and Little Cottonwood Canyons. Up Big Cottonwood are the ski resorts of Brighton and Solitude; up Little Cottonwood are Snowbird and Alta. A bit farther north lie The Canyons, Park City, and Deer Valley, three fine resorts located up Parleys Canyon, just a forty-five-minute drive from Salt Lake City. Going north another forty miles, there are three more

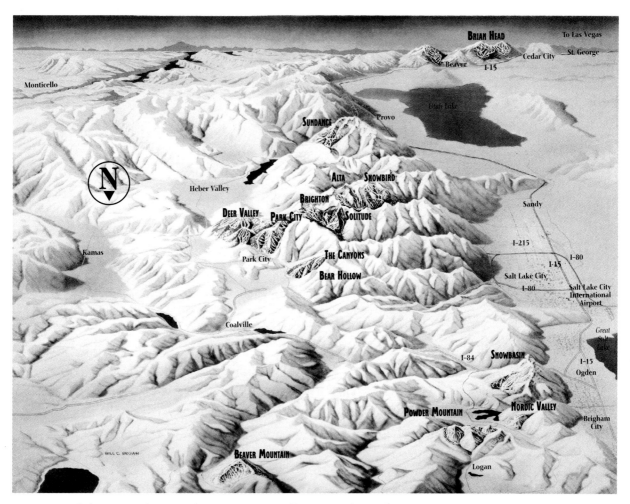

Map of the Wasatch Front ski areas, 1998. Illustration by Bill C. Brown. Photo courtesy *Ski Utah*.

prominent ski areas—Snowbasin, Powder Mountain, and Nordic Valley. Even farther north are Sun Valley, Idaho, and Jackson Hole, Wyoming. In Provo Canyon is Sundance, and south towards Cedar City, Utah, is Brian Head.

Utah may be well known as the Mecca of the Mormon religion, but the truth is, when newcomers arrive in Utah, the first question most commonly asked by the locals is not "Are you Mormon?" but rather "Do you ski?"

SUN VALLEY, IDAHO

In Idaho, what was to become one of the nation's largest and best-known ski resorts was taking shape in the 1930s. According to an article written by Deanne Thompson in the January 30, 1986, issue of the *Idaho Mountain Express,* Averell Harriman was quoted as saying, "As chairman of the board [of the Union Pacific Railroad], I was trying to develop

industry in the West, which would not only promote traffic for the railroad, but promote the territory as well. One of the things that I had learned when I was in Europe—I was a banker and traveled there—was that my banker friends went off skiing in the wintertime to places like St. Moritz and Austria in the mountains. There were no ski resorts in the West. There were lots of people skiing, but there was no resort in the sense of having a St. Moritz or places with hotels and people owning property nearby. I thought that was something we should develop in the West. So I employed Count Felix Schaffgotsch, who as an Austrian . . . had a lot to do with development of resorts in Austria. I asked him to come over and explore the Union Pacific territory for a place where we could start a resort."

Schaffgotsch spent most of 1935 and part of 1936 searching throughout the West. A few of the places he visited were Alta, Utah; Jackson Hole, Wyoming; and

Left: Count Felix Schaffgotsch, circa mid-1930s.
Right: Averell Harriman, circa late 1930s.

Aspen, Colorado. At the recommendation of Union Pacific's Idaho representative, William Hynes, Schaffgotsch visited several places there. When he reached the little mountain ranching town of Ketchum, Idaho, he fell in love with the surrounding area and called Harriman to let him know that he had found the place to build his dream resort. Schaffgotsch felt it had all the necessary assets: excellent dry snow, scenic mountains, and a mild climate. Plus it had one additional attribute—the Union Pacific Railroad passed by the town of Shoshone, only fifty-five miles south of Ketchum.

Harriman agreed with Schaffgotsch's recommendation; however, before proceeding further, he had a businessman from Florida look over the terrain. At first, Steve Hannagan, who had put Miami Beach on the map, was not positive about the area because he was not used to snow and cold. But when the sun came out, that made all the difference. It was Hannagan who recommended to Harriman, "Do it on a big scale or don't do it at all—and call it Sun Valley." Shortly after, the Union Pacific purchased ranchland owned by the Brass family near Ketchum. In the spring of 1936, work started on the Sun Valley Lodge. Harriman also asked Union Pacific engineers to figure out how to transport the skiers up the mountain. James Curran, a Union Pacific bridge engineer in Omaha, Nebraska, originated the idea of using chairs. Harriman put him in charge of lift construction. Curran came up with the chair idea from watching a monocable conveyor system used to load banana boats. Instead of hooks to carry bananas, he substituted chairs to carry skiers. The idea worked, and Harriman approved construction of the world's first chairlift. According to national ski historian Allen Adler, there were "actually two chairlifts involved, one on Dollar Mountain and the other on Proctor Mountain."

Sun Valley opened on December 21, 1936. Through extensive promotion, such movie stars as Claudette Colbert, Errol Flynn, Robert Young, Loretta Young, Clark Gable, and Gary Cooper were attracted to the resort. Shortly after the opening, a film called *Sun Valley Serenade* celebrated the resort's ice skating and skiing, and greatly increased the resort's popularity. Author Ernest Hemingway relocated to make his home in Sun Valley. The word was out—Sun Valley was the place to be.

In 1939 the chairlift on Mt. Baldy was opened to the public, giving advanced skiers a chance at a real mountain run. The prestigious Harriman Cup ski race was organized and ran every year until 1965. Recreational activities came to a halt during World War II, while the U.S. Navy used Sun Valley for hospital and recuperation facilities. After the war Sun Valley reopened as an exclusive destination resort. By the end of the 1997–98 ski season, Sun Valley offered skiers seventeen lifts and more than seventy-seven ski runs laid over two thousand acres.

Dick Durrance receiving the prestigious Harriman Cup from Mrs. Averell Harriman, circa 1937.

Sun Valley Lodge, as viewed from Dollar Mountain, circa mid-1940s.

Evelyn Engen, doubling for the double of Barbara Stanwyck, is carried down the mountain by her husband, Alf.

Alf Engen and Ralph Bellamy, circa 1945. Alf doubled for several Hollywood stars for movies made in the 1940s.

Alf Engen was still a bachelor when he first arrived in Ketchum, Idaho, in 1937. At that time (1935–42), he was employed by the Forest Service in planning and developing winter sports recreational areas throughout Utah, Idaho, Wyoming, and other points encompassing Forest Service Region 4. His first year at Sun Valley involved overseeing the construction of a ski-jumping hill at Ruud Mountain. That following winter (1937–38) Alf was put on loan from the Forest Service to the Union Pacific Railroad, retained by Harriman to represent Sun Valley in a public relations capacity when he competed in tournaments around the country. He was also courting, so whatever free time he had was spent driving between Sun Valley and Centerville, Utah.

Alf and Evelyn were married on December 23, 1937, in Centerville and left immediately after the reception for Sun Valley in their Chevy coupe. A blinding snowstorm was in progress, causing so many delays that they did not reach Sun Valley until the following evening. Upon arrival, they were greeted by a band and a large crowd of well-wishers, and given a room in the Challenger Inn, which became their first home.

Over the next several years, Alf continued to represent Sun Valley during winter months and work for the Forest Service, overseeing development of selected ski areas during the summer. According to Evelyn, the summer of 1939 was particularly interesting. As the Forest Service foreman of a CCC group, Alf was assigned the job of overseeing the cutting of timber when the Warm Springs Run was put in at Sun Valley on Baldy Mountain. "The entire summer was spent living in a tent. That was an experience I shall never forget."

During the early 1940s Alf participated in the filming of Hollywood movies, doubling for such stars as George Brent and Ralph Bellamy. In the film *Northern Pursuit*, Alf doubled for Errol Flynn as the hero in the story, while Corey Engen doubled for the actor playing the part of the villain. Evelyn also became involved in the movies during the filming of *My Reputation*. Barbara Stanwyck's double, who was to be carried off the ski hill by my father, was so frightened that she refused to do it. So Evelyn jumped into Alf's arms and became the double for Stanwyck's double.

The Alf Engen family left Sun Valley and returned to Utah in 1942 so that Alf could help in the develop-

Alf Engen, Forest Service foreman and senior supervisor of CCC Company 3240, circa 1942.

ment of the Snowbasin area. They lived in Huntsville and Ogden during the war years, then returned to Sun Valley in 1945.

During this time, Alf, Evelyn, and Alan lived in the Sun Valley Lodge, next door to Gary Cooper. Alan remembers how big Cooper looked and that he allowed Alan to tag along with him on many occasions. He also has fond recollections of the good times fishing in the backcountry with his parents and Walter and Eleanor Prager.

The family's Sun Valley years between 1945 and 1948 were full of wonderful experiences, but upon Alf's return from coaching the 1948 U.S. Winter Olympic Ski Team in St. Moritz, Switzerland, they went back to Salt Lake City. There, Alf joined Sverre at Alta and, shortly after, became the ski-school director.

BRIGHTON, UTAH

Utah's Brighton sprang from totally different roots. It began as a hotel, long before skiing became popular, and was named after William S. and Catherine B. Brighton, who moved to Utah from Iowa City in 1857. In 1870, through the Homestead Act, they acquired

an eighty-acre piece of land near Silver Lake in Big Cottonwood Canyon. Because of the extensive mining in Alta, Park City, and American Fork Canyon, William Brighton saw a good business opportunity because Brighton was centrally located between these camps. He built a two-story hotel in 1874 to accom-modate travelers, and by 1890 the location had become well known. In 1893 William and Catherine replaced the first hotel with a second, much larger one, which they named the Brighton Hotel. Catherine died of heart failure shortly after its completion in July 1894. The pass that separates Brighton and Alta

bears her name—Catherine's Pass. Nine months later William died of blood poisoning. James H. Moyle, a young attorney, became administrator of the Brighton estate and bought the property.

According to Utah ski historian Alexis Kelner, William Brighton and his brother "were probably among the first to use skis at Brighton. As skis, bindings, and overboots were not available commer-cially, most had to be fashioned at home."

During the 1920s the Wasatch Mountain Club often visited Brighton on its summer and winter outings and in 1928 built a lodge. In December 1935,

CCC camp at the mouth of Big Cottonwood Canyon, circa late 1930s.

because of increased interest in Alpine skiing, the Wasatch Mountain Club sponsored its first Alpine competition on the north slope of Mt. Millicent.

K. Smith and a group of Salt Lake businessmen constructed a thirteen-hundred-foot T-bar lift in 1939. Art Johansen was the first ski-teaching professional at Brighton. In 1941 a rope tow was added. In 1943 Zane Doyle purchased the Brighton ski area. Following World War II, he redesigned the original T-bar and constructed the Millicent chairlift in 1947. K. Smith became ski-school director.

From the late 1940s through the 1960s, Brighton was a center for many competitive Alpine skiing events. The Utah High School State Skiing Championship, known as the Knutson Cup (named after businessman and avid supporter Art Knutson, who donated the large trophy), usually was held at Brighton. Another favorite local race at Brighton was the *Salt Lake Tribune* Ski Classic. Jim Gaddis, who became one of America's premier Alpine racers, frequently won this annual event during the 1950s and early '60s. As of the 1998–99 ski season, Brighton offers skiers high-speed quad lifts, two triple chairs, and three double chairs, with a total uphill capacity of eleven thousand skiers an hour.

PARK CITY, UTAH

The mid-1930s saw the start of recreational skiing in Park City. Located some thirty miles from Salt Lake City, Park City was first explored by Mormon settlers in the 1840s. In 1869 three soldiers from Col. Patrick

E. Connor's company found an outcrop of quartz containing large amounts of silver and some gold. By 1880 Park City was a thriving place with three hundred buildings. The town's turbulent history includes a disastrous fire in 1898 that, fanned by canyon winds, almost destroyed the mining community.

Because of deteriorating metal prices at the end of World War II, Park City's economy skidded downhill. To reverse the gloomy situation, the United Park City Mines Company Board of Directors studied the possibility of converting property to recreational use, including downhill skiing. With eleven thousand acres of potential ski terrain to work with, Park City Mines commissioned the Salt Lake Office of National Planning and Research to conduct a feasibility study in 1958 to see whether the area could support year-round recreational facilities. The study concluded that Park

Young skiers on Creole Hill above Park City.
Photo courtesy Park City Museum.

The Snow Train making its way toward Snow Park (now Deer Valley),
circa 1930. Photo courtesy Mel Fletcher.

Old Snow Park ski run, circa mid-1940s. Photo courtesy Park City Museum.

City could compete successfully with such towns as Aspen, Colorado, and Jackson Hole, Wyoming. The result was a massive infusion of low-interest loans from the federal government.

Park City established the Park City Recreation Committee to oversee the management of the recreational efforts. It named its first recreational facility Treasure Mountain, which opened in December 1963 and continued to operate under the ownership and management of the United Park City Mines Company throughout the remainder of the 1960s.

In 1969 Royal Street Development Company of New Orleans bought the Park City resort, and a new organization—the Greater Park City Company—was formed to manage the properties. Because of rising interest rates and the Arab oil embargo of 1973–74, the company could not meet its obligations and sold the resort to Alpine Meadows of Lake Tahoe, Inc., headed by Nick Badami. About 1995, Badami sold the Park City ski area to Ian Cummings. Currently under Cummings' direction, the name has been changed to Park City Mountain Resort, and it operates as a world-class facility, contributing greatly to Utah's economy.

DEER VALLEY, UTAH

Skiing in the Deer Valley area, located about a mile from Park City, dates to the mid-1930s. In an effort to promote skiing in the Salt Lake City region, the Salt Lake Junior Chamber of Commerce decided to charter a train to transport skiers to various recreational sites along the Wasatch Front. They named it the Snow Train, and the area that is now Deer Valley was one of the first places visited. On February 16, 1936, the first Snow Train departed the Denver and Rio Grande Station in Salt Lake City with approximately five hundred skiers bound for Parleys Canyon. The train remained at the area during the day so skiers could return to the train periodically to warm up. In late afternoon the train returned to Salt Lake with many happy but tired skiers. The Snow Train ran for a number of years with marginal success. The program was discontinued at the outbreak of World War II.

In an attempt to energize interest in Park City skiing after the war, Otto Carpenter and Robert Burns constructed a T-bar lift in an area above Park City commonly called Deer Valley, and they named the area Snow Park. It opened December 8, 1946, with free tow rides for any skier. During the summer of 1947, Burns and Carpenter converted it to a chairlift and also

added another lift in 1948.

Mel Fletcher organized the Snow Park Ski Club to promote skiing in the area and raise money for a proposed new ski-jumping hill near Thayne's Canyon, not far away. Unfortunately, neither the ski area nor the ski club had an easy time in the late 1940s and early '50s. Fletcher was so disappointed with the lack of interest in skiing in Park City that he wrote an article in the *Park Record* newspaper on March 20, 1947, in which he said, "Park City is fortunate in having the finest snow conditions in the country but the city is also unfortunate in the fact that it can not, or will not, recognize or make use of nature's gift."

Fortunately, that is no longer true. Royal Street Development Company turned its interest to developing the Deer Valley resort in the 1980s, and the area is now a world-class resort attracting an elite clientele. Deer Valley ended the 1997–98 season with three high-speed quads, one fixed-grip quad, nine triple quads, two double-quad lifts, and seventy-three trails laid over 350 acres. Both Deer Valley and Park City will be Olympic venues in 2002.

ALTA, UTAH

Park City, Snow Park, and Brighton were not the only areas in Utah under consideration as ski resorts. In 1935 Alf Engen recommended that the Forest Service consider Alta for development. Because of the Forest Service's interest in ski-area development, it had retained Alf to visit Alta during the winter and evaluate the former mining town as a potential ski area. He stayed with a couple of brothers named Jacobson. Based on Alf's recommendations and George Watson's deeding of surface rights, development of Alta as a ski area began.

In 1937, under the leadership of Joe Quinney, a group of Salt Lake businessmen formed the Salt Lake Winter Sports Association. The association's goal was to establish a modestly priced ski area for the local population, so it laid plans to construct a chairlift at Alta. The association made a deal with the Michigan-Utah Mines to purchase the aerial tram that hauled ore down Little Cottonwood Canyon in the early 1900s. Association members raised ten thousand dollars for this purchase and awarded Utah ski promoter Mark Strand the contract to build the supports and install the lift up the face of Collins Gulch. The first lift towers were built of timbers once used to brace mine shafts.

Collins chairlift, Alta, circa 1940.
Photo courtesy Utah State Historical Society.

The Forest Service issued the initial permit to construct the chairlift to the Salt Lake Winter Sports Association on October 19, 1938, and Alta officially opened as a ski area in December. On Sunday, January 15, 1939, the Collins lift, America's second chairlift, operated for the first time, carrying 350 people up the mountainside at a cost of 25 cents for a single ride or $1.50 for a full day. From January 1939 through April 1940, eighty-six thousand skiers rode this chairlift, which was operated by Fred Speyer.

In 1939 two public shelters were opened. The first was the Snowpine day lodge. The original building had been used as part of the Bay City Mine and then was converted to a general store and post office in the late 1870s. After the stock market crash of October 1929, owner Howard Stillwell closed the doors to the building and moved away. The old store sat abandoned from 1929 through 1937. When the Salt Lake Winter Sports Association and the U.S. Forest Service decided to develop Alta into a ski area, the Forest Service had the WPA renovate the old store into a public shelter for those who skied the lower mountain. For the upper mountain, the original Watson Shelter, constructed of logs and granite, was dedicated on November 19, 1939. It was named in honor of "Mayor" George Watson and offered food and warmth to skiers using the Collins lift.

During that winter the Salt Lake Chamber of Commerce announced that the Denver and Rio Grande Railroad would invest twenty-five thousand dollars to develop Alta as a ski area, including construction of the Alta Lodge, which opened in 1940. Alta's first master plan was approved by the Forest Service on April 11, 1940. A ski school had been in operation since 1938, when Karl Fahrner became the first ski-school director. In 1940 Dick Durrance replaced Fahrner as director, but it was not until January 1, 1942, that formal approval was given by James E. Gurr, Forest Service supervisor, to operate the ski school within the confines of the Alta ski area.

In 1944 several people generated the idea of selling Utah's unique scenery to increase the tourist business. After lengthy discussions the Utah Department of Publicity and Industrial Development contracted with Twentieth Century Fox to produce a short promotional film. The department designed the film to show audiences around the world that Utah is beautiful and is the center of "ski-nic" America—the winter sports paradise of the West. The film, featuring Alta and the three Engen brothers, was titled *Ski Aces,* cost twenty thousand dollars to make, and consisted of ten minutes of narrated skiing, music, and color. Color film was relatively new in the early 1940s, so the technology was state-of-the-art. In February 1947 the *Utah Industrial Development News* published an article headlined "Utah Film Short Seen by 90 Million People." *Ski Aces* effectively promoted skiing in Utah in the mid- to late-1940s. It was one of the first promotional films for ski tourism in the United States.

Alta today enjoys a reputation as one of the top recreational places to ski, especially suited to those who enjoy powder snow, beautiful scenery, and a low-key approach to further development and expansion. As of the 1990 census, 397 individuals called Alta home. At the end of the 1997–98 season, Alta operated six double and two triple chairlifts and five surface tows; it has twenty-two hundred skiable acres.

There are many people who were instrumental in the development of Alta. As already mentioned, Alf Engen played an early role, as well as Joe Quinney, in the early stages of Alta as a ski area. Several others, however, also made major contributions to its development:

FRED SPEYER grew up in Vienna, Austria, immigrated to Canada, and then moved to Salt Lake City. During the mid- to late-1930s, he spent time coaching his friends in the new Alpine *skisport.* By 1937 he had

Early ski-area development pioneers at Alta, circa early 1950s: (left to right) Bob Card, unidentified person, Chic Morton, Fred Speyer. Photo courtesy Alta Ski Lifts Company.

settled on Alta as the place where he could best use his skiing talents and exceptional aptitude for fixing anything mechanical. He became the first manager of Alta's first chairlift.

CHARLES "CHIC" MORTON was one of the key pioneers in the development of Alta. He came to Alta in 1946 at the encouragement of his good friend Sverre Engen, who knew of a bartending job available at the Alta Lodge. Chic also loved to ski, and Sverre felt this presented an excellent opportunity for the two to ski together on a more frequent basis. Chic took the job, which launched a fifty-year career at Alta. During those years, Chic managed the Alta Lodge during the mid- to late-1950s, ending when he took over as general manager of Alta Ski Lifts from Fred Speyer in 1958. In 1976, Chic assumed further duties as president of the company in addition to being general manager. In 1988, he relinquished general manager duties to Onno Wieringa but retained the title of

president until his passing in 1997.

Over a half-century span, Chic Morton made numerous contributions to the skiing industry—president of the Utah Ski Association, president of the Intermountain Ski Association, and member of the board of directors of the Forest Service Recreation Association. Chic was recognized in 1995 by the University of Utah J. Willard Marriott Library's Ski Archives Program when he was presented the prestigious S. J. and J. E. Quinney Award for Outstanding Achievements and Contributions to the Sport of Skiing.

JANET QUINNEY LAWSON, daughter of S. Joseph Quinney, is a figure who looms large in Utah's skiing history. She became interested in skiing when her father met Alf Engen and started to judge ski-jumping events at Ecker Hill in the early 1930s.

"As a very young girl, I went with Dad and my brother Dave to Ecker Hill," Lawson remembers.

Janet Quinney Lawson with Alf Engen at Utah Winter Sports Park, August 1993.

"While the jumping activities were going on, I would go to nearby Mile Canyon and practice skiing. I jumped a little as well in those days. However, my first serious Alpine skiing was done at Brighton. Alta was not a ski area then so we skied mainly at Brighton and some at Park City. But when Alta opened as a ski area in 1938–39, I skied there from then on. I began to race around the age of fourteen."

Before the outbreak of World War II, Lawson became a top American ski racer. If the Olympic Winter Games had not been canceled in 1940 and 1944, she probably would have been named to the women's squad. During those years she competed in such major races as the Harriman Cup at Sun Valley, the Roche Cup at Aspen, and the Snow Cup at Alta. Twice at Sun Valley, Lawson won the Mary Cornelia Trophy for an important intercollegiate race. She also raced at Snowbasin when it began operating and recalls that "the first Snowbasin lift was started by my mother's brother, Bill Eccles. He and several other Ogden businessmen raised the money and built the lift." Lawson presently serves on the board of directors for Alta Ski Lifts Company.

So Joseph Quinney's legacy continues. Janet plays a significant role in preserving the ski history of the Intermountain West. Quinney's son, the late David Sr., became one of Utah's premier ski jumpers in the 1930s and '40s. Quinney's grandson, David Jr., is also promoting Utah's ski history as a board member for the Alf Engen Ski Museum Foundation.

JAMES "J" LAUGHLIN (pronounced *Lock-lin*) received a number of awards for his role in developing skiing, among them the International Ski History Association Lifetime Achievement Award for his writing in the *Ski Bulletin*. He began skiing in 1935 in Switzerland, later spending a winter in St. Anton, Austria, taking ski lessons in the Hannes Schneider Ski School. At St. Anton he became familiar with the European ski hut program, which he felt was so worthwhile that he introduced it to the United States.

After finishing his schooling at Harvard, he started a publishing firm, New Directions. During the winter of 1940–41, Dick Durrance, the ski-school director, invited him to visit Alta. According to Laughlin, "Dick got me to visit Alta and have a look. It reminded me of Zurs, Switzerland, before it was developed."

The Snow Cup

One of the earliest and most significant ski races in the country, the Snow Cup, was held at Alta. In the 1940s and '50s it was considered almost as important a race as Sun Valley's prestigious Harriman Cup and was one of the major competitive events used to select the U.S. Olympic Alpine Team. Many people think the race was named for Alta's internationally famous deep powder. This is not the case, however. Herbert Snow, a local Salt Lake businessman, underwrote the cost of the four-foot-tall perpetual trophy, so the race was named after him.

Barney McLean and Gretchen Fraser won the first race in 1940. Other winners have included famous names such as Corey Engen, Dick Durrance, Jack Reddish, Marvin Melville, Andrea Mead Lawrence, and Suzy Harris. Jim Gaddis won it three successive years (1962–64) but was not allowed to retire the trophy. Unfortunately, in 1987 the old trophy disappeared, and attempts to locate it have so far not met with any success.

James "J" Laughlin, circa early 1940s.

Laughlin liked what he saw so much that the following year he took over the lease on the Alta Lodge and eventually bought out the interest of the Denver and Rio Grande Railroad.

Laughlin played a significant role in Alta's conservative approach to development. He was a primary influence on Alta's ability to remain one of America's premier winter recreational resorts while retaining its unspoiled beauty and unique charm. In an article published in the *New Yorker* in March 1992, Laughlin said, "You've got to keep some places like God made them. . . . If you overdo it, you'll destroy Alta. . . . I take great pride in Alta, because it is the one place that's left that's a little bit like the old skiing." Laughlin died in November 1997.

BILL LEVITT must also be included as a major contributor to Alta's development. While not a native, he is, as he puts it, "one of Utah's most loyal patriots." His interest in skiing started through his affiliation with the Boy Scouts in New York State. At age fourteen, while at a Scout winter camp, he strapped on a friend's wooden skis (without metal edges) and slid down a sloped roadway leading to a lake covered with ice.

Levitt, who has served as mayor of Alta longer than anyone, laughed as he finished the story: "I must have gone a quarter of a mile across the lake before I came to a stop. I thought this was the greatest thing that had ever happened to me. I went back up the hill

Ski Huts Come to America

Although downhill was the most visible manifestation of skiing in Utah, another form of skiing became important in the 1940s. Because of Laughlin's experiences in Europe, he strongly advocated touring—making extensive trips through the backcountry on skis.

After World War II, the National Ski Association formed a special committee, headed by Laughlin, to search for areas appropriate for huts. Laughlin gained strong support from the Wasatch Mountain Club and Felix Koziol, supervisor of the Wasatch National Forest. In 1942 Laughlin wrote an article in the American Ski Annual titled "A Plea for Huts in America." It reads:

> We must have huts in America for high mountain touring. Not just occasional isolated huts here and there, but groups of two and three related huts in our principal mountain areas. Until we have them, the run of American skiers will never know what it means to tour, and, as anyone knows who has toured abroad, touring is the real cream of skiing.

The first huts in Utah were constructed in 1948—two at Alta and one on Snake Creek Pass above Brighton. A long-range plan to build fourteen huts connecting Alta, Brighton, American Fork Canyon, and Park City never materialized.

Sadly, interest in ski touring with overnight stays has diminished. The huts constructed at Alta lasted approximately thirty years. The one on Germania Pass was constructed of prefabricated metal and remained until the 1970s. The other, an old Quonset hut nestled in the trees at the top of the Supreme Lift, still stands. It has not been used for several years and is in poor condition.

and tried it again, but this time something went wrong, and I fell headfirst into a snowbank. That was my introduction to skiing."

Mayor Bill Levitt, Town of Alta

Many years went by before Levitt tried skiing again. His second experience was with a business associate at an area in Vermont called Big Bromley. After being outfitted, he took his first ski lessons and became hooked. Shortly after, he and his wife decided to go west and try skiing during the Thanksgiving holiday. They planned to go to Aspen but found it had marginal snow conditions that year. Freidl Pfeifer, who was the ski-school director at Aspen, recommended they ski Alta because it had plenty of snow.

The Levitts followed Pfeifer's suggestion and immediately fell in love with Alta. He loved it so much that as Mayor Levitt says, "I had to make a choice: buy United Airlines so I could afford to continue visiting Alta on a frequent basis or purchase the Alta Lodge. I decided on the latter and bought the lodge in 1959 from J. Laughlin."

Alta became a Utah township (defined as eight hundred residents or less) in August 1970, and Levitt

Mining tram that ran between Alta and Tanner's Flat, Little Cottonwood Canyon, with the future Snowbird area in the background, circa 1915. Photo courtesy Alta Ski Lifts Company.

was elected mayor in 1971. (The only other Alta mayor was George Watson, who carried the self-proclaimed title from 1937 to 1953). Levitt's contributions have had a lasting effect on the community, which include a volunteer fire department, a police force, a community center, and a modern communications hub for handling emergencies on a twenty-four-hour-a-day, seven-day-a-week basis. Levitt's greatest challenge, and perhaps his most significant contribution, involves keeping Alta low-key and environmentally sensitive.

SNOWBIRD, UTAH

In the early to mid-1950s, G. Ted Johnson visited Alta, working as a handyman for the Rustler Lodge. He had a passion for skiing, especially powder snow. It wasn't long before he joined Alf Engen in the Alta Ski School and became one of the best-known powder-skiing instructors. While teaching part-time, Johnson worked his way into lodge management and cultivated an interest in starting a small ski operation of his own. He took a fancy to Peruvian Gulch, just a mile down Little Cottonwood Canyon from Alta. At this time, the Engen brothers and their wives owned several acres of land between Alta and what was to become Snowbird. They donated part of the land to the Utah Department of Transportation (UDOT) so that a bypass road could be constructed around avalanche-prone Mt. Superior. This allowed skiers to access Alta despite heavy snow conditions. The balance of the land was subsequently sold to Ted and Wilma Johnson.

By the middle 1960s, Johnson had secured title to several former mining properties. His first acquisition was the Blackjack claims, followed by land near Snowbird's present Cliff Lodge. Over the next several years, Johnson quietly continued buying up mining claims. In March 1966 he applied for a special-use permit from the Forest Service to develop Peruvian Gulch/Gad Valley into a year-round recreational resort. His initial plan was to capitalize the project through the sale of thirty limited partnerships. In September 1967 he obtained a permit to proceed with the development of the area he called Snowbird.

As is true in many ventures, planning to raise capital and actually doing it are two different things. Johnson's dream for Snowbird was in serious jeopardy until 1969 when he met Richard D. Bass, the wealthy son of Oklahoma oil magnate H. G. Bass. After viewing a promotional film about Snowbird's development plan, Bass acquired an 80-percent ownership in the

venture and provided the desperately needed funding that pushed the project from dream to reality. Johnson's remaining interest in Snowbird was bought by Bass, leaving him as principal owner.

In December 1971 Snowbird's tram began operation. Since then Snowbird has continued to grow as a year-round resort but has been plagued by financial difficulties. In December 1997, at a Snowbird-sponsored conference, Bass told a large audience with a smile, "I am finally able to see the light at the end of the tunnel. It has been a long time coming." At the end of the 1997–98 season, Snowbird operated a 120-passenger tram, seven double chairlifts, and one high-speed quad lift that served sixty-six runs covering more than twenty-five hundred acres.

One thing that can be said about Bass is that he thrives on challenge. In more recent years, at an age when many people are thinking about retirement, he did what few have ever done: he climbed and stood at the top of Mt. Everest, the highest point on this planet.

SNOWBASIN, UTAH

Relatively unknown outside of Utah but destined for fame, thanks to the 2002 Winter Olympics, is Snowbasin, east of Ogden. In the early 1930s, the citizens of Ogden had a high interest in skiing but mostly as spectators who watched a few professional ski-jump meets at Becker Hill near Huntsville. A group of ski enthusiasts formed the Ogden Ski Club, but they had a problem—lack of suitable terrain. Talk persisted of great skiing terrain behind the lofty peak of Mt. Ogden. After several requests to the Forest Service to examine the site as a potential ski area, Felix Koziol sent Alf Engen, who was the Forest Service recreation advisor, into the high country to investigate. In the early spring of 1936, Alf and Koziol were watching a young group of skiers on the hills just outside Huntsville, where the Trappers Loop Highway is today. Alf remembered the day well. "I pointed toward Mt. Ogden and said, 'Kozy, do you see that mountain over there? That is where a ski area should be built. It has all the fine features necessary. It has good terrain, the exposure is right, and the snow conditions are excellent.' "

Koziol agreed, and in 1938 Alf and a couple of Forest Service associates hiked into Wheeler Basin to inspect the terrain. Alf said the hike was difficult because there were no roads. That notwithstanding, the troupe confirmed that the area was an excellent

Alf Engen selecting a potential ski area,
Snowbasin, circa 1936.

The Forest Service funded construction of a road into Snowbasin during the summer and fall of 1940. Alf was a Forest Service foreman during the summer months and supervised the CCC crew that built the road into the area. He had quite an experience while working on the road. "I had just come around a corner of the hill below the entrance to Snowbasin," Alf recalled. "There facing me eye to eye, not more than a few feet away, was a badger with his mouth open, flashing his fangs and growling fiercely. All I had was a shovel, and no one else was close by. I have very rarely known panic in my life, but that was one occasion where I felt I was truly in big trouble. Luckily, the badger did not pursue the confrontation and allowed me to make a hasty retreat. I have never forgotten the incident." Fortunately, he had no more encounters with the local wildlife.

By the late 1940s the access road, two temporary rope tows, a shelter, and a forty-five-meter jumping hill, later named Bjørngaard Hill, had been built at Snowbasin. The first season was a huge success, capped off with the 1940–41 Intermountain Downhill and Slalom Championships.

The next summer, under the supervision of Alf Engen, the CCC cut ski runs. In the process of clearing one of the runs, the crew stirred up a litter of wildcats. That encounter lead to the naming of the Wildcat ski run. The crew also cleared a very steep run off Mt. Ogden intended to be used for downhill races. The name of that run is Chicken Springs. It will comprise part of the 2002 Olympic downhill course, which is destined to become one of the most challenging in the world.

The 1941–42 *Western Ski Annual* featured this article by Koziol and Arthur Roth Jr.:

place to put a ski area. They brought back photographs that reinforced their findings. As a result, exploratory trips continued for four years, and in 1940 the Forest Service decided to make Wheeler Basin a winter sports site.

Prior to 1934 most of the land in Wheeler Basin was privately owned by the Ostler Land and Livestock Company. According to Ralph Johnston, a local Ogden ski pioneer, "The land was drastically overgrazed by livestock and eroded to the point that every time there were heavy rains, the soil would be washed down Wheeler Creek into Ogden River, causing flood and pollution in the valley. . . . The people of Ogden were concerned, and in 1937 it was decided to do something about Wheeler Basin."

In 1938 a suit was filed by Ogden City for condemnation of the private property. The land was condemned and turned over to the federal government in 1939 to become part of the Cache National Forest, which helped plan the area. The name "Snowbasin" was coined by a member of the Ogden Chamber of Commerce, and it stuck.

> Snowbasin offers one of the few places where two-, three-, and four-way tournaments can be held within the compact limits of the same ski area. According to Alf Engen, *langlauf* courses are excellent across the rolling hills at the intermediate elevations.
>
> The downhill race course is two and one-half miles. Slalom courses of any length and steepness can be set. The main jumping hill will eventually be boosted up to seventy meters. . . . Snowbasin is destined to become one of the best all-around winter playgrounds in the West.

Area illustration of Snowbasin, circa 1946.

Sverre and Corey Engen were granted a permit for the first ski school and concessions for the 1941–42 season. Sverre said in an early article about the area,

Snow Basin [sic] has a combination of many natural advantages that is hard to find. There is plenty of snow, sometimes maybe too much. The altitude is not too high to cause trouble from excessive storms, and the season is plenty long. Being only 30 minutes over a good highway from a city like Ogden, with all its road, rail and air connections, it is probably one of the most accessible major winter playgounds of the west.

The initial operation of Snowbasin was short-lived. World War II caused the Forest Service to close the area, which it did not reopen until 1945. When it reopened, Corey Engen was again area manager, a

position he held until 1953, when he moved his family to McCall, Idaho. On January 20, 1946, Snowbasin dedicated its first chairlift.

Snowbasin covers eighteen hundred acres of skiable terrain and has one double and four triple lifts, which can handle seventy-four hundred skiers an hour. In the year 2002, worldwide attention will be focused on Snowbasin when the Winter Olympics downhill and super giant slalom events for both men and women will be staged.

JACKSON HOLE, WYOMING

Jackson Hole's skiing history dates to the earliest days of this country, when fur trappers made their way into the Rocky Mountains. In 1807 James Colter, a guide with Lewis and Clark, entered the valley— the first reported fur trapper to discover its beauty and natural wealth. Jackson Hole soon became a central rendezvous for fur traders. For generations before that, the Crow and Shoshone Indians had summered and hunted in the area.

Fur traders used handmade skis during winter months while the trappers used snowshoes. In the 1920s, townspeople used handmade skis, along with snowshoes, sled dogs, and horse-drawn sleighs for transportation.

An article in volume six of the 1973–74 *Teton Annual* describes Mike O'Neil, who, during the winter of 1925–26, bought store-made skis and had a black-smith forge some iron bindings that "encased the shoe soles with a strap across the top and around the heel." For ski poles O'Neil used two bamboo fishing poles with criss-crossed ladies' embroidery hoops and leather riveted to the pole at the base. Most of the downhill skiing involved climbing partway up Snow King Hill and coming down straight without turning.

Snow King town hill was known as Ruth Hannah Simms Ski Hill in honor of a wealthy resident who financed the construction of the town's ski-jumping hill. The name of the hill at Jackson was changed in 1938 to Snow King. In 1935 the Forest Service brought in the CCC and had its crews construct ski trails and a small shelter at the top of Snow King Mountain. In 1937 Jackson Hole formed its first ski club and conducted a jumping and downhill tourna-ment. Jimmy Braman won, using wooden skis with metal edges, which had never before been seen by local residents.

In 1939 Neil Rafferty, a member of the Jackson Hole Ski Club, built the first skier rope tow, which had handles attached to the cable. The cable tow was used until the late 1940s, when a chairlift was built that went to the top of Snow King Mountain. Jackson Hole's Snow King now has a Dream Catcher, Wyoming's first high-speed, detachable quad lift.

Late in the 1930s, Alf, Sverre, and Corey went to Jackson Hole for the first time to put on a jumping exhibition promoted by George Lamb, a Salt Lake restaurateur. The road to Jackson was closed during winter months, but the brothers drove to the base of the Idaho side of Teton Pass and got a ride to the top on a mail sleigh. From there they skied down to the Jackson Hole valley. When the jumping exhibition was over, Alf returned over the pass with the mail sleigh to get to another tournament. Sverre and Corey were having so much fun in Jackson Hole that they decided to stay an extra day. When they were ready to leave, the only form of transportation was an open-cockpit airplane, piloted by barnstormer A. A. Bennett. In *Skiing a Way of Life,* Sverre recalls the experience:

I had only flown one time before in Minneapolis, and Corey hadn't yet been up in a plane. They assured us that when we flew with A. A. Bennett we didn't have anything to worry about. The next morning, we were up bright and early and went over to look at the airplane that was covered with canvas and parked at the school ground in the middle of town.

A real winter storm had set in again, and it looked as if it wasn't going to let up. Mr. Bennett said he was willing to try if we were. Since we were scheduled to take part in another jumping tournament, we were anxious to get out while we could.

We loaded our four pairs of skis, suit-cases, and two sets of big elk horns the folks had given us into the little plane, then we crowded in. We started out in the snow-storm and headed for the pass. Corey and I couldn't see a thing, even though we were sitting in the front. Mr. Bennett was in back of us in an open cockpit. From time to time he would slide open a little window and talk to us.

Many times we tried to gain enough altitude to get over the mountain, but each time we had to drift back towards Jackson and try again. Finally we hit the right spot at the right altitude and started over. It felt like the little plane was just standing still shaking itself. We could see the tops of the trees and it seemed as if we could have touched them with very little effort. The door on Corey's side was rattling so hard we were sure it was going to fall off, so he leaned over to my side and hung on for dear life.

When we got to the Idaho side of the mountain, we could see a little better and had a few anxious moments as Mr. Bennett barely cleared a barbed wire fence to land in a field near our car. When we finally came to a stop, Mr. Bennett opened the door and asked us how we were doing. We weren't just sure. It took us a little while to answer, but I sincerely hope it was "thank you very much."

Beaver Mountain, circa 1950s.
Photo courtesy University of Utah J. Willard Marriott Library, Utah Ski Archives.

BEAVER MOUNTAIN, UTAH

In the mid- to late-1930s, skiers from Logan and the surrounding communities traveled Logan Canyon to ski. When they could make it, they often traveled to the summit, which overlooks Bear Lake to the east. They skied in the beautiful, high alpine meadows on both sides of the summit. In the early 1940s, the Mt. Logan Ski Club and the city of Logan funded the construction of a rope tow and later a cable tow at the Sinks, about three miles below the summit on the Logan side. Don Shupe, E. M. Jenson, Stan Chipman, and a few others volunteered to operate the lift, which ran on weekends and holidays. Logan charged a token fee, just enough to pay for the battery and gasoline to run the DeSoto motor that powered the lift.

When the DeSoto engine died, Harold "Harry" Seeholzer and Don Shupe installed an eight-cylinder Chrysler engine that was more suitable for pulling the heavy cable. Skiers used a small metal device to grip the cable as it pulled them up the hill because holding on would destroy a pair of gloves in short order. Children and not-so-strong adults hitched on behind the stronger skiers if they could not hold the weight of the cable. The cable ran over aspen logs so that it would not bury itself in the snow or slice its way to the ground.

In the early 1940s, much of the towing equipment was moved to Beaver Mountain, a spot five miles down the canyon that collected more snow and had a northern exposure. A T-bar lift was built using wooden supports to carry the cable. Seeholzer and his wife, Luella, liked the area so much that they decided to purchase the tow. After Harold passed away in 1968, Luella and the children developed Beaver Mountain into a fine ski area that serves the residents of nearby Bear Lake, Logan, and other communities in Cache Valley. Beaver Mountain offers twenty-six runs within 525 acres and operates three double chairlifts.

Timp Haven (now Sundance) and Mt. Timpanogos, circa 1960s. Photo by Mike Korologos.

SUNDANCE, UTAH

At the time Beaver Mountain was being developed in the mid-1940s, another small area near Provo, Utah, was also getting started. Called Timp Haven after the picture-perfect Mt. Timpanogos towering nearby, this area was started by brothers Ray and Paul Stewart and their wives, Ava and Hilda. Paul, nicknamed "Speed," was also in the sheep business. Several generations of Stewarts had grazed their sheep on two thousand acres up Provo Canyon. He became particularly interested in the open slopes near Mt. Timpanogos, both for grazing sheep and for developing a winter sports recreational area. The first lift to go in was a rope tow, followed by a T-bar, a forty-meter ski-jumping hill, and a twenty-two-hundred-foot single chairlift. Stewart continued to run his small ski operation during winter months every day except for Sundays. Timp Haven flourished, supported primarily by local skiers living in the Provo area.

In August 1968 the Timp Haven resort, involving approximately twenty-four hundred acres of private land, was sold to Hollywood actor Robert Redford and four others—Stanley Collins, Hans Estin, Robert M. Gottschalk, and Michael P. Frankfurt. Not long after purchasing the property, the owners changed its name to Sundance. Many improvements have been made to this area since the late 1960s, and Sundance is now considered to have some of the finest resort accommodations in the Intermountain West.

SOLITUDE, UTAH

Robert M. Barrett, an eccentric and one-time bean farmer in southwest Colorado, developed Solitude. When Utah was in the throes of a uranium boom in the 1950s, Barrett was a bulldozer operator, or catskinner, in southeastern Utah for Charlie Steen, Moab's legendary uranium baron. With big earnings derived from his involvement in uranium mining,

Robert M. Barrett, original owner of Solitude, circa 1960s. Photo by Mike Korologos.

Barrett purchased a number of properties, one of which contained several thousand acres in the Honeycomb and Solitude Fork areas in Big Cottonwood Canyon near Brighton. He developed a strong interest in skiing and decided to develop a ski area on the land. He named the new area Solitude, but it was to have a troubled history.

In 1958 Solitude opened with a base lodge, a mid-mountain restaurant, a Pomalift, and two chairlifts. Barrett was very generous but prone to doing things the way he wanted, regardless of whether he had the technical knowledge required. As a result, over a period of ten years, he had a number of unfriendly encounters with the Forest Service regarding various issues: lack of construction permits, failure to protect the watershed, and safety problems concerning the lifts. By mid-1968, Barrett lost his special-use permit and decided, after much frustration, to divest his interest in the ski area. For a short period of time, Barrett's two daughters, Judy Tschaggeny and Patty Barrett, took over the reins of Solitude. In late 1968 the area was acquired by Paul Hunsaker.

The area reopened in January 1969 under a permit issued by the Forest Service to the Solitude Recreation and Development Corporation. On January 2, 1970, an accident involving a cable-clamp failure on one of the lifts caused several skiers to be thrown out

of the chairs, resulting in injury to five of them, one seriously. On January 6, after an investigation by the Utah Passenger Tramway Safety Board, the lift was closed. Ken Burns, the area manager, quickly corrected the problems, and the 1969–70 season ended favorably. Unfortunately, over the next several years, more lift problems arose because of poor original design. During the early 1970s, more than a dozen significant problems occurred, resulting in the termination on March 31, 1974, of the second-generation Solitude ski-area operation.

In July 1975 a new Solitude venture began to unfold under the direction of Richard A. Houlihan. It involved a complete renovation of the lodge complex through private equity and replacement of the lifts under separate financing. Over the next decade, many improvements were made. Today, it is owned by Gary Seelhorfe and enjoys a fine reputation as one of the growing ski resorts in the Intermountain area, with sixty-three runs spread over twelve hundred acres. It has one high-speed quad lift and two triple and four double chairlifts.

BRIAN HEAD, UTAH

During the 1950s a small ski run up Cedar Canyon, near Cedar City in southern Utah, was used primarily by students from nearby Southern Utah University, then known as the College of Southern Utah. The run was served by a short rope tow. In the early 1960s, as part of a real-estate development project, this area was turned into a ski resort and named Brian Head. According to George Hartlmaier, who helped construct the first lift, "Alf Engen from Alta, Ernie Blake from Taos, New Mexico, and John Herbert of the Forest Service were asked to visit Brian Head to offer their expert opinions on where the most ideal ski terrain was located and where to build an additional lift." Said Hartlmaier, "They spent a couple of days donating their time in evaluating and recommending the best place to put in a second lift." After the lift was built, "Alf, Stein Eriksen, Wayne Nichol, Sid Jenson, and several others officially opened the two slopes, which were named Upper and Lower Engen's Face. These two runs are the most enjoyed and challenging on the mountain."

Several years later Hartlmaier attempted to build another ski resort near Brian Head. A corporation was formed, and skiing terrain considered for the area was named Engen Mountain. "This ski area never

Alf Engen and George Hartlmaier at Brian Head, circa 1960s. Photo courtesy George Hartlmaier.

materialized, but the name of the mountain remains in honor of the ski legend Alf Engen," Hartlmaier says. "Alf will be remembered as one of my greatest friends and teachers of skiing. I will never forget him."

POWDER MOUNTAIN, UTAH

Powder Mountain in the Ogden Valley officially began operation as a ski area in 1972, according to Dr. Joe Arave, historian for the Utah Ski Archives. It was initially developed by Dr. Alvin Cobabe on land owned by him and his father. In 1958, while Alvin Cobabe was attending medical school, he and some friends were riding horses near the present location of Powder Mountain. Byron Nesbitt commented that the terrain was suitable for skiing. The idea stuck, and before long, Cobabe started investigating the possibilities of starting a small ski area. He discussed the idea with Chic Morton of Alta and Nelson Bennett in Yakima, Washington, who provided him with good input.

By 1959 Cobabe had installed a small rope tow in an area called Wolf Creek and operated it for the next decade, primarily for the locals. By the early 1970s, interest had grown to expand the area further, and a Thiokol lift began operation on Washington's Birthday

1972. By the end of the year, Timberline Lift was open, and two lodges—the Sundown Lodge and Timberline Lodge—were constructed in 1972 and 1973. Three years later, the Hidden Lake Lift was installed by Borvig of New York.

Powder Mountain offers expansive terrain and excellent conditions for those who enjoy skiing deep snow, which might be the reason for the ski area's name.

NORDIC VALLEY, UTAH

Dr. Joe Arave reports that Nordic Valley began operation in the late 1960s as part of a real-estate development by landowner Art Christiansen. Initially one large lift was built, then a small beginner lift was added later. In 1978 Nordic Valley was sold to a large group of investors—Ski Associates Inc. That group retains ownership of the area, with a number of the owners being past members of the initial start-up operation. Nordic Valley currently enjoys a niche in night skiing, which makes up approximately half of its business.

THE CANYONS, UTAH

The Canyons ski area is a stone's throw away from the Utah Winter Sports Park and only a few minutes' drive from Park City. It's so close to Park City, in fact, that when it debuted as a fledgling ski resort three decades ago, it was initially called Park City West.

According to John Durham, who was the weekend ski-patrol director at the area for twenty years, the initial principals were Bob Autry and Don Redman, who operated the area from its opening in 1968 until the mid-1970s. In approximately 1970–71, the name was changed to Park West. Durham said, "Somewhere around 1975 to 1977, because of ongoing financial difficulties, the Ford Motor Credit Union acquired ownership for a short period of time, and sold their interest to Jack Roberts about 1977." Roberts retained ownership of Park West until he sold it to Jerry Gillaman in the late 1980s. During his period of ownership, Gillaman leased the operation to Wayne Ragland, who managed Park West until it was sold to Ken Griswold and Michael Baker about 1991. Griswold, in turn, changed the area's name again to Wolf Mountain.

In 1997, Griswold sold Wolf Mountain to the American Skiing Company, headed by Les Otten. In very short order, one of the first tasks was to give

Park City West (now The Canyons), circa 1969.
Photo courtesy University of Utah J. Willard Marriot Library, Utah Ski Archives.

the resort another new name—The Canyons. So, for historical purposes, four names had been given to this particular resort. The Canyons is touted to become one of the largest ski resorts in the country by the year 2000. Otten, often described as the "Bill Gates of skiing," has an impressive track record in ski-resort acquisition. In addition to being a major investor in Steamboat Springs, Colorado; Heavenly Valley Ski Resort, California; and The Canyons, it is estimated that Otten owns approximately 75 percent of all Maine's ski businesses, along with 50 percent of Vermont's and 27 percent of New Hampshire's.

Otten continues to set his sights on ever-greater challenges. The Canyons operates nine lifts, seven built in 1997–98, including one high-speed gondola, three high-speed detachable quads, three fixed-grip quads, and two double chairs. How fast The Canyons will grow into a megaresort remains to be seen, but certainly no one is betting against its bright future.

UTAH WINTER SPORTS PARK, BEAR HOLLOW, UTAH

Following a successful statewide referendum vote in 1989, the Utah legislature approved forty

million dollars in sales tax revenues for construction of winter and summer sports training facilities at Bear Hollow. Construction of the Utah Winter Sports Park began in May 1992 under control of the Utah Sports Authority. The sports authority has a three-part mission: 1) to promote amateur athletics throughout the state; 2) to enhance the state's image as a winter sports center; and 3) to foster economic development and prosperity. The sports park became part of a commitment to the U.S. Olympic Committee, with the goal of not only winning the Olympic host-city nomination in 1998 or 2002 but also helping transform Utah into a winter sports training center for aspiring Olympians.

First to be constructed were four Nordic ski-jumping hills (90-, 65-, 38-, and 18-meter hills), a paved road and utilities into the sports park, a day lodge, and a 110-by-90-foot pool where freestyle athletes can practice inverted aerial maneuvers in one of the finest facilities in the world.

In 1994, construction of the combined bobsled/luge track began, a year before the announcement that Salt Lake City had been awarded the 2002 Olympic

Day lodge, Utah Winter Sports Park, 1995.

Winter Games. Since the announcement, significant
planning efforts have gone into effect that will transform the sports park into a world-class facility for
accommodating the Olympic Nordic jumping, bobsled,
and luge events. In 1999, ownership and control of
the Utah Winter Sports Park transfers to the Salt Lake
Olympic Committee (SLOC). After the Olympics,
SLOC will turn over operation of the sports park to
the Utah Athletic Foundation, a private nonprofit
organization approved by the state legislature in 1994.

The park is located thirty miles east of Salt Lake
City via I-80 and Highway 224 to Bear Hollow Drive.
The park borders The Canyons ski area and is approximately five miles from Park City. Another interesting
feature about the sports park location is that the
storied Ecker Hill, where Alf Engen set several world
professional ski-jumping records, is only about a
mile west as the crow flies. So to some degree, Utah's
ski-jumping past and future are interwoven.

Changing Times and the Land

During the late 1930s and '40s when these ski
areas were being developed, the approval process for
construction of lifts and lodges as well as developing
the ski runs was less complex than current procedures.
Environmental concerns were not a high priority in
those days, and all that was required was a letter to the
forest supervisor outlining the need for development
and how it would be accomplished. If the Forest
Service agreed, a formal letter was quickly sent autho-
rizing the work. Fifty or sixty years ago the citizenry
was not as sensitive to the necessity of protecting the

environment as we have now become. The country
was sparsely inhabited; nature seemed in no danger
from developing ski areas.

In our more enlightened times, the process is far
more complex for ski-area owners who operate on
Forest Service land. An Environmental Impact
Statement (EIS) document must be prepared, following
a proposed Master Development Plan (MDP) that
contains in-depth information as required by the U.S.
Department of Agriculture. In this document, specific
topics must be addressed, including purpose and need,
proposed action and alternatives, affected environment
analysis, and environmental consequences. Once the
document has been prepared, copies must be mailed
out to interested parties throughout the country for
review. When the comments are fed back to the Forest
Service, all information is evaluated and, after further
discussions and actions as appropriate, a decision is
made on what is approved or not approved. This can
take several years at a minimum, depending on the
proposal being evaluated. However, it does not always
end there because there is a provisional opportunity for
an appeal process to be initiated, which can involve
litigation and must ultimately be resolved in the courts.

While this process can be very lengthy and costly,
it is intended to make everyone involved think carefully about what is being done and how it potentially
affects the mountain environment and ecology. This is
good, but it can also lead to a high level of frustration
for those involved. As we move toward the twenty-first
century, the very words "ski resort" is being replaced
with "destination resort community." New development must, by necessity, continue to undergo scrutiny
in order to balance the desire to create giant destination resort locations with the need to protect our
remaining natural resources for future generations.

SKI INSTRUCTION

In the early days of skiing, who could give lessons and what theories of skiing and teaching would be pursued were open questions. During the late 1940s, however, as more and more people took to the slopes, the need for quality instruction became painfully apparent. Members of the Intermountain Ski Association (ISA), recognizing this need, were prime movers in creating the Professional Ski Instructors of America (PSIA).

Internationally, Austria was the first country to give examinations for ski teachers. In 1928 it initiated a testing program that certified individuals to teach. The examinations covered ski teaching, skiing ability, and knowledge of mountaineering, equipment, and first aid.

In the late 1930s, many U.S. officials and ski instructors recognized the need for testing to protect the public from incompetent instruction. In 1937 the United States Eastern Amateur Ski Association formed a Ski Teachers Certification Committee of individuals with ski-teaching experience, under the direction of Dr. Raymond S. Elmer. He appointed Professor Charles Proctor of Dartmouth College as the chief examiner and Walter Prager and Benno Rybizka as assisting examiners. The first ski-certification examination in the U.S. took place in 1938 at Woodstock, Vermont. Twenty applicants took the exam and seven passed. Other regions formed similar associations and made plans for ski-teacher certification during the early 1940s but no national standards existed.

Lois Engen teaching class composed of young ski enthusiasts Bonnie Speyer, Rob Speyer, and Bruce De Boer, circa 1947. Photo by Ted Hansell.

CERTIFIED SKI TEACHER
I. S. I. A.

LOOK FOR THE BADGE

Intermountain Ski Instructors Assn.

First Intermountain Ski Instructor's Association poster, circa early 1950s. Poster courtesy Bill Lash.

As a result, the National Ski Association of America Certification Committee was established in 1961 at Whitefish, Montana.

U.S. Forest Service Influence

The Forest Service had a significant effect on ski-teaching certification, particularly in the western United States. After World War II, the Forest Service realized that people throughout America were taking up Alpine skiing in national forests in almost explosive numbers. Although there was a need for teaching these new skiers how to ski safely, each instructor at

that time had his or her own method of teaching, and the techniques often presented conflicting approaches. Those teaching could basically ski and present any technique as long as it could be communicated effectively. However, this caused significant problems for those wishing to learn how to ski. There were almost as many different techniques being offered as there were instructors skiing.

The Intermountain Ski Association (ISA), with Forest Service prompting, recognized the problem. In 1946–47, the association adopted the National Ski Association certification process. Felix Koziol, supervisor of the Wasatch National Forest, and Sverre Engen, who headed the ski school at Alta, made the first attempts at creating a unified teaching and certification process. On February 16, 1949, the *Deseret News* ran an article that urged the new skiing public to obtain lessons from an ISA-certified instructor "to be certain of having proper instruction."

On December 5, 1949, the ISA conducted its first instructor examination at Alta. Three levels of certification were offered: apprentice instructor, instructor, and master instructor. The fee to take the examination was $10, with an annual renewal fee of $2.50. The following year the ISA changed its instructor categories to two levels—associate certified, which was designated by a blue pin, and certified, which merited a white pin that was often called the "White Badge."

This first certification system rectified some of the inconsistency in individual teaching approaches, but it had two significant deficiencies. First, only one exam was given annually in the late fall. No other avenue existed for instructors to formally discuss teaching methods. Second, throughout the country several major ski-teaching techniques existed, each emphasizing different approaches. Some ski areas promoted the Arlberg Technique developed by Hannes Schneider, which focused on rotating the upper body. Others offered the French Ski Technique developed by Emile Allais, which emphasized the lower body. Then in the late 1940s and early '50s, a technique called Reverse Shoulder was introduced by Dr. Kruckenhauser of Austria, which promoted twisting the upper body in an opposite direction to the legs and skis.

One official let it be known that if consistency in ski teaching could not be agreed upon, the Forest Service might elect to do its own certifying of teachers

The first *Deseret News* Ski School instructors staff, December 1948:
(left to right, front row) Tom Trua, Gordon Allcott, Michael-Ann Healy, Bob "Pepi" Smith,
Gary Peterson, Jack Reddish; (back row) Bob Beck, John Belden, Sverre Engen, Lois Engen,
Felix Koziol, Harold Van Pelt, Carolyn Harris, Evelyn Engen, Alf Engen.

in ski areas operating under special-use permits. To avoid a potential conflict, Bill Lash, who taught skiing at Alta while attending the U of U, and others in the ski-teaching profession decided that it was in their own best interest to establish national norms of ski instruction. To solve the dilemma, a new teaching protocol was introduced at Alta in the spring of 1958 called the American Technique. In 1961 the Professional Ski Instructors of America was formed as a national organization. It was agreed by all member ski schools throughout the country to officially adopt the new technique as the standard. This single change is viewed as the major contributor to standardization and uniformity of ski-teaching methodology, resulting in happier customer satisfaction and a more efficient certification process.

Deseret News Ski School

In 1948, following the first postwar Olympic Winter Games at St. Moritz, interest in downhill skiing increased rapidly in the Intermountain area. The *Deseret News* in Salt Lake City saw an opportunity to increase its readership, and talked with such pro-fessional skiers as Olympian Jack Reddish and Alf and Sverre Engen about looking for ways to increase interest in skiing. Wilby Durham, then assistant general manager of the newspaper, came up with the concept of forming a free ski school and convinced the Engens to get the program off the ground.

The idea resulted in Durham, Alf, and Sverre staging the first *Deseret News* Ski School session in December 1948, just before the Christmas holiday, on the Bonneville Golf Course in Salt Lake City. "The first session was originally supposed to be at Alta, but we got snowed out," Durham remembers. "Therefore, since we were committed, we quickly looked for an alternative site, and the Bonneville Golf Course was the option we selected."

The Professional Ski Instructors of America: Utah's Influence

JUNIOR BOUNOUS

Two of the most influential figures in skiing and teaching during that early period were Junior Bounous and Bill Lash. Junior started skiing at a young age in

Wayne Nichol teaching his son Larry how to ski, circa 1953. Photo courtesy *Deseret News*.

Junior Bounous, assistant ski-school director at Alta, getting input from Alf Engen, circa 1955.

the early 1930s on his family's farm near Provo, Utah. His first skis were, as Bounous explains, "a pair of what we could call skates or skis. It was one barrel stave cut into two pieces, with toe straps. My father had shaped it a little so it was narrower at the back." Because very few people skied in those days (other than professional ski jumpers and a limited number of hardy members of the Wasatch Mountain Club), Bounous did not have anyone to teach him, so he taught himself, beginning on a small hill on his family's farm.

By the time Bounous reached high school, he was into ski jumping and cross-country skiing. "I developed an interest in getting into the backcountry, climbing with skins on my skis, and visiting some of the places I would hike during the summer months," he recalls. In 1944 Bounous heard about a cross-country ski race being held near Deer Creek Reservoir in Wasatch County near Heber City.

"I entered, and I remember it was Gordon Wren who was the champion. I did poorly in that race, but it gave me my first taste of ski competition and kicked off an interest in cross-country skiing, which complemented my experience as a half-mile runner in high school," Bounous says. "Not long after, I heard about the Intermountain cross-country tournament being held in Brighton. My good friend Earl Miller from Provo encouraged me to enter with him. This was good because it introduced me to Jim Shane, Harold Goodro, and other Wasatch Mountain Club members. I won that race and continued to win the Intermountain cross-country division title for several years. My first loss came when Corey Engen beat me. Corey was, at

that time, training for the 1948 U.S. Olympic Team, and he cleaned my clock."

About the same time (1946–47), Bounous set a goal to pursue cross-country skiing so he could be competitive at the national level. He sought out Alf Engen to help him with his technique with ski jumping. During these sessions Bounous became interested in more than competing—he became interested in teaching others to ski.

Bounous was certified as an ISIA instructor in the late 1940s by the ISA. He went to work for Alf at Alta and quickly rose to assistant director, a position he held until 1958 when he accepted the job of ski-school director at Sugar Bowl, California. He returned to Utah with his family in 1966 to become part owner and head of the ski school of the Timp Haven ski area in Provo Canyon. When Timp Haven (now Sundance) was purchased by Robert Redford, Bounous continued as the ski-school director until 1970, when he was hired to lay out the ski runs and direct the cutting crews at a new resort called Snowbird in Little Cottonwood Canyon. Soon, he was appointed Snowbird's ski-school director, a position he held for the next twenty years.

Bounous's contributions to the ski-teaching profession as a leading force in developing the PSIA, writer of numerous articles on skiing, author and coauthor of several ski books, and master instructor, earned him a place in the National Ski Hall of Fame in 1996. He has been called "the Cal Ripkin of skiing," as a tribute to his longevity, just as Ripkin was labeled the "Ironman" of major-league baseball for his record-setting number of continuous games played.

BILL LASH

Bill Lash has influenced professional ski teaching about as much as any individual since Hannes Schneider developed and promulgated the Arlberg Technique. Lash began skiing in 1940 at Magic Mountain near Twin Falls, Idaho. He passed all the requirements for full certification from Alf Engen in 1950. During the early 1950s, Lash attended the University of Utah and directed the ski program there where he became interested in ski-instructor training. At the same time, he and several others formed the Intermountain Ski Instructors Association (ISIA).

"A number of ski instructors had been skiing at Alta on December 9, 1950," Lash recalls. "In the morning all certified teachers assembled and taught in

Bill Lash, ski-school director at Solitude, circa 1960s. Photo courtesy Mike Korologos.

the *Deseret News* Ski School. In the afternoon we skied with Alf. At the end of the day, we would meet in the Sitzmark Room of the Alta Lodge. Felix Koziol, Forest Service supervisor for the Wasatch Mountains, was there and suggested it was time for a separate ski-instructors group to be formed. After some discussion, someone suggested the name Intermountain Ski Instructors Association, and it stuck."

On November 10, 1951, an election of officers was conducted, again at the Alta Lodge, and Lash was elected president of the ISIA. Bounous was elected vice-president and Chuck Rowan secretary/treasurer. In April 1952 Lash met at Squaw Valley with ski instructors from the Far West Ski Association and the Rocky Mountain Ski Instructors Association to discuss the need for a national professional ski-teaching organization. As a result, several ski-school directors and instructors met in Estes Park, Colorado, in June 1952, and moved to develop the National Council of Ski Instructors of America. According to Lash, this council coordinated ideas and developed procedures that could be used by the separate divisions within the National Ski Association but allowed all

divisions to select their own technique.

In 1957 Lash was appointed to head the National Ski Association Certification Committee. He worked six years to assemble for the first time a national meeting of ski instructors from the country's seven regions. The meeting was held at Alta, Utah, and hosted by Alf Engen. This weeklong meeting involved discussions about national certification standards. The participants also thoroughly evaluated all current ski-teaching techniques.

Ski philosophy and instruction were in turmoil because of revolutionary techniques, driven by the influence of the newest Olympic ski champions— Stein Eriksen and Toni Sailer—and the advent of a new Austrian approach called *wedeln*. These methods constituted a radical departure from the long-revered Arlberg Technique, which advocated a forward stance and power to initiate the turn while the Austrian *wedeln* featured a taller stance, more finesse, and less reliance on strength to turn.

Lash had experimented with various techniques ski schools used to train instructors. He incorporated the best philosophies and methods into the new ISIA. When he had the basic teaching methodology formalized and accepted at the local ski areas, he decided to broaden the base. He photographed the Alta meeting sessions and, in 1958, wrote and published a book entitled *Outline of Ski Teaching Methods*. This was the first complete ski-instructor's manual distributed throughout America. It analyzed the differences between the Arlberg, Swiss, and modern Austrian ski techniques.

The Alta meeting prompted annual follow-up gatherings of ski-school directors in 1959 at Arapaho Basin, Colorado, and 1960 at Brighton, Utah. At the Brighton meeting, the certification committee, under Lash's leadership, conducted the first national exam for instructors involving all seven U.S. regions. Through the efforts of Lash, the PSIA was formed at Whitefish, Montana, in May 1961. Lash served as its president for eight years. During his presidency he edited and published *The Official American Ski Technique,* which went through three editions—1964, 1966, and 1970. For his many contributions, Lash was inducted into the National Ski Hall of Fame in 1983.

Bill Lash and Junior Bounous are but two of the many fine skiing instructors across the country who have made significant contributions to ski-teaching development. ❄

chapter eight

BRIDGING THE OLD AND THE NEW: The Collegiate Influence

While skiing was becoming a national recreation and continuing to be a major Olympic winter sport, it was also growing on the intercollegiate level. In many ways, intercollegiate competitive skiing and, to some degree, collegiate recreational skiing formed a bridge between skiing in the 1930s and skiing as viewed today. Over the years, many Olympic and world-class skiers have come from collegiate competition, and collegiate recreational skiing has also provided a resource for training future ski professionals through special training programs.

The University of Utah formed its first ski team

A new development in the Salt Lake area is at the University of Utah where **plans are being pushed for formation of a sponsored ski team.** *In past years the school skiers have not been organized, although some of the nation's top racers have been students.*

But now the school athletic board is considering a sizable fund to back a collegiate team to compete throughout the country.

—*Dick Movitz*
Western Skiing, *December 1946*

in 1947, and it consisted solely of men. What a start they had! They won the overall U.S. collegiate title their first year in a competition held at Sun Valley, Idaho. Sverre Engen coached the team, which included Jack Reddish, Dick Movitz, Dev Jennings, Steve Nebeker, Bill Beesley, Dick Kirby, George Romney, and Bill Hawkins. Beesley won the downhill; Movitz, the slalom; and Reddish, the combined title. As a group, they beat the best collegiate ski teams in the country, including Dartmouth and Middlebury Colleges.

In 1949 the team, coached by Friedl Lang, consisted of Mel Dalebout, Jim Crockford, Jim Murphy,

Six members of the first University of Utah Ski Team, 1947: (left to right, front row) Dick Movitz, Bill Beesley; (back row) Dick Kirby, Steve Nebeker, Coach Sverre Engen, Jack Reddish, Dev Jennings. Missing: George Romney and Bill Hawkins.

Above: Alan Engen,
U of U Ski Team,
Brighton, Utah, 1959.

Left: Part of the U of U
Ski Team, 1959–60:
(left to right) Dick
Mulder, Bennett Larson,
Jim Gaddis, Alan
Engen, Brad Smith,
Coach Pres
Summerhays.
Missing: Darm Penny
and Dave Wilson

Dave Christenson, Al Grice, and Lee Weiss. During the early to mid-1950s, the University of Utah Ski Team continued to attract outstanding skiers. Dick Mitchell captained the team and won the national collegiate downhill in 1953. Another outstanding skier during that time was Spence Eccles, who skied for the University of Utah and gained All-American honors. Darrell "Pinky" Robison also represented the University of Utah in ski competition and was a member of the 1952 U.S. Olympic Alpine Ski Team. Other outstanding skiers on the U of U Ski Team during the early 1950s included Mike Reddish, Don Irvine, Bill Meyer, and Tom Warnock.

Beginning in the mid-1950s and continuing through the early 1960s, Preston Summerhays coached the men's team while Alf Engen coached the women's. Ute skier Marvin Melville, who was also an Olympic competitor later, distinguished himself in March 1959 by winning the National Collegiate Athletic Association (NCAA) downhill and slalom. In 1960 Jim Gaddis and Alan Engen were the only two University of Utah skiers who qualified for the NCAA championships at Bozeman, Montana. Gaddis won his first NCAA title there, while Engen finished third. On the women's ski team, Manya Baumbacher and Betty Lou Sine were outstanding performers during the late 1950s and early '60s.

During the 1959–60 ski season, a U of U teammate lost his life in a collegiate downhill accident at Beaver Mountain in Logan, Utah. On February 27, 1960, Bennett Larson, Darin Penny, Dave Wilson, Brad Smith, Jim Gaddis, and Alan Engen had gone with Coach Pres Summerhays to compete in a western regional collegiate ski tournament. The start of the downhill was far above the highest chairlift terminal and required about a half-hour hike. The top of the course was fast and had one turn that fell away into a bank of aspen trees. Gaddis and Engen had made their runs and were waiting for Penny and Larson to make their runs. Penny fell and hit a tree but was not seriously hurt; he injured his rib cage and was taken to the hospital. Larson did not arrive at the finish gate. Because no one had seen him fall, it was presumed he was between the top of the lift and the start of the course.

Gaddis and Engen went to look for him. After climbing about a quarter of a mile above the top lift terminal, they found him lying against the side of an aspen tree off the course. He was semiconscious when

they arrived but soon passed out. Bennett had hit the tree headfirst. Bob Beck, ski coach of Montana State College, arrived shortly after and administered mouth-to-mouth resuscitation several times, which kept Larson alive until he got to the hospital. He never regained consciousness, however, and died early the following morning from a fractured skull and internal injuries. Everyone was devastated. Bennett Larson lost his life to a sport he loved, representing the highest level of collegiate competitive spirit.

During the 1960s the University of Utah belonged to the Rocky Mountain Intercollegiate Ski Association, one of five major athletic affiliations in the United States. Through the 1960s, Association events considered for the national intercollegiate title were downhill, jumping, slalom, and cross-country. In 1965, under the coaching of Marvin Melville, the University of Utah Ski Team finished second in the NCAA championship with the finest showing for a University of Utah team since 1946. Utah was only 2.2 points (out of a possible 400) behind the NCAA champions, Denver University. According to Melville, this was the finest group he ever coached at the University of Utah.

Outstanding Members, U of U Ski Team, 1950s and '60s

Over the years a number of individuals who have excelled in intercollegiate sports at the local and national level have competed for the University of Utah. Three of the finest are Jim Gaddis, Marvin Melville, and Bill Spencer.

JIM GADDIS—NCAA ALL-AMERICAN

Jim Gaddis started skiing at age eight in the late 1940s on the Salt Lake Country Club golf course. Neither of his parents skied, but as a Christmas gift, they bought him a pair of five-foot wooden skis with leather toe straps and without metal edges. The following year, he tagged along with his older brothers when they went to Alta or Brighton to ski. They dropped him off in the morning on the beginners' slope and immediately headed to higher terrain. Gaddis had no choice but to fend for himself. He had no money to take lessons and no one to ski with so he did the only thing he could: watched how others skied and taught himself. At age ten, Gaddis entered his first race at Alta, sponsored by the *Salt Lake Tribune*. He recalls the race with a smile: "My time was four minutes, fifty-nine seconds," he says. "The winning

Jim Gaddis, early 1960s.
Photo courtesy Jim Gaddis.

time was around forty-five seconds. They started us at two-minute intervals and by the time I got on the course, it had big ruts, and I was soon passed by another racer who said, 'Get out of the way, jerk!' Anyway, I managed to finish the race but came in dead last."

Originally, Gaddis raced just for fun with no thoughts of becoming a top competitor. But at age fourteen, he began beating everyone in his age class and doing well in higher classes. In high school he was one of the best in the Intermountain region and a national junior competitor during the mid- to late-1950s. Alan Engen remembers one experience that he and Gaddis had as high school racers:

Jim had just obtained his driver's license and borrowed his parents' car so several of us could attend a ski race in Pocatello, Idaho. Keith Lange, our coach, teammates John Mortensen and Jane Coombs, Gaddis and I piled in the car early one Saturday morning and headed for the race. Everything went fine until just before we reached the Utah/Idaho border, where in the darkness we came upon a divided highway. "I didn't see it [the divided highway] in time and ended up going into the divider space separating the highway, rolling

the car one or two times," Gaddis remembers. "The car came to rest upside down in the barrow pit."

Fortunately, no one was hurt. Everyone climbed out of the car through the windows and proceeded to look for the skis, which had been on the rack on top of the car. Because the car was upside down, we thought the skis had been demolished. We rolled the car back on its wheels and, to our surprise, found no skis. The top of the car had been crunched down almost to seat level. After a search, we found the skis, still intact in the ski rack, on the other side of the highway in a snowbank. Thankfully, they survived the rollover unscathed.

As dawn neared, we could see a gas service station about a half mile away. Gaddis and I crawled back inside the car, put our feet against the roof, and with all our strength pushed the top out so we could have some head room. With one person steering, the rest of us pushed the car to the gas station. After some work, we got the car started. The decision then was whether to continue to the race or head back to Salt Lake. After some deliberation, we unanimously decided the race had priority. We plugged the disintegrated side windows with cardboard and, peering out through the shattered windshield, drove on to Pocatello.

By the time we arrived at the ski hill, the competition had started. Coach Lange had to do some creative talking to get us entered, but he succeeded. We had to start dead last in both heats, however. When the race was over, Gaddis was in first place. I finished second and John Mortensen third—a clean sweep! We collected our awards, got back into the car, and coaxed it back to Salt Lake.

The car's frame was so far out of alignment that the vehicle oscillated on the highway almost sideways. When we arrived at the Gaddis home, the car engine died in the driveway and would not start again. His parents' insurance company appraised the car as a total loss, and it was hauled away to the scrap heap.

The following year, several members of this group elected to attend the University of Utah. Gaddis received a full athletic ski scholarship and over the next four years excelled in almost every intercollegiate ski competition he entered, twice winning the NCAA championship as well as the national giant slalom championship. According to Alan Engen, his teammate during those years (1959–63), no one's competitive spirit and determination excelled Gaddis's.

Though his qualifying results appeared to have been good enough, Gaddis was not named to the 1964 U.S. Olympic Alpine Ski Team because of injuries—three broken legs and chronic shoulder problems—and disagreements with the U.S. Olympic ski coach, Bob Beattie. A formal protest was submitted by the Intermountain Division of the USSA to the U.S. Olympic Association but to no avail. In a letter dated June 27, 1963, by Bob Beattie to Hack Miller, sportswriter for the *Deseret News,* Beattie said, "I think it is important to understand that Jim Gaddis is considered by me, personally, to be a fine young lad, an excellent skier, and a great credit to Salt Lake City. . . . The responsibility for his not having been selected rests with me."

MARVIN MELVILLE—U.S. OLYMPIC ALPINE SKIER

Marvin Melville started skiing in 1945 at the age of ten. "My dad and I went to the Army/Navy surplus store and bought two pairs of white army skis, the kind with the hole in the tip," he remembers. "We went to Alta and started sliding down the hill. That is my first recollection of skiing."

After a couple of years, Melville began to develop an interest in competitive skiing. When he began ski racing, he had no aspirations of becoming a top-level racer. "I think that evolved over time," he says. "I think initially that goal was far beyond my comprehension. Probably after I had been in competition at the local junior level for some time, the thought began to emerge. I would have been about high school age."

After Melville graduated from high school, several universities invited him to ski for them. He chose the University of Utah. During the years he skied there, he was named an All-American and competed in all events (downhill, slalom, cross-country, and jumping). In 1959 he won the national collegiate downhill, slalom, and combined titles, and he tried out for the 1956 Olympic team.

"It was kind of a quirk of fate," he says about

Marvin Melville, Estes Park, Colorado, 1955. Photo courtesy Marvin Melville.

making the team. "When I entered college, no one was eligible to ski for the university his freshman year, and I was also having to deal with the possibility of the military draft. During my second year in college [1955], several U of U Ski Team members—including Spence Eccles, Bill Meyer, Bill Bennett, and me—went back East to take part in the NCAA championship. We stayed an additional week after the competition to participate in the 1955 Olympic trials.

"I was able to obtain good seeding in the trials primarily because I had won the Snow Cup earlier in the 1955 season. In those days the Snow Cup at Alta was considered one of the biggest ski races in the country. My winning the Snow Cup that year, which was the year Jill Kinmont was seriously injured in the race, allowed me to have a good start position. That Snow Cup race, by the way, was the first time I ever beat Olympian Jack Reddish, and it became a memorable event in my life."

Only two men from the western part of the United States made the 1956 U.S. Winter Olympic Alpine Ski Team: Marvin Melville and Buddy Werner from Steamboat Springs, Colorado. "Following my selection on the 1956 Olympic team, I traveled to South America to train during our summer months in the U.S. and then went into the army for two years," Melville remembers. "Three weeks after the 1956

Olympics were held in Cortina, Italy, I broke my leg in an international race in Switzerland. Following my military tour of duty, which ended in 1957, I tried out and made the 1958 U.S. Federation Internationale de Ski Team, which went to Badgestein, Austria, for the world championship. Following that experience, I returned to school at the University of Utah and completed my competitive eligibility for the ski·team."

In 1959 Melville, Jim Gaddis, Alan Engen, Robert Nelson, Darm Penny, and John Mortensen were selected to represent the Intermountain Ski Association at Squaw Valley for the 1959 North American Alpine Ski Championship. This was considered the test run in preparation for the upcoming Olympics. It was also one of the qualifying races for selecting the 1960 U.S. Olympic Team.

"I did well in the championship," Melville recalls. "Following the North American championship, Alan Engen and I went on from the Intermountain area to compete at the Harriman Cup in Sun Valley and the U.S. nationals at Aspen, Colorado. Ogden's Alan Miller, who was skiing for Denver University, was another outstanding ski racer who competed in the Olympic trials in 1959. After all the competition results were compiled for the season, I was selected as a member of the 1960 U.S. Olympic Men's Alpine Ski Team and competed at Squaw Valley, California, in the downhill."

During the years Melville skied for the United States in international competition, 1956–60, one of his closest friends was Wallace "Buddy" Werner. Werner was considered the finest American-born male Alpine skier in the United States. Melville and Werner skied and competed together for several years, and Werner was best man at Melville's wedding. In April 1964, however, following the Olympics at Innsbruck, Austria, Werner lost his life in an avalanche in St. Moritz, Switzerland.

Melville finished his competitive career after the 1960 Olympics. In 1961 Melville, Bill Spencer, and Al Hansen started the Alpine Training School (ATS), a program for junior racers.

"We went to each of the local high schools and tried to recruit the best racers for our new program," Melville says. "We would bring them together once or twice a week and work with them. Eventually, I bought a bus so I could haul them to and from ski races. That became my introduction to coaching and was probably one of the main reasons I became interested in taking over the ski-team coaching position at the

University of Utah. I take a lot of pride in the ATS program and feel we did some innovative programs that proved beneficial for local junior ski racing."

Melville started to coach at the University of Utah in 1963. Pres Summerhays, who had been the coach of the ski team since 1955, was ready to turn the job over to someone else. Melville took the job for the next three years until his father, Alton, passed away in 1966.

"My proudest memory as a coach at the University of Utah was in 1965 when a team of only eight members placed second in the NCAA Championship," Melville observes. "Almost every man on the team competed in all four events (downhill, slalom, jumping, and cross-country). The team consisted of Frithjof Prydz, who was probably the finest ski jumper in the country at that time; David Engen, Bjorn Loken, Pete Karns, Matz Jensen, Ladd Christensen, Rich Groth, and John Miller. They were truly an outstanding group, both as athletes and goodwill ambassadors."

While Melville was coach at Utah, he was asked by U.S. Olympic Coach Bob Beattie to become his assistant for the 1964 U.S. team. For the 1963–64 winter season, Melville wore two coaching hats, a sizable undertaking! During the latter part of the 1960s, Melville served as chairman of the United States Ski Association (USSA) Alpine Competition Committee and in 1970 represented the U.S. at the World Ski Championship in Italy and the FIS Ski Congress in Innsbruck, Austria. After Melville's administrative responsibilities for the USSA at the world championship, he hung up his boards for about twenty-five years and did not actively ski until 1986, when he got back into masters-level competition. Melville enjoyed that for a few years and eventually took over the reins as the national masters chairman for the USSA, a position he held from 1992 to 1994.

BILL SPENCER—U.S. OLYMPIC BIATHLON SKIER

Another University of Utah ski champion and Olympian was Bill Spencer, who specialized in biathlon. The history of biathlon dates back four thousand years, to the time when the oldest rock petroglyph drawings were made. In the early 1700s, Norway's military defense was, to a large degree, built on skills that used both skis and weapons. In 1767 one of the units guarding the border between Norway and Sweden organized the first recorded competition involving the skills used in modern biathlon. This

Frithjof Prydz, member of the U of U Ski Team, mid-1960s.

Frithjof Prydz—
World-Class Ski Jumper

In 1962 the University of Utah Ski Team attracted the talents of world-class ski jumper Frithjof Prydz of Norway. During the four years he attended the university, he won the NCAA ski-jumping title three times and was named an All-American. After he finished his ski career at the University of Utah, he returned to Norway and became a world-class jumper on its Olympic team. Because of his successes and the overall achievement of the ski team, other Norwegian athletes have been enrolled at the University of Utah.

competition combined a skiing course with shooting a rifle at a target forty to fifty paces away. In 1912 the Norwegian military held the first official annual seventeen-kilometer biathlon race called the *forvarsrennet*. This race unveiled the concept of subtracting time from the biathlete's ski time for each target hit.

After World War II, Sweden became the primary advocate of the biathlon and sponsored several events, called *sidfeltskytting*. In 1958 the first World Biathlon Championship was held at Saalfelden, Austria. Two

years later the International Olympic Committee made the biathlon an official event at the 1960 Olympic Winter Games at Squaw Valley, California. As of 1996, approximately sixteen thousand world-class biathletes, representing forty to fifty countries, actively participated in the event.

Utah's Bill Spencer knows as much about the biathlon as anyone, being active in the sport as a competitor, coach, and official since 1959. Spencer started skiing after he, along with his parents and brother, moved to Provo, Utah, from Alabama in 1948. He became active in the Boy Scouts, where he made a pair of skis for a merit badge and got interested in the sport.

Spencer became active in the junior Reserve Officers Training Corps (ROTC) at his Salt Lake high school and began shooting with the rifle team. A few years later, he joined the Utah National Guard and heard about a sport being promoted that involved both skiing and shooting—the biathlon.

At that time Spencer was attending the University of Utah, where he was a member of the ski team as a cross-country specialist. He became very interested in biathlon because he felt he had developed strong skills in both cross-country skiing and shooting. Very few people knew about the sport, and Spencer had a difficult time getting information; however, he discovered that the U.S. Olympic Committee had

Bill Spencer running in the biathlon,
1968 Winter Olympics, Grenoble, France.
Photo courtesy Bill Spencer.

The Biathlon

The biathlon combines two skills: cross-country skiing and rifle shooting. Biathlon cross-country courses range from 7.5 to 20 kilometers and typically are laid out in color-coded loops, each having a relatively even distribution of uphill, downhill, and level terrain. In addition, special challenges such as sharp turns put an extraordinary demand on the athletes' muscular and cardiovascular systems.

But cross-country running on skis is only part of the competition. After the biathletes are at or near maximum ski-running effort on the loops, they must shift into a shooting mode, requiring them to fire a rifle accurately at a small target fifty meters away. The biathletes fire five shots within thirty seconds from the time they ski to the firing line and drop their ski poles. For every shot that misses the target, one minute is added to the biathlete's running time. These factors make the biathlon one of the most demanding and physically taxing of all athletic competitions.

approved the biathlon as an event in the 1960 Squaw Valley games.

To prepare for these Olympics, the United States held the North American Alpine Ski Championship at Squaw Valley, and representatives from several countries attended. Spencer knew that the U.S. Olympic Committee had selected several members of the University of Utah Ski Team to participate in the pre-Olympic Alpine events, but the U.S. Olympic Committee had not selected anyone to represent the United States in Nordic competition. Spencer decided to give it a try. He packed his cross-country ski equipment and his deer-hunting rifle, caught a Greyhound bus, and headed for California for the competition.

At Squaw Valley, Spencer met several Russian skiers, one of whom spoke English. Nikolai Anikin asked Bill if he was going to McKinley Creek where the biathlon activities would take place. Spencer answered yes, and the Russians took him along. They taught Spencer how to wax for the competition and gave him several other key pointers. He credits the Russians, who at that time were not very friendly toward the United States, with getting him started in biathlon. Those same athletes remain his friends to this day.

Spencer also befriended members of the U.S. military from the Tenth Mountain Division stationed at Camp Hale, Colorado, where tryouts for the Olympic biathlon team were held in early 1960. Spencer barely missed making the team but decided to put all his energies into getting on the Olympic team in 1964. As a member of the U.S. Army, he went to Alaska to train, and won his way onto the 1964 and 1968 Olympic teams.

In 1973 the military closed its Alaska winter-training facility, and Spencer requested that the biathlon equipment in Alaska be sent to the Vermont National Guard because that was the location where he was being reassigned. The army accepted his request, and the United States continued to have a biathlon team, thanks to Spencer and others who started a training center in Vermont. Soon, he was hired as overall coordinator for biathlon activities and has stayed involved ever since.

Spencer has participated in numerous changes in biathlon equipment. The heavy, cumbersome, big-bore rifles have been replaced by small-bore .22-caliber rifles. The biathlon range has also changed: the first competitions involved a course in which competitors shot at several ranges; now only one range is used.

The biathletes run several loops, returning to the same range to shoot at metal knock-down targets. These changes encouraged more countries to participate in the sport because the big-bore rifles, which fired shells for longer ranges, prevented some countries from hosting competitions.

Women biathletes first competed in this event in the Olympics in 1992, and according to Spencer, the U.S. women's team often ranks higher than the men's team in international competition.

Spencer sees the opportunity for biathlon events to be held indoors in a skating rink using laser rifles, so that more spectators can enjoy the action. The competitors would run several short spurts around the rink and shoot at an indoor range. The Eko rifle, being developed in Finland, will eliminate bullets, powder, noise, and the danger associated with the weapons now being used. This environmentally friendly system uses an infrared light and small video camera to record shooting results.

Pat Miller

Since Pat Miller became head coach of the University of Utah Ski Team in 1976, the results have been impressive. He enjoys a reputation as one of the "winningest" university ski coaches in U.S. history. Under his leadership the ski team won the men's NCAA title in 1981, its first since 1947. Following that title, his combined men's and women's ski team won eight more NCAA championships (1983, 1984, 1986, 1987, 1988, 1993, 1996, 1997). In 1993 Miller was named the Rocky Mountain Intercollegiate Ski Association's coach of the year. His outstanding accomplishments, both as athlete and coach, have made him a significant part of intercollegiate ski history.

He was born in 1948 in Syracuse, New York, but moved to Maine shortly after his birth. There, Miller started skiing at a young age, competing almost every weekend during the ski season in both Alpine and Nordic disciplines. In 1965 at age sixteen, he won the National Junior Cross-Country Championship at Bend, Oregon. According to Miller, winning that race did more than anything else to help focus his skiing goals.

He and his brother Jim, older by ten months, decided in 1966 to attend Fort Lewis College in Durango, Colorado. There, Miller trained with the U.S. Ski Team and competed on the national Nordic combined team from 1968 until 1974, under the direction of Coach Adolph Kuss.

During the years 1968 to 1974, while attending Fort Lewis College, Miller competed as a member of the national Nordic combined team under Coach Kuss, and was named an All-American in 1970. Following college, Miller observed that it was time for him to start thinking about a new direction, and coaching provided a good option. Said Miller, "It was very fortunate for me that, at the time I was making the decision to leave active competition, an assistant ski coach opportunity opened at the University of Utah for someone to oversee the jumping and cross-country teams. I was thrilled to hear I had been selected to fill that opening. The ski-team coach at that time was Phil Klingsmith. My original intention was to stay at Utah long enough to obtain my master's degree and then move on. Well, my plans obviously changed," he grins.

In 1976 Miller took over as head ski coach for the University of Utah Men's Ski Team. In 1982 he became director of skiing for both men's and women's programs. Up to that time, the University of Utah sponsored separate men's and women's teams. The men's program operated under sanction of the NCAA, and the women functioned under the auspices of the Association for Intercollegiate Athletics for Women

---

NCAA Changes

In 1975 and 1980 NCAA officials made some significant changes in ski competitions. They eliminated the downhill event (1975) and ski jumping (1980), partly because of the excessive risk involved and partly because of the expense and time required to train and compete in the events. The NCAA placed three competitors with the giant slalom and cross-country relay. In another change, the NCAA combined the men's and women's ski teams at the end of the 1982 season.

In 1996 the NCAA reduced the number of competitors at the national intercollegiate championships from 160 to 148, allowing a team to have only three skiers per discipline, or a total of twelve. According to U of U Coach Pat Miller, "With this change you are going to see smaller, very specialized ski teams, recruiting only from national and Olympic team programs throughout the world."

Coach Pat Miller (center) being hoisted to the shoulders of members of the U of U Ski Team, winner of the 1981 Men's NCAA championship at Park City, Utah: (left to right, on shoulders) Roo Harris [head Alpine coach], David P. Gardner [president, U of U], Pat Miller; (standing) Bjorn Gefle, Oyvind Solvang, Trygve Mikkelsen, Bernt Lund, John Higgins, Mark Halvorson, Albert Innamorati, Per Chr. Nicolaisen, Henning Ruud, Scott Hoffman, Monte Straley. Photo courtesy Pat Miller.

Willy Schaeffler—The Vince Lombardi of Skiing

Willy Schaeffler is another ski pioneer who advanced the sport. With Bill Lash and others, Schaeffler helped organize the Professional Ski Instructors of America. But Schaeffler is best remembered as one of the finest ski coaches in the history of intercollegiate competition. German born, Schaeffler immigrated to the United States in 1948 and coached the ski team at Denver University. He was sometimes referred to as the "Vince Lombardi of skiing" because of his tough coaching approach and the success of his championship teams. He coached the Denver University Ski Team until 1970. During his eighteen years at Denver University, Schaeffler's teams won thirteen NCAA championships.

(AIAW). In 1982 the AIAW disbanded, and the women's competition became part of the NCAA program. This change, according to Miller, "altered the structure of the competitive ski programs with emphasis being placed on overall discipline balance."

The top intercollegiate ski power in the 1960s was the University of Denver under Coach Willy Schaeffler. During the 1970s the power moved to the University of Colorado under Coach Bill Marolt. In the 1980s and into the '90s, under the direction of Coach Miller, the University of Utah has dominated the intercollegiate competitive ski scene, placing in the top three NCAA competitive rankings every year since 1979, winning the All-Conference title sixteen times, and producing 214 All-American skiers and 258 All-Conference skiers. ❄

REBIRTH OF SKI JUMPING IN UTAH: Alf's Dream

chapter nine

By the 1949 U.S. National Ski-Jumping Championship at Ecker Hill, interest in ski jumping as a spectator sport had already started to diminish throughout the Intermountain West as downhill and slalom skiing began to grow. Advances in ski equipment and clothing made skiing more enjoyable and easier to do and learn. Such technological improvements as edged and waxless skis and new bindings also made skiing more popular.

In Utah during the 1930s and '40s, people loved to watch the daring performances on Becker and Ecker Hills. Ski jumping is not a sport for many people; few are brave enough or disciplined enough for the

To be good in almost any sport, I think a person has to get comfortable with being in the air. This is what makes the Utah Winter Sports Park at Bear Hollow so special. It teaches kids the basics of being in the air, starting at a very young age. I love the little kids! To see them jumping at Bear Hollow brings back many memories of my childhood and the happiness ski jumping brought to me. I think that with this facility, there is no reason why Utah cannot develop a future world ski-jumping champion right here.

—Alf Engen
Interview with Larry Warren,
Utah Winter Sports Park at Bear Hollow, Utah, 1993

years of extensive training required. In addition the sport demands physical ability and focused courage. Jumpers must be able to ride cushions of air by forcing their bodies to resemble airfoils. They must be trim and lithe. Ski jumping simply isn't an average Saturday-morning occupation. And as skiing changed from a spectator to a participation sport, ski jumping in Utah declined.

By the 1980s most of the ski jumps in and around Utah that had been built in the late 1940s had either been dismantled or had deteriorated from lack of use. Utah's first major jumping facility, Becker Hill, had been torn down in the mid- to late-1930s. Today, Pineview Reservoir covers the bottom half of the old hill.

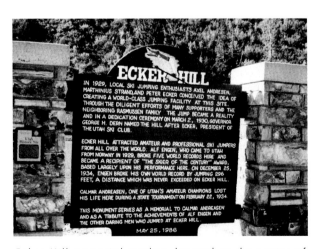

Ecker Hill memorial marker, located at the center of Pinebrook Estates south of Jeremy Ranch and I-80.

Use of Ecker Hill was discontinued in the early 1960s. Today, private homes in Pinebrook Estates surround the hill and only part of the old judges' stand and takeoff can barely be seen. Because of Ecker Hill's contribution to Utah, a historical marker has been placed on the outrun next to the road leading into Pinebrook. A monument also stands as part of a tribute to the jumpers who competed at this international site. But that is all that remains—a marker, a monument, and memories!

Other smaller jumping hills, such as those at Snowbasin and Sundance ski areas and the one at Spruces in Big Cottonwood Canyon, were torn down or abandoned in the 1960s and '70s. With a few exceptions, the original jumping facilities from the 1930s and '40s exist only in photographs.

Summer Ski Jumping

In place of the old Nordic ski jumps, another sport began to emerge—jumping in the summer on hills constructed of steel scaffolding. The Intermountain region played an important role in its development.

Summer ski jumping began in the United States during the early 1950s. All the events used crushed ice to create a sliding surface. The finely ground ice was usually applied with a blower mounted on a truck parked near the underhill. Usually the ice had to be laboriously hand-carried in sacks to parts of the hill where the blower could not reach. One event was held near Portland, Oregon, in June 1952, but the participants jumped only at night because the crushed ice melted too fast during the day.

In Utah, summer ski jumping began in September 1953 at the Utah State Fairgrounds in Salt Lake City. Art Theobald, who ran the fairgrounds, wanted a gala attraction and felt that a summer ski tournament would attract an audience. Theobald contacted Alf and Sverre Engen, and they almost single-handedly erected a jumping hill from ninety tons of steel scaffolding and sixty thousand pounds of lumber. When finished, the jumping hill stood approximately 110 feet high at the top of the inrun. They covered the inrun and landing with hay and blew several layers of crushed ice on top, creating the inrun, takeoff, and landing surface.

It was very difficult to keep enough crushed ice on the hill in the summer heat. The original blower was not large enough to layer sufficient ice onto the landing area, so special arrangements had to be made to locate a larger machine. One was finally obtained from the Hygeia Ice Company in Sugarhouse, but the jumpers still had to carry crushed ice in buckets up the hill to cover the inrun because the blower could not throw ice all the way to the top. Despite these challenges, the tournament went off on schedule, and everyone had a great time—spectators as well as jumpers.

Pleased with the success of the exhibition at the fairgrounds, the Norseman Ski Club decided to sponsor a summer ski jump. The club suggested a site not far from the mouth of Emigration Canyon, along the Wasatch Mountains. The hill was constructed and named Norseman Hill in honor of the Norwegians who had pioneered ski jumping in Utah. Only a few competitive tournaments were held on the hill, the first one in August 1955 on a new product called Summer Snow. Only a handful of jumpers participated, but the

Summer ski-jumping hill at the Utah State Fairgrounds in Salt Lake City, 1953.

event did attract a number of spectators who wanted to see crazy people ski jumping during the summer.

One of the most unusual jumping events ever held, again organized by the Norseman Ski Club, was the indoor exhibition in Salt Lake City's Rainbow Rendezvous ballroom, a popular place for special events and dancing.

The jumping hill was built in two large rooms, separated by a wall with a window. Because of very limited space, the inrun was short and went all the way up to very hot, cramped quarters in the steel-beam rafters. From this confined space, the skiers jumped through the window. They placed heavy drapes in front of the window, leaving only a small opening to jump through. When the jumpers started from the dark rafters, they could see nothing but the narrow opening in the curtains. The crowd below saw nothing until the jumpers suddenly appeared through that small opening.

All of those who were scheduled to jump were concerned that the short inrun did not allow sufficient

Alan Engen participating in the indoor ski jumping at Jerry Joneses' Rainbow Rendezvous ballroom, November 10, 1955.

space to get up enough speed before the takeoff. To remedy this, they rigged up a two-person pulley to propel each other down the dark inrun. One person held onto one end of a rope and jumped fifteen or twenty feet off a platform; the falling weight then yanked the jumper down the inrun with enough momentum to allow him to land safely on the outrun.

The spectators were both thrilled and impressed, but they knew nothing of the confined starting place or the rope-pulley system; however, they quickly learned about the difficulties of landing on a very short outrun. Bales of hay covered with straw were positioned at the end of the outrun. Some of the jumpers went right through the hay bales into an adjoining room. Fortunately, no one was injured when flying out of the steel rafters or plowing through the hay bales. All of the jumpers knew they were stretching their luck, even though they acknowledged it was great fun; but in those days, they considered such recklessness no more than a good chance to test their agility. Now, the old Rainbow Rendezvous ballroom is gone, having been torn down in the 1960s.

These exhibitions worked so well that they decided to follow up with an exhibition in Sugarhouse Park in late September 1958. The underhill was a natural hillside, but a scaffold was needed for the inrun and takeoff, which the jumpers built in two weeks. The event was scheduled to last two days, with both afternoon and evening performances. Local newspapers and the radio were used to publicize the event.

Everything went well until two nights before the

first tournament, when a severe storm driven by fierce winds hit the area. The wind blew the scaffold over. When the jumpers, headed by Dick Simons, arrived at the park the next morning, all that was left was a pile of twisted metal. After considerable discussion the jumpers decided to rebuild the scaffold, but they had to do it in one day!

Working nonstop all that day and night, the steel hill was again ready to jump by 8:00 A.M. the next morning. Only the young, strong, and optimistic would have undertaken such a task. They jumped on schedule for two days without further incident.

The next significant summer-jumping exhibitions we're held at Mt. Baldy, California, where Alf and Alan performed double jumps for the spectators. The inrun, covered with Merrill Nielson's Summer Snow, was only about three feet wide, so they had no room for error. The double jumps worked, and they jumped together for several summers in the late 1950s and early '60s at Mt. Baldy, becoming a featured attraction in Southern California and drawing crowds that ranged from a hundred to a thousand visitors each time they jumped.

Normally the two put on a jumping exhibition in the morning around 11 A.M. and another in midafternoon on weekends. During the weekdays, Alf ran a summer ski school with Summer Snow for visitors wishing to learn to ski.

Jon Engen, Alf's younger son, learned to jump on Summer Snow and went on to become a very fine competitor. As they gained confidence jumping on Summer Snow, they began trying challenging stunts to add spark (sometimes literally) to the exhibitions, such as jumping through a large round hoop set on fire. Initially they performed this stunt one at a time, but soon four or five of them came through the hoop right after each other, thrilling the crowds.

The jumpers held the most spectacular and dangerous of the Summer Snow exhibitions at the Los Angeles County Fair in Pomona, California. A very large scaffold jumping hill was built in the middle of the horse-racing track, with the top of the inrun 130 feet high. Many guy wires held the scaffold in place, but when any breeze came up, the inrun swayed alarmingly back and forth. This made jumping very dicy because the jumpers had to time things perfectly or they would take off sideways—not a healthy situation.

When the hill was under construction, none of the union laborers were willing to go up that high to

Alan Engen performing a spread-eagle exhibition jump, Mt. Baldy, California, circa 1959.

Skiers climbing the summer ski-jumping scaffold at Sugarhouse Park, September 1958.

erect the steel scaffold. So Alf, Sverre, Alan, and several other jumpers decided to do it themselves. They had no protection, no hard hats or safety belts. They climbed more than a hundred feet up, added new steel frames, and hoped no one would make a mistake and slip—it was a long way down!

When they finished building the hill, the difficult job of spreading the Summer Snow on the running surface remained. They had to carry bag after bag of Summer Snow up the hill, thousands of pounds; then they had to spread the stuff with shovel and rake to evenly cover the inrun, takeoff, and landing hill.

Finally someone had to test-jump the hill to make sure it was safe. No one had ever jumped on Summer Snow on a hill this size. They were not certain the Summer Snow would glide in the humid ocean air as it did in the dry air of Utah, which allowed it to provide a consistent surface with no speed resistance or drag.

After much discussion it was decided that Alf and Alan should test-jump. They climbed to the top of the inrun with their jumping skis. The day was bright and clear with very little smog, so they could see all over the fairgrounds. Alan offered to make the first jump, but Alf said, "Absolutely not!" He did not want his son to take any unnecessary risks. Merrill Nielson, who was standing with a flag on the knoll of the hill, waved Alf on. He immediately took off down the inrun, approached the takeoff, sprang into the air, and then disappeared out of sight, floating down the hill. A second or two later, he emerged on the flat section of the outrun and stopped in the bales of hay at the end. There was a deep sense of relief that Alf had made the jump with no apparent difficulty.

Now it was Alan's turn. Nielson waved the red flag, and Alan started down the inrun. It was steeper and longer than any of the artificial hills he had

jumped on before, so the acceleration and speed were much greater. Says Alan, "I focused on the end of the takeoff. The next thing I remember is feeling the air cushion develop beneath my skis as I laid out over them. What a sensation! When I came to a stop at the end of the outrun, the first person to greet me was Dad. He asked how I liked the hill, and I replied that I could hardly wait to get to the top for another practice leap. He laughed and said he felt the same way. We were now in business for the exhibition."

The Los Angeles County Fair jumping exhibitions ran for seventeen consecutive days, beginning September 16, 1960. On weekdays the jumpers performed the exhibition jump only once in the after-noon, after the horse races. On weekends, however, they held two performances, one in early afternoon and the other at night, starting about 8:30 P.M. The night jumping was quite spectacular, especially when they jumped through fire hoops. Crowds for all the events ranged in the thousands. On more than one occasion, recorded attendance was in excess of fifty thousand people.

They jumped from 120 to 150 feet, depending on the speed of the hill. Because of the humidity, speed varied from day to·day; because of air pollution, they occasionally needed oxygen between jumps.

Ski Jumping Makes a Minor Comeback

A brief resurgence in Nordic winter ski jumping occurred in the early 1960s when the Solitude ski area built a forty-meter hill. Solitude was just getting started, and the University of Utah Ski Team used the area as its home-base training facility. Several members of the team—including Jim Gaddis, Robert Nelson, John Mortensen, and Alan Engen—worked at the Solitude ski resort during the summer, cutting and grooming new ski trails. During the summer they requested that Solitude construct a jumping hill so they could train on it to prepare for

Top: Scaffold for summer ski jumping, L.A. County Fairgrounds, Pamona, California, 1960.

Middle: At the takeoff with Alan Engen, Alf Engen, Dick Simons, and Sverre Engen, L.A. County Fair-grounds, Pomona, California, 1960.

Bottom: Alf and Alan Engen perfoming a double jump at L.A. County Fairgrounds, Pomona, California, 1960.

Keith Lange performing a well-executed gelande jump. Photo courtesy Keith Lange.

collegiate competition.

Bob Barrett, the first owner of Solitude, hired Alan to do the design work for a hill that Barrett wanted to build. Alan used Sun Valley's Ruud Mountain and Alta's Landes Hill plans as a reference in designing the Solitude jump. Several significant collegiate tournaments were held on the hill in the 1960s. However, the hill had one challenging aspect: it had a relatively short outrun, and if jumpers were not able to slow down fast enough, they ended up going over a bank and into the parking lot about fifty feet below. Perhaps that had some influence on the decision not to continue jumping there anymore, and eventually this jump was torn down and the space converted to a public ski run.

Gelande—The Alpine Skier's Counter to Nordic Ski Jumping

As more and more people migrated to Alpine skiing, a new form of ski flying, known as *gelande,* became popular. The term *geländesprung* comes from the German noun *gelande* and verb *springen,* and means "terrain jump." A *geländesprung* is performed

on Alpine skis rather than the wider and longer Nordic jumping skis, and uses ski poles.

In the early days of skiing, a single long pole was used for balance and speed control. After World War I, an Austrian colonel by the name of Georg Bilgeri invented dual ski poles. From that time on, skiers wishing to perform a *geländesprung* could do so with much more control because they could push off with two poles with baskets.

The *geländesprung* remained a fancy skiing maneuver, particularly popular with expert skiers at Alta during the 1940s, '50s, and early '60s. Some of the better-known jumpers included ski instructors Keith Lange and Junior Bounous and Canadian Jim McConkey. Each of them would jump off large cornices, cliffs, almost anything where they could get plenty of air. A rocky outcrop at the base of Mt. Baldy's main chute at Alta is named McConk's Rock in honor of his spectacular leaps from that pinnacle, and a larger one a few hundred yards to the west is named Bounous's Rock.

Keith Lange perhaps epitomized "gelandemania." He made gelande into an art form by springing off

THIRD ANNUAL NATIONAL GELANDE CONTEST

Photo by Tom Piotchan, Alta Peruvian Lodge

ALTA, UTAH . . . APRIL 22-23
CLASSES FOR PROFESSIONALS AND AMATEURS

AWARDS:
First Professional - $200 - Rosemount Boots
Second Professional - $100 - Head 360 Skis
Third Professional - $50 - Fiber-Glass Poles

Entry Fee: $5 Professional — $2.50 Amateur

TROPHIES IN AMATEUR CLASSES

SPECIAL LIFT RATES AND 20 PERCENT REDUCTION OF
LOW-SEASON RATE AT THESE ALTA LODGES: ALTA
LODGE, ALTA PERUVIAN, GOLD MINER'S DAUGHTER
AND RUSTLER.

Poster advertising the National Gelande
Championship at Alta, with Jon Engen as the
featured gelande jumper.

every bump in sight. The phrase "big air" had a special meaning for Lange. His extraordinary athletic feats sometimes resulted in spectacular falls, which pleased the watching bystanders. But that did not matter to him. He just got up, shook off the snow, and away he went.

Sometime during the 1962–63 ski season, Alf and a number of gelande specialists decided to take the gelande a step farther and make it a competitive event. Alta was chosen as the site and held its first gelande tournament on an old mine dump at the base of High Rustler. Approximately fifty top Alpine and Nordic skiers entered the event, billed as the First Annual Gelande Ski Championship.

The jumps were constructed differently from Nordic ones. The takeoff had a sharp upramp, or lip, which propelled the jumper high into the air. The jumper soared thirty to fifty feet above the landing slope. Later, the professional gelande-jumping tour changed this format, making the jump more Nordic-like, with the jumper following the contour of the hill.

Gelande style points were awarded on the following basis: 1) jumper in the air with legs tucked under; 2) poles at the side, not swinging; 3) body relaxed; 4) back relatively upright and straight; and 5) skis parallel and together. This form was completely different from that of Nordic jumpers, who jumped with straight legs, the body leaning well forward over the skis in flight, and without ski poles.

Alan Engen won the first gelande tournament at Alta, which was held near the end of the ski season on April 22, 1963. He broke two pairs of skis in the process because he outjumped the hill. Other jumpers also broke skis that day. Jim Gaddis, who was at that time one of the nation's top Alpine racers, finished second. Nordic ski jumper Dick Simons came in third.

The 1963 gelande tournament at Alta was considered very successful, but no competition was held the following year. In 1964 a formal proposal was submitted by Jim Gaddis, who was working for Alta at that time, to make gelande jumping an annual national event. The Alta Ski Lifts Company agreed to sponsor the first national competition, which was held in the spring of 1965. A large traveling trophy, formally named the Alta, Utah, National Gelande Cup (later shortened to Alta Cup) was introduced that year to identify and honor the winner. The first recipient of this award, appropriately enough, was Keith Lange. Jim Gaddis had actually won the event but, because he was the head tournament official, declined the first-place prize, and it was awarded to Lange.

The Alta Gelande Committee decided to move the jumping site to a larger mine dump, located between Corkscrew and Nina's Curve near the base of the Collins chairlift, so that the jumpers would have a longer landing hill and could go farther. It also was a better location for spectators.

Jon Engen was considered one of the most stylish gelande jumpers in the early years. He came as close as any jumper to achieving the ideal form set by the style rules in those days. His image became a model for other jumpers and was even used on a special gelande medal in 1989.

The Alta Ski Lifts Company continued to host the National Gelande Championships each spring from 1964 to 1974. In April 1969 the contest generated so much interest that the fifth annual event was televised on ABC's *Wide World of Sports*.

Daredevil exhibitions make their way into recreational ski sports as demonstrated by
Alf Engen jumping the road to Alta, using a freshly run avalanche as a takeoff. Photo by Tom Plofchan.

Doug MacIsaac executing the Nordic V style of gelande ski jumping. Photo courtesy Doug MacIsaac.

Changes in Gelande Jumping

By the early 1970s, the national gelande-jumping event had grown to more than two hundred contestants in five classes, ranging in age from eight to over fifty. Professionals (those competitors who jumped for a cash prize) began to look at Nordic ski-jumping hills on which to compete. In 1974 the gelande format was officially changed to a pro-tour concept on regular ski-jumping hills. The rules allowed gelande jumpers to employ a style very similar to Nordic jumping, except that they carried ski poles and used regular Alpine skis. Modern-day gelande jumpers must tuck just prior to the end of the flight. Other than that, they look very much like a Nordic jumper.

To minimize the potential for serious injury, the designated gelande-hill captain decided where the jumpers would start, which in turn determined how fast the jumper would be traveling at takeoff. The goal was to have enough speed to easily clear the knoll of the hill but not go beyond a preestablished critical point. On the Alta mine dump, jumpers were able to fly safely about 175 feet.

In the years when the championship was held at Alta, relatively few injuries occurred. But, those few who were injured, plus a few other events involving inappropriate behavior by the jumpers and unruly reactions by some of the spectators, caused Alta Ski Lifts Company to discontinue the gelande competition after 1974.

David Wren, son of Olympic ski jumper Gordy Wren from Steamboat Springs, introduced the latest Nordic V style, which enables jumpers to fly much farther. In 1976 the gelande distance record was set

by Paul Hitchcock at 229 feet. In 1979 David Wren exceeded this record by twenty feet. During the 1980s gelande jumps moved to the large ninety-meter ski-jumping hills. In 1982 Bart Lockhart performed a near-perfect gelande jump on Steamboat Spring's Howelsen Hill and set a new record of 96 meters (315 feet). In 1992 Jeff Wogrin flew 320 feet on Howelsen Hill and, in 1997, 328 feet. As of 1998, this distance has not been exceeded and is considered the world record.

Doug MacIsaac, Mike Wogrin, and Jeff Wogrin were the organizers of the professional gelande tour. MacIsaac won the National Gelande Championship three times (1979, 1982, 1985), and is considered among the all-time greats of gelande ski jumping.

The old-style gelande tournament did come back to Alta one more time in 1989 as part of their fiftieth anniversary celebration. The contest used the original gelande rules. Sixty-four jumpers participated in the two-day competition on the same mine dump used in the 1960s. Karl Jakobsen of Park City, Utah, won the overall professional class, followed by Phil Lamothe from Montana. Third place went to another outstanding Alpine skier, Steve Bounous, Junior's son. In the veteran class (age fifty and over), some of the early gelande winners participated, with the top professional spot going to Gene Christiansen of Alta, followed by Junior Bounous in second place, and Alan Engen in third.

Stein Eriksen performing his famous forward somersault with layout. Photo courtesy Stein Eriksen.

Stein Eriksen

The story of gelande jumping—in fact, the story of skiing—in Utah would not be complete without mentioning one of the world's greatest champions— Stein Eriksen. He was born on December 11, 1927, in Oslo, Norway. His father, Marius Sr., owned a large sporting-goods store and was himself a champion skier in Norway in the early 1900s. He was also a famed athlete and represented Norway in the 1912 Olympic Games in Stockholm, Sweden, as a member of the gymnastics team.

Stein Eriksen established himself as a ski champion in Norway at a very young age. In 1952 he won gold and silver medals in the Olympic giant slalom and slalom races in Oslo. He instantly became a national hero because he was the first Norwegian ever to win an Olympic Alpine skiing event.

The following year, Sun Valley Ski School invited

> ### Back Flip Accomplished on Skis
> As far as can be determined, the first recorded "standing" full backwards somersault on skis was accomplished in 1960 by Rodney Hurick at Alta, Utah. Ski-movie producer Sverre Engen captured the jump on camera and used it in his 1961–62 film Ski Spectacular.

Eriksen to come to America as a guest instructor. While there, he astounded the world with his unique Reverse-Shoulder Technique and also by performing the first forward somersault with a full layout on skis. Although skiers had performed somersaults in earlier years, no one had combined it with a "swan dive" prior to Eriksen's acrobatic feat. He may very well lay claim

Stein Eriksen, Alf Engen, and Alan Engen, April 1995. Photo by Dr. William W. Miller.

to being the father of the inverted aerials that we see in competition today. He was a fine acrobat/gymnast and in the 1950s and '60s could do things on skis that amazed the best athletes in the world.

In 1954 Eriksen reentered international competition. He won the giant slalom, slalom, and combined events at the world championship in Aare, Sweden. This again put him into the record books as the first Alpine skier to win triple gold medals in world-championship competition.

With his two Olympic and three world-championship medals solidly in the international official records, Eriksen decided to leave active competitive racing and pursue a professional skiing career. He fulfilled ski-school directorships at Boyne Mountain, Michigan; Heavenly Valley, California; and Aspen Highlands, Colorado. In 1979, under prodding from one of his longtime friends, Edgar Stern, he came to Utah, where he directed the ski school at Park City for three years and then became director of skiing. When the initial planning started for changing the old Snow Park ski area into a world-class resort called Deer Valley, Eriksen became integrally involved and has remained there ever since.

Eriksen is a ski legend by everyone's standards. At the end of each ski season, he and another ski legend, Alf Engen, always got together to discuss old times and the friendship they had enjoyed over the span of four decades. In a 1996 reunion, Eriksen talked a little about his early years and some of the positive influences in his life.

"When I was growing up in Norway," he said, "I remember having many Norwegian ski champions come to our house because they were close friends of my father. Legends such as Thorleif Haug, Sigmund Ruud, Birger Ruud, and Reidar Andersen were among many top athletes who visited. I can remember seeing how happy they all were and how much fun they were having enjoying the sport they loved.

"I said to myself, 'That is what I want to do! I want to be a part of that wonderful life.' And so it was that I went that direction. I have never regretted the decision. Skiing has been very good to me, and I, in turn, have tried hard to give something back to the sport just like Alf Engen has done.

"Alf has always been my personal hero. I have somewhat patterned my ski career after him. Like Alf, I came to America from Norway and through the years have attempted to show the same friendly warm feeling toward everyone. I can't remember Alf ever having a bad day. I think to be successful in this business, you must truly care about people." ❄

chapter ten

LET OUR GAMES BEGIN!
The 2002 Olympics

Contrary to popular belief, Pierre de Coubertin was not interested initially in having winter sports as part of the Olympic agenda. There were, after all, no snow-related events played on the sweltering fields of Olympia, Greece. Neither was there any classical image to provide incentive to include winter events in the Olympic program. However, because of the growing interest and participation in winter athletics, particularly in the northern countries, it was finally agreed that there should be winter Olympic games held in addition to the summer ones. Chamonix, France, was selected to host the first Olympic Winter Games in 1924.

Now over seven decades later, Salt Lake City, Utah, is being given the opportunity to carry the Olympic flag and light the Olympic torch, which will burn ever so brightly throughout the 2002 Winter Olympics.

For many athletes, being selected as a member of the U.S. Olympic Team is the ultimate achievement and honor. Despite criticism of the modern Olympic Games—the politics that divide rather than unite nations, the quest for million-dollar endorsements—most athletes compete for the challenge, the thrill of meeting the world's best in open, friendly competition.

The main issue in life is not the victory but the fight; the essential is not to have won but to have fought well.

To spread these precepts is to pave the way for a more valiant humanity, stronger, and consequently more scrupulous and more generous. . . . May joy and good fellowship reign, and in this manner, may the Olympic torch pursue its way through the ages, increasing friendly understanding among nations, for the good of a humanity always more enthusiastic, more courageous, and more pure.

—Baron Pierre de Coubertin
Founder of the Modern Olympic Games

Although the world knows that Salt Lake City will host the 2002 Olympic Winter Games, it may not be aware that it took many years and several attempts to achieve that honor. Perhaps the first person to have a vision of Utah hosting the Olympics was Mark Strand. After the 1932 Olympics at Lake Placid, New York, Strand proposed that, because of Utah's growing international prominence in ski jumping and great snow conditions, there was surely no better spot to hold the Olympics than Salt Lake City. The biggest drawback for Strand was the lack of financial support, so his dream did not garner any serious attention.

The idea continued to pop up periodically throughout the 1940s, '50s, and early '60s. Then sometime around the mid-1960s, the Olympic dream attracted more serious discussion. According to John W. "Jack" Gallivan, then publisher of the *Salt Lake Tribune*, it began one evening over a bottle of Jack Daniels in the basement of Utah governor Calvin Rampton's home. Max Rich, former Utah National Guard adjutant general, was there also. An Olympic bid, they thought, would be a great help to Utah's rapidly growing ski industry. As a result, Governor Rampton appointed a special committee to start a campaign to get the ball rolling with the goal of hosting the 1972 Olympics in Salt Lake City.

Special Salt Lake City Olympic Award given to (left to right) Joe Quinney, Alf Engen, and Felix Koziol, circa 1975, for their involvement and support of the 1973 attempt to gain the 1976 bid for the Olympics in Salt Lake City.

The committee was composed of Jack Gallivan; Max Rich; Gene Donovan, president of Prudential Federal Savings and Loan; H. Deveraux (Dev) Jennings, member of the 1948 U.S. Winter Olympic Team; M. Walker Wallace, president of the Downtown Planning Association; Glenn Adams, Ogden attorney; and Felix Koziol, former supervisor of the Wasatch National Forest.

Although Utah was named the U.S. candidate for the 1972 games, Sapporo, Japan, was chosen as the host. In 1973 Salt Lake lost the U.S. Olympic nomination to Denver, which subsequently withdrew from international contention to host the 1976 Winter Games. Innsbruck, Austria, was eventually chosen as the site. In 1985 Salt Lake again lost the bid to become the U.S. candidate, this time to Anchorage, Alaska, which then lost in the final selection to Albertville, France.

To make matters worse, during the 1970s and '80s, only limited Nordic winter ski jumping occurred. Becker and Ecker Hills and all the other old jumping sites were long gone. Alpine skiing dominated the Intermountain region.

Then something happened to change that bleak outlook. Even after all the past attempts and close calls, Utah decided to put in a bid for the 1998 Olympics. To do this, a suitable jumping site had to be built. John Bower—a four-time national Nordic combined champion, Olympic team member, and Nordic program director for the U.S. Ski Team—headed a committee charged with making recom-

mendations for a jumping site during the winter of 1992–93, under the overall direction of the Utah Sports Authority.

Alf and Alan Engen became members of the committee. After several potential sites had been carefully studied and wind-tested for two years, in 1990 the committee selected Bear Hollow near Park City for the Winter Sports Park. The committee then chose John Bower to manage the construction and maintenance of the complex in preparation for winning the 1998 Olympic bid.

The Utah Winter Sports Park as then proposed would have two small jumping hills (18 and 38 meters) so young people could learn how to jump, and two larger hills (65 and 90 meters) for competition. A fifth hill (120 meters) would also be constructed if Salt Lake City were chosen to host the Olympic Winter Games. In addition a world-class freestyle (inverted-aerial) jumping facility and a bobsled/luge track would also be constructed at the sports park. The overall cost estimate for the complex was forty-five million dollars, including the bobsled/luge runs, which require costly refrigeration systems.

No. 109   Winter, 1993

Utah's Jumping Again

Bear Hollow Takes First Leap on Olympic Path

Photos by Alan Engen

A resurgence of ski jumping is under way with the new ski jumping facility at the Utah Winter Sports Park in Bear Hollow Canyon northeast of Park City. Bear Hollow is located just off I-80 at Kimball's Junction on U-224 and is visible to motorists approaching Park City from the east on I-80.

A winter sports complex was part of a move to lure the Winter Olympics to Utah. John Bowers, ski jump complex manager, said the selection and construction of a jumping complex was not a choice, but a requirement for bidding by Salt Lake City for the 2002 Olympic Winter Games.

Bear Hollow was one of five sites extensively investigated over a two-year period; four sites were in Summit County and one in Wasatch County. Snow conditions were recorded and wind studies were made of each of the areas.

The six-member investigation committee included John Bowers, a former Olympic ski jumper and former director of ski jumping and Nordic combined for the U. S. ski team. Other members included Neil Richardson, chair for the Salt Lake Olympic Bid Committee's technical committee; Neal Stowe, director of State Facilities Construction and Management; Charles Winters, Utah Sports Authority; Alf Engen,

Alf Engen and John Bowers, L. to R, view take-off of the 90 meter jump.

acclaimed jumper in the 30s and 40s, former director of the Alf Engen Ski School and current Director of Skiing, Alta, Utah; Alan Engen, former downhill and Nordic competitor, businessman and current director of the Alf Engen Ski School, Alta, Utah.

"The criteria for the selection of the jumping complex," John Bowers said, "were based on the relative protection of the jumping facility, visibility and proximity of routes of access."

Out of the five sites studied,

The 90 meter Olympic-caliber hill at Bear Hollow was first tested by the country's top jumpers on December 12-13.

Bear Hollow was selected because the area best filled the criteria required for a jumping complex. The Bear Hollow site is aerodynamically sound and environmentally satisfactory. Bear Hollow has desirable wind conditions; the big jump hill is protected by two ridges from dangerous cross winds and by trees that further disperse the

winds; the hollow has trees that outline the jumps; the jump line has the advantage of the ridges' natural contour. Furthermore, the jump did not require huge concrete structures.

The Bear Hollow complex has on site four Olympic-caliber jump hills (18, 35, 70 and 90

Continued on page 2

News clipping highlighting the resurgence of ski jumping in Utah, 1993.

John Bower winning the Holmenkollen Nordic combined event in Norway, circa 1960s.

John Bower

John Bower is a former member of the U.S. Ski Team (1962–68), including two Olympic teams, and was the first American to win the prestigious King's Cup (Nordic combined championship) at the Holmenkollen Ski Festival in Oslo, Norway. "Winning Holmenkollen was a great way for me to end my competitive ski career," Bower says. "The fact that I won was a surprise not only to me but to everyone else as well. I think the Norwegians were more excited than I was. No one expected an American skier to win this tournament. I think because of this fact, I perhaps got more attention than someone else might have from another country, like Germany, Finland, or even Norway. It was just so unusual for this to happen!

"But what this one event did for me was open doors that would never have been possible otherwise. I gained some notoriety and was even invited to the White House. Winning this particular tournament was certainly a beneficial way for me to end my competitive career, though possibly not as prestigious as winning an Olympic medal."

After nearly forty years of sporadic Nordic ski jumping in the Intermountain West, a renaissance began with the construction of the Utah Winter Sports Park at Bear Hollow. The drive to bring the 1998 Olympic Winter Games to Salt Lake City sparked this reawakening. When the games were awarded to Nagano, Japan, many Utahans became even more determined to bring the Olympics here. To help ensure that the next drive was successful, construction began on the bobsled and luge at the sports park. In addition, the complex began holding national tournaments on its 90-meter jumping hill, encouraging young people to use these outstanding facilities. And come

the young jumpers did, sparking a resurgence of interest in jumping.

On January 9, 1993, the Utah Winter Sports Park opened with a special ceremony and competition ski jumping on the 90-meter hill (K90) as part of the Utah Winter Games. Tim Tetrault from Norwich, Vermont, a member of the U.S. Ski-Jumping Team, won the first event, flying ninety meters (more than 270 feet).

Salt Lake City's loss to Nagano spurred the state and the U.S. Olympic Committee to try again and bid for the 2002 games. Effort was launched to make sure Utah's facilities were considered top-notch, and in the summer of 1993, Bear Hollow became a training site

The Salt Lake Tribune

VOLUME 250 NUMBER 35
TODAY'S READERSHIP: 339,680

SATURDAY
June 17, 1995

©1995, THE SALT LAKE TRIBUNE
SALT LAKE CITY, UTAH 84111

UTAH CHOSEN AS 2002 WINTER SITE

Let Our Games Begin!

Three Tries and 30 Years Later, the IOC Says S.L. Right Place

By John Keahey
THE SALT LAKE TRIBUNE

BUDAPEST, Hungary — Tom Welch's 8- and 12-year-old sons gave their dad a Hungarian good-luck charm Friday. It had colorful, clutchable beads — the kind a person in need of comfort can get his or her fingers around.

"I put it in my pocket. I had my hands on it," said the Salt Lake Olympic bid president, his voice hoarse with emotion, his tear-filled eyes trying to focus as he made his way, two steps a minute, through a jam of more than 100 Utahns — each trying to get his attention, to clutch his arm, to give him a hug.

Just moments before, members of that crowd — many hoarse and wet-eyed as well — heard the words "Salt Lake City" roll from the lips of Juan Antonio Samaranch, 75, president of the International Olympic Committee (IOC).

Friday's pronouncement by the slight, immaculately tailored Samaranch in this ancient East European city gave the 2002 Winter Olympics to Utah.

They were words that Welch and a small group of trusted Olympic-bid insiders have waited years to hear.

The victory came in the third bid out of five tries made — on and off — over three decades. Salt Lake City has gone before the international body as the U.S. Olympic Committee's choice for 1972, 1998 and 2002. It was rejected as the U.S. candidate for 1976 and 1992.

The 2002 victory was decisive.

Of the 90 IOC members voting, Salt Lake City got 55 votes on the first ballot, well above the 46 needed. Competitors Sion, Switzerland, and Ostersund, Sweden, received 14 apiece, and Quebec, Canada, managed seven.

Members of the Salt Lake City Olympic Bid Committee appear to cheer the news that Utah was selected as the site of the 2002 Winter Games.

This front page says it all! June 17, 1995.

for the U.S. ski-jumping and freestyle teams. Several exhibitions and competitions were held for the public during the summers of 1993 and 1994.

After the success of the 1995 National Ski-Jumping Championship at Bear Hollow, all attention was focused on the upcoming announcement of the city to host the 2002 Winter Olympics. Rumor had it that Utah had the nod, but the state had been close before. In the international arena, positions can change in a moment.

The months before the announcement were tense. Though some people didn't want the Olympics, many others were eager for this once-in-a-lifetime opportunity. The city mounted a large sign on the corner of State Street and Fourth South to count down the days to the announcement. Time seemed to crawl and fly at the same time. Much had been

accomplished, but there was a lot left to do.

On June 16, 1995, it looked as if half the city gathered around the City and County Building in downtown Salt Lake to hear the announcement. One of the local television stations erected a huge screen so the crowd, estimated at forty thousand, would be able to see as well as hear the announcement.

Then the dream became reality. Juan Antonio Samaranch, president of the International Olympic Committee (IOC), proclaimed from Budapest, Hungary, that Salt Lake City had been selected to host the 2002 Olympic Winter Games. All the hard work contributed by so many people for so many years had finally paid off.

Chairman Tom Welch, Frank Joklik, and the other members of the Olympic Bid Committee had done a magnificent job of selling the advantages of Salt Lake

Eleven-year-old Lindsey Van, current world champion for girls in her age class, accepts congratulations from (left to right) Sverre, Alf, and Corey Engen, Utah Winter Sports Park, Bear Hollow, September 1996. Photo by Dobber Price.

as a host city. With its selection, Salt Lake City became an international city. Competitive skiing in Utah, whether in the air or on the ground, is certain to become once again an international stage for those world-class athletes who possess a passion for the sport.

Since the modern Olympic movement was started in 1896, the games have been held in the United States only six times: in Los Angeles twice, Lake Placid twice, Squaw Valley, and Atlanta. That averages one time every 1.6 decades. For any city, town, or village to have an opportunity to play host to the International Olympic Games even once is a distinction of historic magnitude and imposes an obligation and commitment of commensurate proportions. So now we all await the 2002 Olympics. And what then? What will happen in ski jumping, this now obscure Nordic sport that once dominated winter competitions? Time has changed ski jumping. The V style that Alf worked so hard to correct is now considered state-of-the-art. Ski jumpers using this style now exceed six hundred feet, twice the length of a football field.

Before the 1980s, using the V style would have caused serious point deductions on form because the jumper's skis are in a wide V rather than close together. In 1988, however, Sweden's Jan Bokloev started jumping this way and immediately got the world's attention because he flew much farther than the competition. By the early 1990s, the Austrians, Germans, Japanese, Finns, and Czechoslovakians had switched over to the V style. In 1992 the international rules were changed, eliminating deductions for using the V style, much to the dismay of the Norwegians, who strongly felt the new style was inferior aesthetically to the traditional form. But the V style gives the flyer a more favorable aerodynamic position with less resistance, thus promoting greater distance, and in this age of Faster, Higher, Stronger, it appears to be here to stay.

The question now is, Where do we go from here? John Bower has a unique perspective as a champion and committee chair for the Utah Winter Sports Park. "Ski jumping is changing technically," he says. "There are increasing limitations on equipment, and it is becoming very competitive. I think the biggest change, however, will be the emergence of women as a significant factor in jumping competition. Physiologically, women are well suited for ideal flight, being relatively small, compact, and light. I think the U.S.

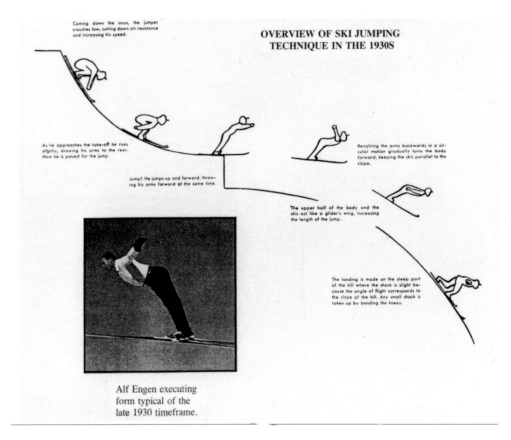

OVERVIEW OF SKI JUMPING
TECHNIQUE IN THE 1930S

Coming down the inrun, the jumper crouches low, cutting down air resistance and increasing his speed.

As he approaches the take-off he rises slightly, drawing his arms to the rear. Now he is poised for the jump.

Jump! He jumps up and forward, throwing his arms forward at the same time.

Revolving the arms backwards in a circular motion gradually turns the body forward, keeping the skis parallel to the slope.

The upper half of the body and the skis act like a glider's wing, increasing the length of the jump.

The landing is made on the steep part of the hill where the shock is slight because the angle of flight corresponds to the slope of the hill. Any small shock is taken up by bending the knees.

Alf Engen executing form typical of the late 1930 timeframe.

Comparison: ski-jumping style of the 1930s vs. that of the '90s.

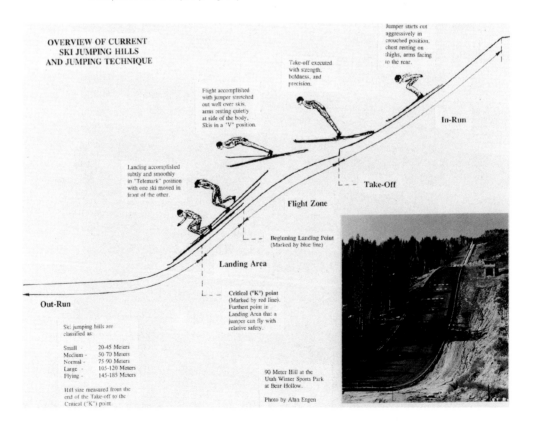

OVERVIEW OF CURRENT
SKI JUMPING HILLS
AND JUMPING TECHNIQUE

Jumper starts out aggressively in crouched position, chest resting on thighs, arms facing to the rear.

Take-off executed with strength, boldness, and precision.

Flight accomplished with jumper stretched out well over skis, arms resting quietly at side of the body, Skis in a 'V' position.

In-Run

Landing accomplished subtly and smoothly in "Telemark" position with one ski moved in front of the other.

Take-Off

Flight Zone

Beginning Landing Point
(Marked by blue line)

Landing Area

Out-Run

Critical ("K") point
(Marked by red line).
Furthest point in
Landing Area that a
jumper can fly with
relative safety.

Ski jumping hills are
classified as:

Small   20-45 Meters
Medium -   50-70 Meters
Normal -   75-90 Meters
Large -   105-120 Meters
Flying -   145-185 Meters

Hill size measured from the
end of the Take-off to the
Critical ("K") point.

90 Meter Hill at the
Utah Winter Sports Park
at Bear Hollow.

Photo by Alan Engen

Jumper executing the modern V style, Utah Winter Sports Park, Bear Hollow, Utah, July 1994. Photo by Alan Agle.

What It Feels Like to Jump

In 1962 Heini Klopfer, designer of the largest jump in the world at Oberstdorf, Germany, was asked what it is like to fly six-hundred-plus feet on skis. The worst part, he said, is that just before beginning to jump, you get *startfieber*, a gripping in the stomach that makes it difficult to swallow or talk. Some jumpers even feel nausea.

This is not so much fear, Klopfer says, but simply a result of extreme concentration prior to starting down the inrun. Once the jumper starts, the *startfieber* leaves as he quickly accelerates to sixty miles an hour. Eyes are fixed on the end of the takeoff. When the jumper reaches just the precise spot and moment, his legs uncoil powerfully in a forward dive that thrusts his entire body out over the skis. At this moment, Klopfer says, the jumper gets herrliches gefuhl, "the glorious feeling." At first the air buffets the jumper, but that quickly subsides and all that is left is a feeling of complete release from the pull of gravity. The ski flier lies on a cushion of air, which carries the jumper far down the hill many meters from the end of the takeoff. The jumper keeps his arms quietly by his side but uses his hands like an airplane rudder, guiding the flight of the jump. Most ski jumpers agree that a good jump gives a supreme high and creates a feeling of wanting to get back to the top of the hill for another ecstatic encounter.

Atop Mt. Ogden, Snowbasin, where the 2002 Olympic downhill course starts, March 1998: (left to right) sportswriter Craig Hansell, Dale Miller, Alan Miller, Darm Penny, Jim Gaddis, M. Earl Miller, Alan Engen, Brad Smith, and Kent Mathews, Snowbasin's general manager. Photo courtesy Jim Gaddis.

is perhaps leading the way in this area. Here at Bear Hollow, we have an eleven-year-old girl named Lindsey Van who is the current world champion for girls in her age class. It will take a while for the European countries to fully embrace women ski jumpers, but in my opinion, it will happen.

"I also think summer ski jumping will develop to a point where it is equal to the winter. It is certainly safer jumping on artificial surfaces during summer months. I think you will see more and more world-level competitions held during the summer. Here at Bear Hollow, this is already occurring."

Throughout its centuries of history, skiing has changed from a utilitarian tool, to an activity embraced by a relatively few hardy souls, to a sport enjoyed by millions of people from all walks of life throughout the world. During the last decade of the twentieth century, skiing contributed approximately five hundred million dollars annually in direct revenue to Utah's economy through purchases for lodging, lifts, ski lessons, transportation, food, clothing, ski equipment, and related items. Utah ranks among the top-ten states in ski participation. Without question, the ski industry in Utah contributes significantly to the overall economy. The awarding of the 2002 Olympic Winter Games to Salt Lake City magnifies the importance of this sport to the Intermountain West and the contributions of all Utah's early ski pioneers, including those of Alf, Sverre, and Corey Engen.

The sport of skiing is not static. It will continue

to evolve, driven by economic pressure, technological advances, and the ever-present human desire to conquer new challenges, to excel, and to explore new ways of testing the limits of what our bodies are able to achieve. As an example, in recent years Freestyle skiing has become an Olympic sport involving aerial and mogul competition. In 1998, the U.S. produced three Olympic gold medalists in Freestyle competition—Jonny Mosely in moguls, and Eric Bergoust and Nikki Stone in aerials. Ballet skiing also has come into its own, and Alan Schönberger, one of the world's finest ballet skiers, has made it into a business, traveling throughout the country with his show. Then there is the explosive growth in the sport of snowboarding, also a new addition to Olympic competition. The November/December 1995 issue of *Ski Tech* magazine indicated that the number of active U.S. snowboarding participants had grown to 2.1 million by the end of 1994, and that was in less than ten years, compared to many more years to get the sport of recreational skiing to that level back in the 1930s, '40s, and '50s.

Alf Engen once told Max Lundberg, his assistant ski-school director, "Watch for new ideas, new moves, and changes in equipment. Try them all, and when you find something good, grab onto it right away." With change will come new opportunities, some not even contemplated yet. The one absolute about skiing's future is that as long as the world has snow, someone will want to slide on it or fly over it, and only time will reveal how many ways this can be accomplished. ❄

EPILOGUE

Just before dawn on a clear midsummer day in 1997, the phone rang, shattering the silence of the moment and more; the voice on the other end uttered the words no one who ever knew Alf Engen wanted to hear: "He is gone." Gone physically, but never absent from their hearts, minds, and memories. A passage in the book *Leaves of Gold* applies to Alf quite well:

Mortal death is not final. It is but a step toward a fuller and freer and more glorious life, glimpses of which the Gods have given us to lighten the burden of the worldly-laden. Grieve not too much for this valiant son; he made his

Most all young men have a sports hero. I was no different, but my model of athletic excellence happened to be my father. In my eyes, no one could run faster, kick a ball farther, fly higher or farther, ski faster, or was stronger physically than Alf Engen.

He epitomized what every young boy sees in a champion, namely quiet but indisputable inner determination to achieve excellence beyond expectation. And achieve excellence he did! The history of skiing in America includes my father, and he is truly a living legend.

—Alan Engen
The Instructors Edge,
vol. 13, no. 1 (fall 1991)

race and the victory is won. But live as he did, faithful, kind, and true, that you may be worthy and ready for the day when the Gods need another and look down with a smile, and point their finger at you.

It was always Alf's desire to see his beloved mountains cherished and enjoyed. When he was interviewed by television commentator Larry Warren for the 1989 documentary *Ski Riders of the Wasatch,* he said, "Have some fun now! I hope to see all of Utah on skis. I have loved it so much! I like to share the pleasures of skiing and be out in these beautiful mountains. Utah is so blessed with beautiful mountains!"

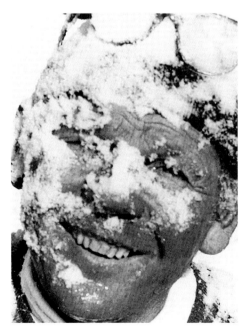

Alf Engen: "I love the pleasures of skiing!"

It is most likely that the history of skiing will certainly include the name Alf Engen. But while his achievements are recognized worldwide, he will probably be best remembered for his optimistic outlook on life and his great love of people, especially children. Over the span of eighty-eight years, he passed on a legacy of love—the love of skiing in the beautiful outdoors—to countless people throughout the world. When the final chapter is written on Alf, he deserves the title *"Ski Meister* of the Twentieth Century." Perhaps the inscription on his gravesite marker provides the most concise description of his life:

Born of Viking heritage; educated by the school of life experiences; molded to world-class greatness through competitive achievement and tempered by a heart filled with love and compassion for all people.

Ski heil!

The Alf Engen Ski Museum: Safeguarding Utah's Ski History

The story continues. Utah has been selected to host the 2002 Olympic Winter Games, and the role the Intermountain region plays in ski-jumping history is destined to go well into the twenty-first century and beyond. The events described in this book are only a brief moment in time, a time that is memorable as the golden years of ski jumping and skiing in the Intermountain West. To everyone who enjoys skiing or has an interest in its history, may reading this book evoke a full gamut of feelings and thoughts: laughter, sadness, amazement, learning, and genuine enjoyment. If it accomplishes even some of this, it will be considered a success.

On the morning of October 30, 1997, three short months after Alf's passing, a meeting was held at the Utah Winter Sports Park to decide on the spot for the Alf Engen Ski Museum. In attendance were representatives from the Salt Lake Olympic Committee; the Utah Sports Authority; the Edwards, Daniels and Associates architectural firm; and the Alf Engen Ski Museum Foundation.

Six years of intensive review to determine the best place for the museum had preceded this meeting. Many hours of discussion and consideration were given to a number of potential locations. In the end, however, everyone felt that the Utah Winter Sports Park site at Bear Hollow near the day lodge was the most appropriate location. Here, those who love the sport of skiing or who are merely curious can learn about the glory days, about all those skiing barnstormers of yesterday, in the company of Utah's latest ski champions. As this book concludes, the pieces are now in place to bring the ski museum to reality in time for the 2002 Olympic Winter Games. ❄

The Alf Engen Ski Museum Site was selected in October 1997: (left to right) Ed Sweeney, Randy Montgomery, Alan Engen, Jon Engen, Jerry Anderson [SLOC], Peter Emerson [architect, EDA], Burke Cartwright [architect, EDA], Barbara Amidon, David Amidon, Mike Korologos, John Bower, Janet Lawson, Ranch Kimball [SLOC], Joe Arave, Jim Gaddis, Greg Thompson, Jody Schrontz, Marty Volla [SLOC], David Quinney, Duane Schrontz.

Alf Engen. Illustration by Mark Summers, commissioned by Washington Mutual Bank, 1997. Original artwork displayed at the Utah State Historical Society Museum, Salt Lake City, Utah.

Biographical Sketches: Prose on the Pros

Early Professional Ski Jumpers

HALVOR BJØRNGAARD was born in Norway and immigrated to America in the mid-1920s. After joining the professional jumpers in 1930, he moved to Ogden, Utah, and represented that city on the tour. Besides a genuine love of life and ski jumping, he loved to ride his Harley-Davidson, which cost him his life in an accident north of Ogden.

EINAR FREDBO, born in Asker, Norway, was a Norwegian junior jumping champion in 1926. He finished third in the world championship in 1928 at Holmenkollen outside Oslo and fourth in 1929, before immigrating to the United States. He settled in Salt Lake City, Utah, after joining the professional jumping tour in 1930. He was known among ski experts as one of the most graceful jumpers in the world, holding his arms virtually motionless as he soared off the jump. Fredbo holds the record for the longest jump ever made on Ogden's Becker Hill—203 feet in January 1931. He placed third in the National Ski-Jumping Championship in Red Wing, Minnesota, and third in the National Ski-Jumping Championship on storied Ecker Hill (1937). As an electrician and foreman with the Salt Lake County Street Department, he accidentally contacted a high-tension wire and was electrocuted in 1947—a tragic loss for the jumping group.

ANDERS AND LARS HAUGEN served as co-captains of the professional jumping team. Anders had been a member of the 1924 U.S. Olympic Team before joining the professional jumpers. Lars, at forty-seven, was the oldest member of the group and was called the "father of professional ski jumping in America" by his peers. He immigrated to America in 1908 and won the U.S. National Ski-Jumping Championship several times before turning professional.

HALVAR HVALSTAD immigrated to the United States from Norway in 1923, and joined the professional jumping team in 1930. He was one of the best jumpers in the country, and was nicknamed "Dynamite" because of the terrific spills he occasionally took, though he never seemed to get hurt.

ALF MATISEN of Norway arrived in the United States in the mid-1920s as an established ski jumper. Although he never won a professional tournament, he was one of the most consistent of the ski flyers, nearly always placing near the top third of the field. He did not stay with the professional group more than a couple of years and left jumping.

TED REX was born in Detroit, Michigan, and won the U.S. Professional Ski-Jumping Championship (1930). He was known as the "smiling skier" because he always wore a broad grin.

STEFFEN TRØGSTAD was born in Elverum, Norway, and arrived in America in 1927. He won the U.S. National Ski-Jumping Championship (1928) in Coleraine, Minnesota, and turned professional in 1930. He was described by his peers as "among the most graceful jumpers in the world" in his prime.

SIG ULLAND was born in Norway, immigrated to America, and settled in Mt. Shasta, California. During summer months he worked as a forest ranger. During the winter he was one of the leading members of the professional jumping team. He was a powerful jumper who won several professional tournaments.

Significant Intermountain West Skiers

During the past fifty years, several people have contributed significantly to the development and growth of skiing in the Intermountain West. Skiing was promoted through competitors, equipment innovators, professional ski instructors, ski-area developers, snow-safety experts, book authors, and film producers.

The competitive achievements of these ski legends played an important role in focusing attention on the sport, which led to further development and substantial economic benefit for Utah. Recognizing this as only a partial listing of outstanding skiers, it does represent the caliber of great competitors who made a unique contribution to the ski world at the national or international level through the 1960s. All of these people have been recognized nationally and most are in one or more skiing halls of fame.

JUNIOR BOUNOUS captured the National Cross-Country Championship (1947) and National Gelande Championship during the 1969–70 ski season. He was the first assistant director of the Alf Engen Ski School at Alta and played an integral role in the formation of the Professional Ski Instructors of America during the 1950s. He served as the ski-school director at Sugar Bowl in Northern California, Timp Haven (now Sundance) in Provo, and Snowbird. He was inducted into the PSIA Intermountain Ski Hall of Fame (1989) and given special recognition by the Utah Ski Archives (1991). He was inducted into the National Ski Hall of Fame (1996), and is currently the director of skiing at Snowbird.

JOHN BOWER was a member of the U.S. Ski Team from 1962 to 1968, including two Olympic teams. He became the first American to win the prestigious King's Cup (Nordic combined championship) at the Holmenkollen Ski Festival (1968) in Oslo, Norway, and was inducted into the National Ski Hall of Fame (1969). He is currently director of the Utah Winter Sports Park at Bear Hollow and serves as a board member of the Alf Engen Ski Museum Foundation.

DICK DURRANCE attended Dartmouth College in the 1930s, and won the U.S. collegiate championship all four years in both Alpine and Nordic skiing, becoming America's first collegiate four-event champion. During active competition, he retired the prestigious Harriman Cup at Sun Valley, winning it three times, was the national Alpine slalom champion (1935), national downhill champion (1937, 1940), and the national Alpine combined champion (1937, 1939, 1940).

In Utah, he became Alta's second ski-school director (1940–42) and headed the instructors group that taught 150 paratroopers of the 503rd Parachute Battalion to ski when they arrived at Alta for training in 1942.

He was a member of the 1936 U.S. Olympic Alpine Ski Team at Garmisch, Germany, and also made the 1940 Olympic Ski Team, which never competed because of the war. After World War II, Durrance remained active in skiing, was the principal organizer in 1950 of the FIS World Alpine Ski Championship at Aspen, Colorado, served as chief of race for the 1960 Winter Olympics at Squaw Valley, California, and became a well-known documentary and commercial film producer and photographer. He was inducted into the U.S. National Ski Hall of Fame (1958) and the International Ski Hall of Fame (1986), and was named a founder of U.S. Skiing (1994).

SPENCER ECCLES competed in a series of national and international competitions during the 1950s. He placed fourth in the NCAA downhill (1956) and fifth in the U.S. national downhill and three-way combined races. He was named to the team for the FIS World Championship (1958) in Austria. That same year, he placed in the top five in the Canadian National Championship and third in the U.S. National Championship. He was inducted into the

University of Utah Crimson Club Hall of Fame. Eccles is currently chairman and chief executive officer of First Security Corporation and a prime mover in preparing for the 2002 Winter Olympic Games.

ALF ENGEN was one of the finest all-around skiers ever. He was born May 15, 1909, in Mjøndalen, Norway, the oldest of the three world-famous Engen brothers. Alf was sixteen times U.S. ski champion in jumping, cross-country, downhill, or slalom. He was also the North American ski-jumping champion in 1937; a world ski-jumping record-setter, once breaking the world record twice in one day; and coach of the 1948 U.S. Olympic Ski Team. Specific awards he has received include Skier of the Century (1950); Helm's Hall of Fame (1954); National Ski Hall of Fame (1956); Utah Sports Hall of Fame (1970); Intermountain Ski School Director of the Year (1974); Professional Ski Instructors of America, Intermountain Division Hall of Fame (1989); and one of the Founders of American Skiing (1994). He also appeared in eight full-length movies.

Because of his mastery of skiing deep powder snow and teaching others how to ski it, he was known as the "father of the American powder-skiing technique." He directed the Alta Ski School for forty years, and is the namesake for one of America's ten most acclaimed ski runs, Alf's High Rustler, at Alta.

Alf significantly furthered the sport of skiing throughout the world and Intermountain West, helping to establish over thirty major ski areas in the United States: Utah's Alta, Brighton, and Snowbasin; Idaho's Bogus Basin and Magic Mountain; and Wyoming's Snow King Mountain in Jackson Hole. One of his greatest contributions to skiing was helping to start the *Deseret News* Free Ski School in 1948, and serving many years as its director. Over 225,000 people have started skiing through this unique program, continuing to fuel the growth of the ski industry in the region.

COREY ENGEN was born on March 30, 1916, the youngest of the three Engen brothers. Over his competitive career, Corey won more than five hundred medals and trophies in all skiing disciplines (jumping, cross-country, downhill, slalom, and giant slalom). He was captain of the 1948 U.S. Olympic ski-jumping team and placed third in the jumping portion of the Olympic classic combined event (involving both jumping and cross-country) and twenty-sixth overall.

Corey directed the ski schools at Snowbasin, Utah, and Brundage Mountain in McCall, Idaho, teaching countless skiers. For many years he coached young skiers, some of whom went on to greatness. His teams won eleven national championships. He received the Russell Wilder Memorial Award (1963), presented by the National Ski Association for furthering the sport in the minds and hearts of the youth of America. He was elected to the National Ski Hall of Fame (1973) for devoted service to the sport of skiing, received the Pacific Northwest Ski Educational Foundation Award (1985) in appreciation of his contribution to the youth of America, and was elected to the Northwest Hall of Fame of Winter Sports (1987) at Mt. Hood.

Throughout his many years in Idaho, Corey remained active in civic affairs. For his many contributions to the state, he was honored as the Idaho Statesman.

SVERRE ENGEN was born in January 1911 in the small Norwegian community of Mjøndalen. He is one of the most colorful of the early ski pioneers. During his illustrious eight-decade career, he has been among the best ski jumpers in America; a well-known ski instructor; a ski-school director at Alta, Utah; an author of two books and many articles on skiing; an accomplished musician and actor; owner of a ski area in California; manager of several ski lodges; the first snow ranger in America, establishing snow-safety procedures that are still being followed; and a successful ski-movie producer. Sverre traveled for many years throughout North America and Europe promoting skiing by giving lectures and showing countless adults and children the ski films he had shot and produced.

During World War II, he served with the Tenth Mountain Division. Sverre was awarded the Silver Merit Star (1945) by the National Ski Patrol System for outstanding service, won the open senior class of the National Ski-Jumping

Championship (1949) at Ecker Hill, and was inducted into the National Ski Hall of Fame (1971).

STEIN ERIKSEN first competed in cross-country and jumping competition in Norway at age seven. By the time he came to the United States in 1953, he had won the Lauberhorn in Switzerland, the 1952 Olympic giant slalom in Norway, and numerous international titles. He was skiing's first superstar. Since coming to America, Eriksen has been ski-school director or director of skiing at Boyne Mountain, Michigan; Heavenly Valley, California; Aspen Highlands, Colorado; Sugarbush, Vermont; Snowmass, Colorado; and Park City and Deer Valley, Utah. He is in the National Ski Hall of Fame and on virtually every writer's list of ski legends.

GRETCHEN KUNIGK FRASER, born in Tacoma, Washington, began skiing at a young age, winning many championships, including the Snow Cup in Alta, Utah; the Harriman Cup in Sun Valley, Idaho; the Silver Belt; and the national Alpine combined (1941). She won America's first gold medal in the 1948 Olympic ski racing, finishing first in the slalom at St. Moritz, Switzerland. Fraser was inducted into the U.S. National Ski Hall of Fame (1960) and honored as a founder of U.S. Skiing (1994).

JIM GADDIS won the U.S. National Giant Slalom Championship (1962); the National Collegiate Alpine Combined Championship (1960, 1962); the NCAA Slalom Championship (1962); and the Snow Cup (1962, 1963, 1964). He was also an NCAA All-American (1960, 1962).

Gaddis was a member of the board and part of the original 1970 development team of Snowbird; the first executive director and public-relations director of the Alta Ski Lifts Company; a certified ski instructor and member of PSIA; and the head coach and founder of the Park City ski-racing team, the Utah Racing School, the Gaddis Training Organization, and the Utah Ski Racers Foundation. He was also director of the Intermountain division of the U.S. Ski Association (USSA) and the Intermountain-area coaches system. He currently owns Gaddis Investment, Inc., a real-estate sales, investment, and development company. Gaddis was inducted into the Utah Sports Hall of Fame and the University of Utah Crimson Club Hall of Fame.

JIMMIE GRIFFITH was one of the nation's most promising young downhill and slalom racers in the late 1940s and early '50s. He grew up in Ketchum, Idaho, near Sun Valley. From a very early age, Griffith showed great promise as a competitor. Several world-champion skiers who frequented Sun Valley encouraged and trained him. He made the 1952 U.S. Olympic Team—to no one's surprise. Most people thought him one of the strongest of the American contingent. Unfortunately, he sustained an injury while practicing at Alta, Utah, in December 1951 and died the following week of a pulmonary embolism. Other than a multiple fracture to Griffith's right leg, no other severe injures were evident. His death came as a shock to everyone concerned.

DEV JENNINGS was a member of the 1948 U.S. Olympic Alpine Team. He was also a member of the University of Utah Ski Team (1947) and part of the fabled Tenth Mountain Division during World War II. Jennings served as executive director of *Ski Utah* (1961–70); has been a ski entrepreneur, coach, race official, marketer, promoter, and Olympic official; and was inducted into the National Ski Hall of Fame (1989). He currently lives in Waterville Valley, New Hampshire.

KAREN KORFANTA was an outstanding ski racer from the Intermountain region during the 1960s. A member of the 1968 U.S. Olympic Ski Team and the U.S. Alpine Ski Team (1964–70), Korfanta currently manages the race department at the Park City ski area. Since 1986 she has served as chair for the opening of the World Cup International Ski Race at Park City as well as an event coordinator for the Utah Winter Games.

KEITH LANGE is a longtime Alpine/Nordic/cross-country competitor. He won the first National Gelande Championship (1965) in the professional class at Alta, and coached the Intermountain Junior National Ski Team for several years, with several of his skiers going on to represent the U.S. in national and international competitions. He served as a certified FIS and Olympic-level course setter and guest coach for the men's and women's U.S. Olympic Ski Teams. Lange has been a ski instructor at Alta, Utah, for more than forty years and was instrumental in developing PSIA. He served as the national PSIA president (1975–77), was a member and coach of the national PSIA demonstration team, and coached the first Deaf Olympics. Lange was inducted into the PSIA Intermountain Ski Hall of Fame (1995) for his many contributions to skiing and ski teaching over a span of fifty-plus years.

MARVIN MELVILLE was a member of the University of Utah Ski Team (1955–59). He was the NCAA downhill/slalom combined champion (1959), a member of the 1956 and 1960 U.S. Olympic Alpine Teams, and a member of the U.S. FIS Team (1958). He coached the University of Utah Ski Team (1963–66), was assistant coach of the 1964 U.S. Olympic Women's Ski Team, was a member of the California Skiing Rules Committee and USSA Alpine Competitions Committee, and served as the USSA masters racing chairman. He has been inducted into the Utah Sports Hall of Fame and the University of Utah Crimson Club Hall of Fame.

RAY MILLER is the youngest of the three famous Miller brothers from Ogden, Utah—the other two are Alan and Dale—all outstanding athletes who have excelled in the sport under tutelage of their great coach and father, M. Earl Miller. Ray was named Intermountain Junior Racer of the Year (1963–64); was junior national champion and won the Alta Snow Cup (1965 and 1967); was a member of the U.S. Ski Team (1966–68); was named to the NCAA All-American team (1969); and placed fourth at the Solomon World Ski Dealer Championship at St. Moritz, Switzerland (1975). He has been a head ski coach at Snowbasin and Powder Mountain in Utah since 1978.

DICK MITCHELL captained the University of Utah Ski Team in 1953 and won the NCAA downhill the same year. He was a member of the 1956 U.S. Olympic Alpine Team that competed in Cortina d'Ampezzo, Italy. He then completed a distinguished career as a fighter pilot in the air force.

DICK MOVITZ was a member of the 1948 U.S. Olympic Alpine team. He won the U.S. National Slalom Championship (1946), placed second in the Harriman Cup and second in the North American Ski Championship (1948), placed third in the U.S. National Slalom Championship (1947), and was a member of the U.S. FIS team (1950). Movitz acted as a member of the USSA International Competition Committee (1956) and chair of the national organization (1958); he was named to the 1960 U.S. Olympic Winter Games Committee at Squaw Valley, California, and has been inducted into the National Ski Hall of Fame (1970) and the Utah Sports Hall of Fame.

JACK REDDISH was a member of the 1948 U.S. Olympic Alpine Team and placed seventh in the slalom in St. Moritz, Switzerland. The 1940s were the "decade of Reddish" on the American ski scene and in some venues in Europe. His exploits on skis during that period are among the greatest in the history of the sport in North America. He was the Intermountain slalom champion (1940), the Intermountain Class C champion jumper (1940–1945), and the national downhill and combined champion (1948). He won the Harriman Cup (1948), the National Slalom Championship (1950), and the combined (1952). He was also inducted into the National Ski Hall of Fame (1969). After his competitive ski career, he made a success in the movies. He died in 1992.

DARRELL "PINKY" ROBISON was born in Reno, Nevada, and started skiing in 1944. He moved to Salt Lake City, where he attended the University of Utah and skied on the school's team during the early 1950s. He was a member of the 1952 U.S. Olympic Alpine Ski Team that competed in Norway. He won the National Junior Slalom Championship (1948), placed sixth in the National Giant Slalom Championship (1951), and finished tenth in the national down-

hill. Robison placed sixth in the Harriman Cup (1951) and finished eighth in the North American championship that same year.

SUZY HARRIS RYTTING was a member of the 1948 and 1952 U.S. Olympic Alpine Teams. She won the Mary Cornelia Trophy at Sun Valley (1947) and set a course record in the Gold Sun Race there (1948). She was also a member of the 1950 U.S. Women's FIS Team (1949). Rytting was secretary of the Intermountain Ski Association (1952–59). She served as chair of the Salt Lake United States Ski Team fund-raiser and honorary chair of the Jimmie Heuga Ski Race for multiple sclerosis (1987). Because of her outstanding achievements in athletic ski competition over the years, she was inducted into the National Ski Hall of Fame (1988). She is also in the Utah Sports Hall of Fame and the University of Utah Crimson Club Hall of Fame.

BILL SPENCER was born in Russellville, Alabama, and moved to Salt Lake City in the late 1940s. He was a member of the University of Utah Ski Team during the late 1950s and early 1960s. Spencer was named an All-American (1959) in Nordic skiing. He was a member of the 1964 and 1968 U.S. Olympic Biathlon Teams, won the U.S. National Thirty-Kilometer Cross-Country Championship (1965) and the U.S. and Canadian National Biathlon Championships (1966, 1967), and was a member of the U.S. Council Internationale Sports Militaire Ski Team 1964–68, 1973). Spencer was also the team leader for the 1972 and 1984 U.S. Olympic Biathlon Team in two Olympic Winter Games, served as the shooting coach for the 1976 and 1980 U.S. Olympic Biathlon Team, has been a member of the Union International Pentathlon and Modern Biathlon (UIPMB) Technical Committee, a technical delegate for the Olympic Biathlon (1988), and shooting coach and development coordinator for the U.S. Biathlon Association.

RALPH WAKLEY was born in Logan, Utah. A member of the University of Utah Ski Team, he was named an All-American in cross-country (1969). Wakley was a member of the 1968 U.S. Olympic Biathlon Team, finishing twenty-sixth in the twenty-kilometer run, which was the top U.S. finish that year. He was also a member of the U.S. Olympic Biathlon Committee from 1973 through 1976.

MARGO WALTERS started skiing at the age of nine in St. Anthony, Idaho, and moved to Salt Lake City when she was thirteen. Earl Miller, Marvin Melville, and Dick Movitz coached her in her early competitive years. Walters won the Junior National Downhill/Slalom/Giant Slalom Combined Championship (1960), was a three-time winner of the Alta Snow Cup, and as a member of the 1964 U.S. Olympic Alpine Ski Team, she placed twenty-first in the downhill. She retired from competition in 1967 and married George McDonald in 1969.

WALLACE "BUDDY" WERNER grew up in Steamboat Springs, Colorado, and became one of finest Alpine ski racers the U.S. ever produced, directly influencing skiing's development in the Intermountain region. At one point in his racing career, he was ranked among the world's best skiers. He won many national and international ski races, among them the Alta Snow Cup (1957), the Lauberhorn (1958), the North American Ski Championship (1959), and the National Alpine Combined (1959). He was a member of the 1960 and 1964 U.S. Olympic Teams. Following the 1964 Olympics, he and German ski racer, Barbi Henneberger, were killed in an avalanche in St. Moritz, Switzerland, while filming a ski movie.

Appendix I

TIMELINE OF SIGNIFICANT SKIING EVENTS
4000 B.C.–A.D. 2002

Although the following chronology does not include all of ski history, it provides a snapshot of many events that helped shape the sport.

B.C.

4000–2000	Estimated date of petroglyph found at Rødøy, Norway, showing a man on skis.
2500	Estimated date of Hoting ski, discovered in a Swedish peat bog in the 1930s.
1500	Estimated date of petroglyph found at Zalavrouga, Russia, near the White Sea, showing three individuals on skis with a balancing stick.

A.D.

526–550.	Byzantine historian Procopius discusses a race of *skridfinnen*, meaning "gliding Finns."
1206.	Two Norwegian Birkenbeiner soldiers on skis carry King Sverre's infant son to safety.
1452–1610.	Military troops equipped with skis are used by Norway and Sweden.
1716.	First military ski troops are formed in Norway.
1791.	First mention of ski wax, believed to have been some sort of animal fat.
1808.	War between Norway and Sweden is fought with more than two thousand ski troops.
1841.	First mention of skiing in the United States at Beloit, Wisconsin.
1843.	First organized cross-country racing at Tromsoe, Norway.
1845.	First competitive ski-jumping tournament at Troms, Norway.
1849.	Scandinavian sailors, skis in hand, desert ship in San Francisco to look for gold in the Sierra Nevada.
1854.	Norwegian Carl Torstensen introduces skiing to Australia. The following year, he introduces skiing to New Zealand.
1856.	Snowshoe Thompson begins delivering mail on skis between Placerville, California, and Genoa, Nevada.
1859.	First use of skis in Switzerland at Sils Maria in the Engadine.
1861.	The world's first ski club is formed at Kiandra, Australia.
1866.	Sondre Norheim invents first heel-strap ski binding.
1867.	America's first ski club, the Alturas Snowshoe Club, is formed at La Porte, California
1868.	Sondre Norheim demonstrates the first telemark turn in Christiania (Oslo), Norway. In the United States, the first organized, straight-run downhill ski tournament on "longboard snow-shoes" is held at La Porte, California. Bob Oliver wins the tournament with a speed in excess of eighty miles per hour.

1881.	The world's first ski-school session is conducted near Oslo, Norway.
1887.	First ski-jumping tournament in America is held at Red Wing, Minnesota. It is won by Mikkel Hemmestveit with a jump of thirty-seven feet, establishing the first distance record in the United States.
1888.	Fridtjof Nansen crosses Greenland on a pair of skis. Two years later Nansen writes *Paa Ski Over Grönland,* which becomes one of the first significant books on the use of skis. The same year another Norwegian, Ragnvald Huseby, introduces skiing to Austria and Hungary.
1892.	Holmenkollen, one of the world's most famous ski-jumping hills, is built on a hillside overlooking Oslo, Norway. The first tournament is held.
1896.	Mathias Zdarsky starts the Lilienfeld Ski School, the world's first organized ski school, near Vienna, Austria.
1897.	Zdarsky publishes the world's first ski-theory book, *Der Lilienfelden Ski-Lauf Technik.*
1902.	Norwegian consul Petter Ottesen introduces skiing to Japan.
1903.	The Ski Club of Great Britain is formed, and introduces the concept of holiday recreational skiing at various European locations.
1905.	The National Ski Association is founded in Ishpeming, Michigan. Carl Tellefsen is elected the first president. Zdarsky conducts the world's first slalom event on the Muckenkogel in Austria.
1908.	The Norwegian Ski Federation is founded.
1910.	The first International Ski Congress is held in Oslo, Norway.
1911.	The Ski Club of Great Britain conducts the world's first downhill race, the Roberts of Kandahar Challenge Cup, at Montana, Switzerland.
1912.	The Wasatch Mountain Club is formed in Salt Lake City, Utah, by Charles T. Stoney to conduct outdoor group activities in the Wasatch Mountains in the summer and winter. The club plays a significant role in introducing Alpine skiing to the Intermountain region.
1914.	The Intermountain region's first ski-jumping club, the Norwegian Young Folks Society, is formed. The name is changed in 1920 to Norwegian-American Athletic Club, and in 1928 to Utah Ski Club.
1915.	The first ski-jumping tournament in Utah is held near the U of U.
1924.	The I Olympic Winter Games are held at Chamonix, France. Anders Haugen finished third, but nobody knew it for fifty years. He is credited as winning America's first Olympic ski medal. The Federation Internationale de Ski (FIS) is founded.

1928. St. Moritz, Switzerland, hosts the II Olympic Winter Games. Austria initiates an examining process for individuals wishing to become ski instructors.

1929. The America Ski Association is formed to conduct major jumping events. The first professional ski-jumping group is formed and consists of Anders Haugen, Lars Haugen, Alf Engen, Sverre Engen, Halvar Hvalstad, Einar Fredbo, Halvor Bjørngaard, Steffen Trøgstad, Sigurd Ulland, Ted Rex, and Alf Matisen.

1930. Utah's first major jumping hills are dedicated—Becker Hill in January and Ecker Hill in March. The America Ski Association is dissolved, and a new national organization called the Western America Winter Sports Association is formed to enable sanctioned world ski-jumping events to be held in the western part of the U.S.

1931. The first FIS Alpine Championship is held at Murren, Switzerland. Utah's Alf Engen establishes world ski-jumping record at Ecker Hill (247 feet).

1932. Lake Placid, New York, hosts the III Winter Olympic Games.

1933. The first National Downhill Championship is held on Mt. Moosilauke, Warren, New Hampshire. The first rope tow in North America is constructed at Foster's Hill near Shawbridge, Canada.

1934. The first American rope tow is constructed on Gilbert's Hill, Woodstock, Vermont. The world's first T-bar lift is constructed at Davos, Switzerland. Norwegian Sigmund Ruud breaks the 300-foot ski-jumping barrier with a jump of 303.5 feet at Rapece, Czechoslovakia.

1935. The first National Downhill and Slalom Championship is held on Mt. Rainier, Washington.

1936. Sun Valley, Idaho, constructs the world's first chairlift. Garmisch-Partenkirchen, Germany, hosts the IV Olympic Winter Games.

1937. The first official World Alpine Ski Championship is held at Chamonix, France.

1938. The National Ski Patrol System is organized under the direction of Minot (Minnie) Dole. America's second chairlift is constructed at Alta, Utah. The first ski certification examination in the U.S. is taken at Woodstock, Vermont.

1940. Sverre Engen is designated by the Forest Service as America's first snow ranger.

1948. The V Olympic Winter Games are held at St. Moritz, Switzerland. Gretchen Fraser of the United States wins the first U.S. Olympic gold medal in slalom and a silver medal in the Alpine combined. Zeno Colò of Italy sets the first world speed-skiing record of 159.3 kph (98.8 mph).

1952. Oslo, Norway, hosts the VI Olympic Winter Games. Norway's Stein Eriksen wins the Olympic giant slalom. Andrea Mead of the United States wins two gold medals for the giant slalom and slalom.

1956. The VII Olympic Winter Games are held at Cortina d'Ampezzo, Italy. Austria's Anton "Toni" Sailer becomes the first skier to win all three Olympic Alpine disciplines (downhill, slalom, and giant slalom).

1959. The first World Biathlon Championship is held at Saalfelden, Austria.

1960. Squaw Valley, California, hosts the VIII Olympic Winter Games. U.S. Olympian Penny Pitou wins the silver medals in downhill and giant slalom.

1961. The Professional Ski Instructors of America (PSIA) is formed at Whitefish, Montana.

1962. The National Ski Association changes its name to the United States Ski Association (USSA).

1964. The IX Olympic Winter Games are held at Innsbruck, Austria. U.S. Olympians Billy Kidd and Jimmy Heuga win silver and bronze medals, respectively, in slalom. American Olympic skier Wallace (Buddy) Werner loses his life in an avalanche after the games at St. Moritz, Switzerland, on April 2, 1964.

1968. Grenoble, France, hosts the X Olympic Winter Games. Jean-Claude Killy of France wins all three Alpine events (downhill, slalom, and giant slalom), becoming only the second man to accomplish this feat in Olympic history.

1970. Japanese skier Yuichiro Miura makes the world's first successful descent of Mt. Everest on skis.

1972. The XI Olympic Winter Games are held at Sapporo, Japan. U.S. skier Barbara Cochran wins a gold medal in slalom.

1976. Innsbruck, Austria, hosts the XII Olympic Winter Games. Franz Klammer of Austria wins the downhill with a run that has become legendary in Olympic history.

1980. The XIII Olympic Winter Games are held at Lake Placid, New York.

1984. Sarajevo, Yugoslavia, hosts the XIV Olympic Winter Games. Bill Johnson wins an Olympic gold medal in downhill; Debbi Armstrong wins the giant slalom; and Phil Mahre and his brother Steve win gold and silver medals, respectively, in the slalom for the United States.

1988. The XV Olympic Winter Games are held at Calgary, Canada. The super giant slalom is added as an Alpine event for the first time in Olympic competition. The team Nordic combined is also introduced at these games. Matti Nykanen of Finland wins gold medals in both the large and normal hill ski-jumping events, the first ever to accomplish this feat in Olympic history.

1992. Albertville, France, hosts the XVI Olympic Winter Games. Alberto Tomba of Italy wins his third Olympic gold medal in the men's giant slalom.

1994. Lillihammer, Norway, hosts the XVII Olympic Winter Games. Two United States skiers win gold medals: Tommy Moe in downhill, and Diann Roffe-Steinrotter in the super giant slalom.

1998. Nagano, Japan, hosts the XVIII Olympic Winter Games. The following U.S. skiers win gold medals: Picabo Street, women's super giant slalom; Jonny Mosely, men's moguls; Eric Bergoust, men's aerials; and Nikki Stone, women's aerials.

2002. Salt Lake City, Utah, hosts the XIX Olympic Winter Games.

Appendix II
SUMMARY OF OLYMPIC SITES
1896–2002

Summer Games

1896	Athens, Greece
1900	Paris, France
1904	St. Louis, Missouri
1906	Athens, Greece*
1908	London, Great Britain
1912	Stockholm, Sweden
1916	(not held)
1920	Antwerp, Belgium
1924	Paris, France
1928	Amsterdam, Holland
1932	Los Angeles, California
1936	Berlin, Germany
1940	(not held)
1944	(not held)
1948	London, England
1952	Helsinki, Finland
1956	Melbourne, Australia
1960	Rome, Italy
1964	Tokyo, Japan
1968	Mexico City, Mexico
1972	Munich, Germany
1976	Montreal, Canada
1980	Moscow, Russia USSR
1984	Los Angeles, California
1988	Seoul, Korea
1992	Barcelona, Spain
1996	Atlanta, Georgia
2000	Sydney, Australia

* Games not recognized by the
International Olympic Committee.

Winter Games

1924	Chamonix, France
1928	St. Moritz, Switzerland
1932	Lake Placid, New York
1936	Garmisch-Partenkirchen, Germany
1940	(not held)
1944	(not held)
1948	St. Moritz, Switzerland
1952	Oslo, Norway
1956	Cortina d'Ampezzo, Italy
1960	Squaw Valley, California
1964	Innsbruck, Austria
1968	Grenoble, France
1972	Sapporo, Japan
1976	Innsbruck, Austria
1980	Lake Placid, New York
1984	Sarajevo, Yugoslavia
1988	Calgary, Canada
1992	Albertville, France
1994	Lillehammer, Norway
1998	Nagano, Japan
2002	Salt Lake City, Utah

Appendix III
SUMMARY OF OLYMPIC SKI CHAMPIONS
1924–1998

Nordic Skiing

SKI JUMPING (LARGE HILL)

1924	Tullin Thams, Norway
1928	Alfred Andersen, Norway
1932	Birger Ruud, Norway
1936	Birger Ruud, Norway
1940–44	(not held)
1948	Petter Hugsted, Norway
1952	Arnfinn Bergmann, Norway
1956	Antti Hyvärinen, Finland
1960	Helmut Recknagel, GDR
1964	Toralf Engan, Norway
1968	Vladimir Beloussov, Soviet Union
1972	Wojciech Fortuna, Poland
1976	Karl Schnabl, Austria
1980	Jouko Törmänen, Finland
1984	Matti Nykänen, Finland
1988	Matti Nykänen, Finland
1992	Toni Nicminen, Finland
1994	Jens Weissflog, Germany
1998	Kazuyoshi Funaki, Japan

SKI JUMPING (NORMAL HILL)

1924–60	(not held)
1964	Veikko Kankkonen, Finland
1968	Jiri Raska, Czechoslovakia
1972	Yukio Kasaya, Japan
1976	Hans-Georg Aschenbach, GDR
1980	Anton Innauer, Austria
1984	Jens Weissflog, GDR
1988	Matti Nykänen, Finland
1992	Ernst Vettori, Austria
1994	Espen Bredesen, Norway
1998	Jani Soininen, Finland

COMBINED (CROSS-COUNTRY & JUMPING)

1924	Thorleif Haug, Norway
1928	Johan Gröttumsbråten, Norway
1932	Johan Gröttumsbråten, Norway
1936	Oddbjörn Hagen, Norway
1940–44	(not held)
1948	Heikki Hasu, Finland
1952	Simon Slåttvik, Norway
1956	Sverre Stenersen, Norway
1960	Georg Thoma, Germany
1964	Tormod Knutsen, Norway
1968	Franz Keller, Germany
1972	Ulrich Wehling, GDR
1976	Ulrich Wehling, GDR
1980	Ulrich Wehling, GDR
1984	Tom Sandberg, Norway
1988	Hippolyt Kempf, Switzerland
1992	Fabrice Guy, France
1994	Fred Barre Lundberg, Norway
1998	Bjarte Engen Vik, Norway

SKI JUMPING—TEAM

1924–84	(not held)
1988	Finland
1992	Finland
1994	Germany
1998	Japan

COMBINED—TEAM

1924–84	(not held)
1988	East Germany
1992	Japan
1994	Japan
1998	Norway

CROSS-COUNTRY—MEN

10 Kilometers

1924–88	(not held)
1992	Vegard Ulvang, Norway
1994	Bjørn Daehlie, Norway
1998	Bjørn Daehlie, Norway

15 Kilometers

1924	Thorleif Haug, Norway
1928	Johan Gröttumsbråten, Norway
1932	Sven Utterström, Sweden
1936	Erik-August Larsson, Sweden
1940–44	(not held)

1948	Martin Lundström, Sweden
1952	Hallgeir Brenden, Norway
1956	Hallgeir Brenden, Norway
1960	Hakon Brusveen, Norway
1964	Eero Mäntyranta, Finland
1968	Harald Grönningen, Norway
1972	Sven-Ake Ludback, Sweden
1976	Nikolai Bazhukov, Soviet Union
1980	Thomas Wassberg, Sweden
1984	Gunde Svan, Sweden
1988	Mikhail Devyatyarov, Soviet Union
1992	Bjørn Daehlie, Norway
1994	Bjørn Daehlie, Norway
1998	Thomas Alsgaard, Norway

30 Kilometers

1924–52	(not held)
1956	Veikko Hakulinen, Finland
1960	Sixten Jernberg, Sweden
1964	Eero Mäntyranta, Finland
1968	Franco Nones, Italy
1972	Vyacheslav Vedenine, Soviet Union
1976	Sergei Saveliev, Soviet Union
1980	Nikolai Zimyatov, Soviet Union
1984	Nikolai Zimyatov, Soviet Union
1988	Aleksei Prokurorov, Soviet Union
1992	Vegard Ulvang, Norway
1994	Thomas Alsgaard, Norway
1998	Mika Myllylae, Finland

50 Kilometers

1924	Thorleif Haug, Norway
1928	Per Erik Hedlund, Sweden
1932	Veli Saarinen, Finland
1936	Elis Wiklund, Sweden
1940–44	(not held)
1948	Nils Karlsson, Sweden

1952	Veikko Hakulinen, Finland	1952	Lydia Wideman, Finland
1956	Sixten Jernberg, Sweden	1956	Lyubov Kosyreva, SOV
1960	Kalevi Hämäläinen, Finland	1960	Maria Gusakova, SOV
1964	Sixten Jernberg, Sweden	1964	Claudia Boyarskikh, SOV
1968	Ole Ellesaeter, Norway	1968	Toini Gustafsson, Sweden
1972	Pål Tyldum, Norway	1972	Galina Koulacova, SOV
1976	Ivar Formo, Norway	1976	Raisa Smetanina, SOV
1980	Nikolai Zimyatov, Soviet Union	1980	Barbara Petzold, GDR
1984	Thomas Wassberg, Sweden	1984	Marja-Liisa Hämäläinen, Finland
1988	Gunde Svan, Sweden	1988	Vida Venciene, SOV
1992	Bjørn Daehlie, Norway	1992	Lyubov Egorova, EUN
1994	Vladimir Smirnov, KAZ	1994	Lyubov Egorova, RUS
1998	Bjørn Daehlie, Norway	1998	Larissa Lazutina, RUS

40-Kilometer Relay

1924–32	(not held)
1936	Finland
1940–44	(not held)
1948	Sweden
1952	Finland
1956	Soviet Union
1960	Finland
1964	Sweden
1968	Norway
1972	Soviet Union
1976	Finland
1980	Soviet Union
1984	Sweden
1988	Sweden
1992	Norway
1994	Italy
1998	Norway

CROSS-COUNTRY—WOMEN

5 Kilometers

1924–60	(not held)
1964	Claudia Boyarskikh, SOV
1968	Toini Gustafsson, Sweden
1972	Galina Koulacova, SOV
1976	Helena Takalo, Finland
1980	Raisa Smetanina, Soviet Union
1984	Marja-Liisa Hämäläinen, Finland
1988	Marjo Matikainen, Finland
1992	Marjut Lukkarinen, Finland
1994	Ljubov Egorova, RUS
1998	Larissa Lazutina, Russian Federation

10 Kilometers

1924–48	(not held)

15 Kilometers

1924–88	(not held)
1992	Lyuvov Egorova, EUN
1994	Manuela Di Centa, Italy
1998	Olga Danilova, Russia

20 Kilometers

1924–80	(not held)
1984	Marja-Liisa Hämäläinen, Finland
1988	Tamara Tikhonova, SOV
1992–98	(not held)

30 Kilometers

1924–88	(not held)
1992	Stefania Belmondo, Italy
1994	Manuela Di Centa, Italy
1998	Julija Tchpalova, Russian Federation

20-Kilometer Relay

1924–52	(not held)
1956	Finland
1960	Sweden
1964	SOV
1968	Norway
1972	SOV
1976	SOV
1980	GDR
1984	Norway
1988	SOV
1992	EUN
1994	RUS
1998	Russian Federation

BIATHLON—MEN

10 Kilometers

1924–76	(not held)
1980	Frank Ullrich, GDR
1984	Eirik Kvalfoss, Norway
1988	Frank-Peter Roetsch, GDR

1992	Mark Kirchner, GER
1994	Sergei Tchepikov, RUS
1998	Ole Einar Bjoerndalen, Norway

20 Kilometers

1924–56	(not held)
1960	Klas Lestander, Sweden
1964	Vladimir Melanin, SOV
1968	Magnar Solberg, Norway
1972	Magnar Solberg, Norway
1976	Nikolai Kruglov, SOV
1980	Anatoly Alyabyev, SOV
1984	Peter Angerer, GER
1988	Frank-Peter Roetsch, GDR
1992	Yevgeny Redkine, EUN
1994	Sergei Tarasov, RUS
1998	Halvard Hanevold, Norway

30-Kilometer Relay

1924–64	(not held)
1968	SOV
1972	SOV
1976	SOV
1980	SOV
1984	SOV
1988	SOV
1992	GER
1994	GER
1998	GER

BIATHLON—WOMEN

7.5 Kilometer

1924–1988	(not held)
1992	Anfissa Restsova, EUN
1994	Myriam Bedard, Canada
1998	Galina Kukleva, Russia

15 Kilometer

1924–88	(not held)
1992	Antje Misersky, GER
1994	Myriam Bedard, Canada
1998	Ekaterina Dafovska, Bulgaria

22.5 Kilometer Relay

1924–88	(not held)
1992	France
1994	
1998	Russia

30-Kilometer Relay

1924–92	(not held)
1994	RUS
1998	GER

DOWNHILL—MEN

1924–44	(not held)
1948	Henri Oreiller, France
1952	Zeno Colò, Italy
1956	Anton "Toni" Sailer, Austria
1960	Jean Vaurnet, France
1964	Egon Zimmermann, Austria
1968	Jean-Claude Killy, France
1972	Bernhard Russi, Switzerland
1976	Franz Klammer, Austria
1980	Leonhard Stock, Austria
1984	Bill Johnson, USA
1988	Pirmin Zurbriggen, Switzerland
1992	Patrick Ortlieb, Austria
1994	Tommy Moe, USA
1998	Jean-Luc Cretier, France

DOWNHILL—WOMEN

1924–44	(not held)
1948	Hedi Schlunegger, Switzerland
1952	Trude Jochum-Beiser, Austria
1956	Madeleine Berthod, Switzerland
1960	Heidi Biebl, Germany
1964	Christl Haas, Austria
1968	Olga Pall, Austria
1972	Marie-Theres Nadig, Switzerland
1976	Rosi Mittermaier, Germany
1980	Annemarie Moser-Pröll, Austria
1984	Michela Figini, Switzerland
1988	Marina Kiehl, Germany
1992	Kerrin Lee-Gartner, Canada
1994	Katja Seizinger, Germany
1998	Katja Seizinger, Germany

SUPER GIANT SLALOM—MEN

1924–84	(not held)
1988	Franck Piccard, France
1992	Kjetil-Andre Aamodt, Norway
1994	Markus Wasmeier, Germany
1998	Hermann Maier, Austria

SUPER GIANT SLALOM—WOMEN

1924–84 (not held)
1988   Sigrid Wolf, Austria
1992   Deborah Compagnoni, Italy
1994   Diann Roffe-Steinrotter, USA
1998   Picabo Street, USA

GIANT SLALOM—MEN

1924–48 (not held)
1952   Stein Eriksen, Norway
1956   Anton "Toni" Sailer, Austria
1960   Roger Staub, Switzerland
1964   Francois Bonlieu, France
1968   Jean-Claude Killy, France
1972   Gustav Thöni, Italy
1976   Heini Hemmi, Switzerland
1980   Ingemar Stenmark, Sweden
1984   Max Julen, Switzerland
1988   Alberto Tomba, Italy
1992   Alberto Tomba, Italy
1994   Markus Wasmeier, Germany
1998   Hermann Maier, Austria

GIANT SLALOM—WOMEN

1924–48 (not held)
1952   Andrea Mead Lawrence, USA
1956   Ossi Reichert, Germany
1960   Yvonne Rüegg, Switzerland
1964   Marielle Goitschel, France
1968   Nancy Greene, Canada
1972   Marie-Theres Nadig, Switzerland
1976   Kathy Kreiner, Canada
1980   Hanni Wenzel, Lichtenstein
1984   Debbie Armstrong, USA
1988   Vreni Schneider, Switzerland
1992   Pernilla Wiberg, Sweden
1994   Deborah Compagnoni, Italy
1998   Deborah Compagnoni, Italy

SLALOM—MEN

1924–36 (not held)
1948   Edi Reinalter, Switzerland
1952   Othmar Schneider, Austria
1956   Anton "Toni" Sailer, Austria
1960   Ernst Hinterseer, Austria
1964   Pepi Stiegler, Austria
1968   Jean-Claude Killy, France
1972   Francisco Fernandez Ochoa, Spain
1976   Piero Gros, Italy
1980   Ingemar Stenmark, Sweden
1984   Phil Mahre, USA
1988   Alberto Tomba, Italy
1992   Finn Christian Jagge, Norway
1994   Thomas Stangassinger, Austria
1998   Hans-Petter Buraas, Norway

SLALOM—WOMEN

1924–36 (not held)
1948   Gretchen Fraser, USA
1952   Andrea Mead Lawrence, USA
1956   Renee Colliard, Switzerland
1960   Anne Heggtveit, Canada
1964   Christine Goitschel, France
1968   Marielle Goitschel, France
1972   Barbara Cochran, USA
1976   Rosi Mittermaier, Germany
1980   Hanni Wenzel, Lichtenstein
1984   Paoletta Magoni, Italy
1988   Vreni Schneider, Switzerland
1992   Petra Kronberger, Austria
1994   Vreni Schneider, Switzerland
1998   Hilde Gerg, Germany

COMBINED—MEN

1924–32 (not held)
1936   Franz Pfnür, Germany
1940–44 (not held)

1948   Henri Oreiller, France
1952–84 (not held)
1988   Hubert Strolz, Austria
1992   Josef Polig, Italy
1994   Lasse Kjus, Norway
1998   Mario Reiter, Austria

COMBINED—WOMEN

1924–32 (not held)
1936   Christl Cranz, Germany
1940–44 (not held)
1948   Trude Beiser, Austria
1952–84 (not held)
1988   Anita Wachter, Austria
1992   Petra Kronberger, Austria
1994   Pernilla Wiberg, Sweden
1998   Katja Seizinger, Germany

MOGULS—MEN

1924–88 (not held)
1992   Edgar Grospiron, France
1994   Jean-Luc Brassard, Canada
1998   Jonny Mosely, USA

MOGULS—WOMEN

1924–88 (not held)
1992   Donna Weinbrecht, USA
1994   Stine Lise Hattestad, Norway
1998   Tae Satoya, Japan

AERIALS—MEN

1924–92 (not held)
1994   Andreas Schoenbaechler, Switzerland
1998   Eric Bergoust, USA

AERIALS—WOMEN

1924–92 (not held)
1994   Lina Tcherjazova, UZB
1998   Nikki Stone, USA

Snowboarding

GIANT SLALOM—MEN

1924–94 (not held)
1998   Ross Rebagliati, Canada

GIANT SLALOM—WOMEN

1924–94 (not held)
1998   Karine Ruby, France

Appendix IV

HONORED MEMBERS, U.S. NATIONAL SKI HALL OF FAME

1956–1997

The United States National Ski Hall of Fame, located at Ishpeming, Michigan, was established in 1956 by the United States Ski Association to honor those men and women who have made an exceptional contribution to American skiing as competitive athletes and/or ski sport builders. Election is not limited to U.S. citizens but must be based upon significant contributions to American skiing and voted upon by a national committee of respected and knowledgeable individuals in the sport. Listed below are those who have been inducted through 1997 according to information provided by the National Ski Hall of Fame and Ski Museum.

name	year	name	year	name	year	name	year
A		Carruthers, James "Red"	1990	Flaa, James	1974	**I**	
Allen, T. Gary	1992	Carter, Hannah		Foeger, Luggi	1973	Igaya, Chiharu "Chick"	1971
Andersen, Reidar	1971	Locke Caldwell	1973	Fraser, Donald	1972	Iselin, Fred	1972
Anderson, Graham	1984	Chadwick, Gloria	1986	Fraser, Gretchen (Kunigk)	1960		
Armstrong, Debbie	1984	Chaffee, Suzy	1988	Fredheim, Sverre	1973	**J**	
Atwater, Montgomery		Chivers, Howard	1973	Fry, John	1995	Janns, William	1979
"Monty"	1979	Chivers, Warren	1971			Jay, John	1981
Autio, Asario	1966	Clair, John J., Jr.	1970	**G**		Jennings, H. Devereaux	1989
		Clifford, Elizabeth	1978	Gallagher, Michael	1988	Johanson, Sven	1975
B		Cochran, Barbara Ann	1976	Golden, Diana	1997	Johnson, Jannette (Burr)	1970
Bakke, Hermod	1972	Cochran, Marilyn	1978	Goodrich, Nathaniel	1971	Johnson, William "Bill"	1984
Bakke, Magnus	1972	Conniff, Cal	1990	Griffith, James	1971	Johnstone, Robert	1991
Balfanz, John	1980	Cooke, James Negley	1978	Grinden, Harold	1958	Jones, Gregory	1978
Barth, Arthur "Red"	1956	Cooke, Nancy (Reynolds)	1972	Groswold, Gerald	1986	Judson, Dave	1997
Batson, LeMoine	1969	Cooper, Christin	1984	Groswold, Thor	1970		
Bauer, George	1991	Corcoran, Thomas	1978			**K**	
Beattie, Robert	1984	Couch, Edmund	1976	**H**		Kiaer, Alice	
Bellmar, Fred	1988	Cutter, Christina "Kiki"	1993	Hall, Henry	1967	Damrosch Wolfe	1969
Benedikter, Sepp	1977			Halstad, Halvar	1977	Kidd, William "Bill"	1976
Bennet, Nelson	1986	**D**		Halvorsen, Alf	1968	Kidder-Lee, Barbara	1977
Berry, William	1976	Deaver, Sally	1978	Hamilton, Ann (Heggtveit)	1976	Knowlton, Steven	1975
Bertram, Wallace "Bunny"	1981	Dercum, Edna	1991	Hannah, Joan	1978	Knudsen, Arthur	1973
Bietila, Paul	1970	Dercum, Max	1983	Hannah, Selden	1968	Koch, William	1976
Bietila, Ralph	1975	DesRoches, Ralph "Doc"	1977	Harriman, W. Averell	1969	Kohnstamm, Richard	1992
Bietila, Walter	1965	Devlin, Arthur	1963	Harris, Fred	1957	Kotlarek, Gene	1982
Blake, Ernie	1987	Dewey, Godfrey	1970	Haugen, Anders	1963	Kotlarek, George	1968
Blegen, Julius	1968	Dion, Ernest	1984	Haugen, Lars	1963	Koziol, Felix	1974
Blood, Edward	1967	Dodge, Brooks	1978	Hauk, Andrew	1975	Kraus, Hans	1974
Boothe, Jill (Kinmont)	1967	Dole, Charles		Head, Howard	1979	Kreiner, Kathy	1976
Bounous, Junior	1996	Minot "Minnie"	1958	Hegge, Ole	1970		
Bower, John	1969	Douglas, Henry Percy	1968	Heistad, Erling	1966	**L**	
Boyum, Burton	1965	Durrance, Richard	1958	Henderson, Barbara		Lamb, Vernon	1992
Bradley, David	1985			(Ferries)	1978	Lamming, Sigrid Stromstad	1972
Bradley, Harold	1969	**E**		Hendrickson, James	1971	Lang, Otto	1978
Bradley, Steve	1980	Eaton, Edwin	1980	Heuga, James	1976	Langley, Roger	1958
Branch, James "Jim"	1994	Eldred, William	1970	Hicks, Harry Wade	1969	Lash, Bill	1983
Bright, Alexander	1959	Elkins, Frank	1974	Hill, Clarence "Coy"	1974	Lawrence, Andrea (Mead)	1958
Bright, Clarita		Ellingson, Jimmy	1975	Hill, Cortland	1970	Lawrence, David	1966
(Heath) Reiter	1968	Elmer, Raymond	1959	Hirsch, Harold	1990	Leach, George	1969
Broomhall, Wendell		Elvrum, John	1968	Hodler, Marc	1981	Leimkuehler, Paul	1981
"Chummy"	1981	Engen, Alf	1959	Holman, Katherine		Lekang, Anton	1977
Brown, William "Sarge"	1990	Engen, Corey	1973	(Peckett)	1982	Lien, Harry	1969
Bruun, Fred	1970	Engen, Sverre	1971	Holmstrom, Carl	1972	Lindley, Grace Carter	
Bucher, Jan	1993	Engl, Sigi	1971	Holter, Aksel	1956	(McKnight)	1966
Buchmayr, Sigfried	1977	Erickson, E. O. "Buck"	1974	Hostvedt, John	1969	Little, Amos "Bud"	1965
Buek, Richard	1974	Eriksen, Stein	1982	Howard, Frank "Doc"	1987	Little, Earle	1972
				Howelsen, Carl	1969	Livermore, Robert	1977
C		**F**		Hudson, Sally (Neidlinger)	1971	Luby, Susan (Corrock)	1976
Caldwell, John	1983	Farwell, Ted	1992	Hunter, James	1978	Lund, Morten	1997
Carleton, John	1968	Ferries, Charles "Chuck"	1989	Hvam, Hjalmer	1967	Lunn, Sir Arnold	1968

name	year	name	year	name	year	name	year
M		**P**		Schroll, Hannes	1966	Wise, Anthony	1988
MacKenzie, Ron	1971	Pabst, Fred	1969	Seibert, Pete	1984	Woods, Henry "Bem"	1966
MacNab, L. B. "Barney"	1970	Palmedo, Roland	1968	Serafini, Enzo	1977	Woolsey, Elizabeth "Betty"	1969
Macomber, George	1973	Parker, Robert	1985	Severud, Lloyd	1970	Wren, Gordon	1958
Mahre, Phil	1981	Patterson, Peter	1978	Sigal, Albert	1971	Wurtele, Rhoda	1969
Mahre, Steve	1984	Paulsen, Guttorm	1971	Sise, Albert	1983	Wurtele, Rhona	1969
Maki, Rudy	1982	Peabody, Roger	1976	Smith-Johannsen,		Wyatt, Kathy (Rodolph)	1966
Mangseth, Ole	1968	Peabody, Roland	1979	Herman "Jack Rabbit"	1969		
Marolt, William "Bill"	1993	Pederson, Ernest	1968	Sorensen, Harald "Pop"	1973		
Matt, Toni	1967	Perrault, Paul Joseph	1971	Steadman, J. Richard	1989		
Mattesich, Rudolph "Rudi"	1983	Petersen, Eugene	1965	Steinwall, Siegfried	1969		
Maurin, Lawrence	1966	Pfeifer, Friedl	1980	Stiles, Merritt	1975		
McAlpin, Helen		Pfeiffer, J. Douglas "Doug"	1987	Strand, Hans	1975		
(Boughton-Leigh)	1968	Pike, Penny (Pitou)	1976	Strand, Martinius	1958		
McCoy, Dave	1967	Pollard, Harry	1976	Strom, Erling	1972		
McCoy, Penny	1978	Poulsen, Wayne	1980				
McCrillis, John	1966	Prager, Walter	1977	**T**			
McCulloch, Ernie	1969	Proctor, Charles A.	1966	Taylor, Clif	1979		
McKinney, Tamara	1984	Proctor, Charles N.	1959	Taylor, Dorice	1984		
McLane, Malcolm	1973			Taylor, Edward	1956		
McLean, Robert "Barney"	1959	**Q**		Teichner, Hans "Pepi"	1967		
McMahon, Marilyn Shaw	1986	Quinney, S. Joseph "Joe"	1975	Teichner, Helmut	1983		
McNeil, Fred	1957			Tellefsen, Carl	1956		
Merrill, Allison	1974	**R**		Thomas, Lowell, Sr.	1966		
Mikkelsen, Roy	1964	Raaum, Gustav	1980	Thompson, Conrad	1966		
Mikkelsen, Strand	1974	Raine, Nancy (Green)	1969	Thompson, John			
Miller, Earl A.	1994	Rasmussen, Wilbert	1988	"Snowshoe"	1970		
Miller, Warren	1978	Reddish, Jack	1969	Tikalsky, Linda (Meyer)	1982		
Monsen, Rolf	1964	Reid, Robert	1975	Tokle, Arthur	1970		
Morgan, John	1972	Riley, Betsy (Snite)	1976	Tokle, Torger	1959		
Movitz, Richard	1970	Rinaldo, Ben	1985	Torrissen, Birger	1972		
Mullin, J. Stanley	1973	Robes, Ernest "Bill"	1987	Townsend, Ralph	1975		
		Robie, Wendell	1964				
N		Rockwell, Martha	1986	**U**			
Nebel, Dorothy (Hoyt)	1972	Ruschp, Sepp	1978	Ulland, Olav	1981		
Nelson, Cindy	1976	Ruud, Birger	1970				
Nelson, Nels	1971	Ruud, Sigmund	1970	**V**			
Newett, George	1970	Ryan, Joseph	1977	Vaage, Jakob	1976		
Nishkian, Byron	1976	Rybizka, Benno	1991	Valar, Paul	1985		
Norheim, Sondre	1974	Rytting, Suzy (Harris)	1988	Valar, Paula (Kann)	1970		
				Vaughn, Lucille (Wheeler)	1976		
O		**S**					
Obermeyer, Klaus	1997	Satre, Magnus	1963	**W**			
Oimoen, Casper	1963	Satre, Ottar	1967	Watson, George	1969		
O'Leary, Hal	1994	Saubert, Jean	1976	Werner, Wallace "Buddy"	1964		
Olson, Willis "Billy"	1972	Schaeffler, Willy	1974	Wictorin, John	1970		
Omtvedt, Ragnar	1967	Schneider, Hannes	1958	Wigglesworth, Marian			
Overby, Sigurd	1976	Schneider, Herbert	1992	(McKean)	1966		
		Schniebs, Otto	1967	Wiik, Sven	1981		
		Schoenknecht, Walter	1979	Wilson, Eugene	1982		

Bibliography

The writing of the book *For the Love of Skiing* is based on a wide range of information sources, including but not limited to books, magazines, newspaper clippings, documents, voluminous photographic material, and oral interviews. The following are some of the key sources, but by no means should be interpreted as inclusive.

BOOKS

Allais, Amile. *How to Ski by the French Method.* New York: New Directions, 1947.

Allen, E. John B. *From Skisport to Skiing.* Boston: University of Massachusetts Press, 1993.

The American Teaching System: Alpine Skiing. Minneapolis: Professional Ski Instructors of America, Inc (PSIA), 1993.

Atkeson, Ray, Gordon Butterfield, and Robert W. Parker. *Ski and Snow.* New York: U.S. Camera Publishing Corp., 1960.

Bass, Dick, and Frank Wells. *Seven Summits.* New York: Warner Books, Inc., 1986.

Bays, Ted. *Nine Thousand Years of Skiing.* Ishpeming, Michigan: National Ski Hall of Fame Press, 1980.

Bergsland, Einar. *Pa Ski.* Oslo, Norway: H Aschehoug & Co., 1946.

Berry, William B. *Lost Sierra—Gold, Ghosts & Skis.* Soda Springs, California: Western America SkiSport Museum, 1991.

Burton, Hal. *The Ski Troops.* New York: Simon & Schuster, 1971.

Cohen, Stan. *The Games of '36.* Missoula, Montana: Pictorial Histories Publishing Co., Inc., 1996.

———. *A Pictorial History of Downhill Skiing.* Missoula, Montana: Pictorial Histories Publishing Co., Inc., 1985.

Commemorative Publications. *Chamonix to Lillehammer: The Glory of the Olympic Winter Games.* Salt Lake City: Mikko Laitinen, 1994.

Durrance, Dick, as told to John Jerome. *The Man on the Medal.* Snowmass, Colorado: Durrance Enterprises, Inc., 1995.

Engen, Sverre. *Skiing a Way of Life.* Salt Lake City: Scotlo Enterprise, 1976.

Engler, Bruno. *A Mountain Life.* Alberta, Canada: Alpine Club of Canada, 1996.

Eriksen, Stein. *Come Ski With Me.* New York: George J. McLeod Limited, 1966.

Hovelsen, Leif. *The Flying Norseman,* 2nd ed. Ishpeming, Michigan: National Ski Hall of Fame Press, 1983.

Jay, John. *Ski Down the Years.* New York: Universal Publishing & Distributing Corporation, 1966.

Johnsen, Theodore A. *The Winter Sport of Skiing.* Originally published in Portland, Maine, 1905. Reprinted in New Hartford, Connecticut: International Ski History Association, 1994.

Kelner, Alexis. *Skiing in Utah—A History.* Salt Lake City: n.p., 1980.

Lang, Otto. *A Bird of Passage.* Helena, Montana: Sky House Publishers, an imprint of Falcon Press, 1994.

Lund, Morten, Bob Gillen, and Michael Bartlett. *The Ski Book.* New York: Arbor House Publishing Company, 1982.

Lunn, Arnold. *The Story of Ski-ing.* London, England: Eyre & Spottiswoode, Ltd., 1952.

Muench, Marc, Peter Shelton, Steve Cohen. *Ski the Rockies.* Portland, Oregon: Graphic Arts Center Publishing Company, 1995.

Needham, Richard. *Ski Fifty Years in North America.* New York: Harry N. Abrams, Inc., Publishers, 1987.

The Official American Ski Technique. Minneapolis: Professional Ski Instructors of America, Inc. (PSIA), 1964.

Palmedo, Roland, trans. *The New Official Austrian Ski System.* New York: A.S. Barnes & Company, 1958.

Pfeifer, Friedl. *Nice Goin.* Missoula, Montana: Pictorial Histories Publishing Company, Inc., 1993.

———. *The Sun Valley Ski Book.* New York: A.S. Barnes and Company, 1939.

Pfeifer, Luanne. *Gretchen's Gold.* Missoula, Montana: Pictorial Histories Publishing Co., Inc., 1996.

Pooley, Stephen. *The World Atlas of Skiing.* New York: Mallard Press, 1990.

Rayner, Ranulf. *The Story of Skiing.* London, England: David & Charles Publishers, 1989.

Richards, Rick. *Ski Pioneers.* Helena, Montana: Falcon Press Publishing Company, 1992.

Rudd, Sigmund. *Skisport Krysser Verden.* Oslo, Norway: Forlagt av H. Aschehoug & Co., 1946.

———, and Birger Rudd. *Sporene Videre.* Oslo, Norway: Forlagt av H. Aschehoug & Co., 1945.

Schjelderup, Thorleif. *Fra Sproyte Hopp Til Plani.* Oslo, Norway: J.W. Cappelens Forlag, 1950.

Schwartz, Gary H. *The Art of Skiing 1856–1936.* Tiburon, California: Wood River Publishing, 1989.

Shrontz, Duane. *Alta: A People's Story.* Salt Lake City: University of Utah Printing Service, 1989.

Wels, Susan. *The Olympic Spirit—100 Years of the Games.* San Francisco: Collins Publishers San Francisco, a division of Harper Collins Publishers, 1995.

ARTICLES: MAGAZINES, NEWSPAPERS, PERIODICALS

Adler, Allen. "A History of the U.S. Ski Hall of Fame in Ishpeming." *Skiing Heritage,* vol. 10, no. 3 (Third Issue 1997).

———, and Morten Lund. "One of a Kind: Alf Engen." *Skiing Heritage,* vol. 9, no. 2 (Second Issue 1997).

Atwater, Monty. "Progress Report on Avalanches." *American Ski Annual,* 1953.

Auran, John Henry. "Oh, You Call it Haug, and I Call it Haugen, and Let's Call the Whole thing Off." *Skiing Heritage,* vol. 9, no. 1, (First Issue 1997).

Barth, Arthur J. "Paul Bietla." *American Ski Annual,* 1939–40.

Berry, Bill. "Ski Racing Centennial." *Skier,* February 1967.

Beverly, Bob. "The Father of Ski Jumping in Colorado." *American Ski Annual,* 1953.

Binns, Ken. "Ecker Hill and Sun Valley." *American Ski Annual,* 1937–38.

Blakemore, Page. "An Evaluation of the Economics, Geology, Reserves and Potential for Future Exploration of Alta United Mines Company." *N.p.,* 3 March 1994.

"Boise Has Ideal Ski Site Picked Out, Says Champion (Alf Engen)." *The Idaho Statesman,* 3 April 1938.

Brown, Martin. "The Theory of Ski Jumping." *American Ski Annual,* 1936.

Burt, O. W. "Brighton—Cradle of Utah Skiing." *Utah,* December 1946.

Burton, Hal. "Ski Jumpers Are Born That Way." *The Saturday Evening Post,* December 1950.

Cuddeback, Kenneth D. "The First American Downhill Race." *American Ski Annual,* 1942.

Cyr, Oscar. "The All-American Skier." *The Ski Bulletin,* 9 January 1942.

Dallas, Sandy. "Sierra Schussboomers." *Ski,* December 1964.

Dole, Charles Minot. "The National Ski Patrol." *American Ski Annual,* 1939–40.

Dole, Minot. "What Price the National Ski Patrol System." *American Ski Annual,* 1947.

Engen, Alf. "Engen Believes Skiing Has Come to Stay." *The Salt Lake Tribune,* 12 December 1937.

Flaa, James E. "Fifty Years at Ishpeming." *American Ski Annual,* 1937–38.

Gignoux, Paul. "The French Teaching Method of Skiing." *American Ski Annual,* 1948.

"Glimpses of the Past." *Alta (Utah) Powder News,* no. 87 (fall 1987).

Gorrell, Mike. "Canyon History—Discovery of Silver at Alta, 1868." *The Salt Lake Tribune,* 26 April 1994.

Grinden, Harold A. "More Ski History." *American Ski Annual,* 1937–38.

———. "National Ski Hall of Fame Exhibits Span 4,000 Years of Ski History." *American Ski Annual,* 1957.

———. "We Look to 1904 and Ishpeming as the Date and Place." *American Ski Annual,* 1945.

Hildebrand, Joel H. "American Skiers at the Olympics (1936), Men." *American Ski Annual,* 1936.

"History of the Utah Ski Club." *Utah,* vol. 2, no. 12 (February 1937).

Horowitz, Alan. "Moguls Behind the Moguls—Utah's Ski Resort Owners." *Utah Business,* December 1991.

Howard, Frank H. "Safer Skiing." *American Ski Annual,* 1945.

Johnston, Ralph W., compiler. "History of Snow Basin Ski Patrol." *National* #3809, April 1976.

Korologas, Mike. "Getting the Jump on Utah's Ski History." *Continuum,* fall 1993.

——. "Just Call Me Kozy." *Alta (Utah) Powder News,* winter 1989.

Koziol, F. C. "In the Wake of a Snowflake—A New Industry Comes to Utah." *Utah,* December 1946.

——, and Arthur Roth Jr. "Snow Basin Is Born—The Tale of Ogden, Utah's New Ski Bowl." *Western Ski Annual,* 1941–42.

Langley, Roger. "A Brief History of the Nationals." *Utah,* December 1946

Lash, Bill. "The Development of the National Council of Ski Instructors of America." *American Ski Annual & Skiing Journal,* 1953.

——. "An Outline of Ski Teaching Methods." *N.p.,* n.d.

——. "PSIA Intermountain (Intermountain Ski Instructors Association), PSIA-I, ISIA 1950–91." *Instructors Edge,* April 1991.

Laughlin, James. "The Alta Cup Races." *American Ski Annual,* 1946.

——. "Ski Parachute Troops." *American Ski Annual,* 1943.

——. "25 Years of Ski." *Ski,* October 1960.

Lightfoot, J. Austin. "Skiing Pioneers in Idaho." *Sun Valley Ski Club Annual,* 1942.

Lindholm, Fred. "Avalanche." *Skiing News,* vol. XIII, no. 1 (October 1960).

Lundberg, Max. "Words of Wisdom from Alf Engen and the Pope." *The Professional Skier,* fall 1993.

McLeese, Phil. "Winter Sports Drive Opens—New Committee Hopes to Make S.L. Great Recreational Center." *The Salt Lake Tribune,* 14 December 1934.

McNeil, Fred H. "Skiing and National Defense." *American Ski Annual,* 1942.

Miller, Earl. "Ski Club Aids Snow Basin Development." *(Ogden, Utah) Standard-Examiner,* 23 January 1951.

Mills, David C. "California Pioneers on Skis." *American Ski Annual,* 1938–39.

"Monty Atwater, Avalanche Hunter, Dies." *National Patroller,* September 1976.

Movitz, Dick. "New Development at U of U Where Plans Are Being Pushed for Ski Team." *Western Skiing,* December 1946.

Noall, Claire. "Romantic Alta—A Dream Come Into Being." *Utah,* December 1946.

Parkinson, Glenn. "The First Ski Book in America." *Skiing Heritage,* vol. 6, no.1 (winter 1994).

——. "First Tracks—Stories from Maine's Skiing Heritage." *New England Ski Museum Newsletter* 39 (fall 1995).

——. "Ski Museums—Preserving the Past for the Future." *Snow News,* vol. 9, no. 3 (summer 1991).

Porges, Franziska. "Ski Center Alta." *American Ski Annual,* 1946.

Putnam, Jon E. "Instructor Certification Anniversary." *Skier,* March 1968.

Ritchie, Ensign. "Files Show Sports Coverage Began in 1888." *(Ogden, Utah) Standard-Examiner,* 1 January 1988.

"Salt Lake City—The Winter Haven." *Utah,* vol. 2, no. 12 (February 1937).

Schoemaker, Ted. "The Art of Ski Flying." *Skiing News,* February 1962.

Smart, Bill. "Skiing Makes Progress on Landes Memorial Hill." *Utah,* November 1948.

"Snow King—The Town Hill." *Teton Annual,* vol. 6 (1973–74).

Sorensen, Harald. "Ski Patrol—U.S. Army." *American Ski Annual,* 1942.

Strand, M. A. "Winter Sports." *Utah,* vol. 2, no. 12 (February 1937).

Tangren, W. E. "Forest Service Encourages Utah's Winter-Sports." *The (Salt Lake City) Deseret News,* 9 January 1937.

Taylor, Frank J. "Snowshoe Thompson—The Paul Bunyan of the Mountains." *Ski,* November 1959.

Thompson, Deanne. "Interview: Averell Harriman." *The Idaho Mountain Express,* 30 January, 1986.

"Utah Film 'Shorts' Seen by 90 Million People." *Utah Industrial Development News,* vol. 5 (February 1947).

Vaage, Jacob. "Skiing in Norway." *American Ski Annual,* 1947.

Williams, Emily. "Father of Alpine Skiing." *Skier,* March 1967.

Wolfe, Alice D. "American Skiers at the Olympics (1936), Women." *American Ski Annual,* 1936.

OTHER PUBLICATIONS: HANDBOOKS, MANUALS, PAMPHLETS, REPORTS

Gallagher, Dale, ed. "The Snowy Torrents—Avalanche Accidents in the U.S. 1910–1966." U.S. Department of Agriculture (USDA), Wasatch National Forest, January 1967.

The International Ski Competition Rules. Oslo, Norway: Grondahl & Son, 1936.

"Modern Avalanche Rescue." Alta Avalanche Study Center, April 1968.

National Committee on Ski Jumping. *Designing & Constructing Ski Jumping Hills.* Oslo, Norway: Grondahl & Sons, 1939.

The National Ski Patrol System Manual. New York: National Ski Patrol System Editorial Board, chaired by Charles Minot Dole., 1941.

Report of the United States Olympic Committee 1948 Games—XIV Olympiad, V Olympic Winter Games, St. Moritz, Switzerland. New York: n.p., n.d.

Robertson, Ruth Winder. *This Is Alta.* Salt Lake City: n.p., 1972.

Snowshoe Thompson. Minden, Nevada: Carson Valley Historical Society, c. 1991.

Taylor, Edward F., ed. *Ski Patrol Manual of the National Ski Patrol System of America.* Milwaukee: National Ski Patrol System of America, 1952.

"Utah Goes to the Olympic Games—1948." State of Utah, Department of Publicity and Industrial Development, fall 1947.

Williams, Knox. "The Snow Torrents—Avalanche Accidents in the U.S. 1967–71." USDA Forest Service Tech Report Rm-8, March 1975.

OTHER SOURCES: INTERVIEWS, LETTERS, LIBRARIES, MUSEUMS

Bower, John. Taped interview by author. Bear Hollow Winter Sports Park, Park City, Utah, 7 June 1996.

Ericksen, Stein. Taped interview by author. Park City, Utah, 17 April 1997.

Fletcher, Mel. Taped interview by author. Park City, Utah, 20 January 1997.

Gaddis, Jim. Taped interview by author. Salt Lake City, 16 August 1996.

Goodro, Harold. Taped interview by author. Holladay, Utah, 8 August 1996.

Korfanta, Albert S. "Intermountain Division, USSA Letter of Protest Re: Request for an Official Review of the 1964 United States Olympic Alpine Ski Team Selection Procedure." Communication to Alf Engen, 1 July 1963.

Lash, Bill. Taped interview by author. Salt Lake City, 15 June 1996.

Lawson, Janet. Taped interview by author. Salt Lake City, 17 May, 1996.

Levitt, Bill. Taped interview by author. Alta, Utah, 6 August 1996.

Melville, Marvin. Taped interview by author. Sandy, Utah, 10 February 1997.

Miller, Pat. Taped interview by author. Salt Lake City, 27 September 1996.

Movitz, Dick. Taped interview by author. Holladay, Utah, 30 October 1996.

National Ski Museum, Ishpeming, Michigan.

New England Ski Museum, Franconia, New Hampshire.

Rytting, Suzy Harris. Taped interview by author. Holladay, Utah, 17 Oct. 1996.

Spencer, Bill. Taped interview by author. Salt Lake City, 18 September 1996.

Thomas, Edward H., Brig. Gen. (Ret.). Letter to author concerning the history of Company B, 503rd Parachute Battalion training at Alta, Utah, in January 1942, 1 May 1996.

University of Utah J. Willard Marriott Library, Ski Archives, Salt Lake City.

Walker, Jack. Taped interview by author. Alta, Utah, 13 January 1996.

Western SkiSport Museum, Boreal, California.

Index

Nevada, 9, 10–11, 21, 83

New Directions, 100

New England, 58

New Hampshire,
7, 58, 89, 111, 119

New Mexico, 109

New Orleans [LA], Royal Street
Development Company of, 97

New York [state], 16, 17, 43,
52, 69, 75, 101, 110, 127,
141, 145

New York City, 10, 16, 17

New York Post (newspaper),
on Suzy Harris Rytting and
1952 Winter Olympics, 79

New Yorker magazine,
"J" Laughlin on retaining
Alta's beauty/charm, 101

New Zealand, 5

Newsweek magazine,
on Suzy Harris Rytting and
1952 Winter Olympics, 79

Nichol, Larry, 116

Nichol, Vern, 48, 55

Nichol, Wayne, 109, 116

Nicolaisen, Per Chr., 128

Nielson, Merrill, 65, 66, 131, 133

Nina's Curve, Alta [UT], 136

Nine Thousand Years of Skis,
Ted Bays book, 2

Norby, Ole, 24

Norden Ski Club [MI], 14

Nordic: nomads, 1;
competition, 126

Nordic skiing, 5;
and gelande jumping, 135–38

Nordic V style jumping, 138

Nordic Valley, Ogden/Huntsville
[UT], 90, 110

Nordic Winter Festival (1903), 5

Norge Ski Club of Chicago
(sidebar), 19

Norheim, Sondre, 4

Norheim ski binding, 4

Norseman Hill,
Emigration Canyon [UT], 130

Norseman Ski Club, 130

North America, 9, 69;
first rope tow in, 60

North American Alpine Ski
Championship (1959), 124, 126

North Conway [NH], 7

Northern California, 83

Northern Pursuit (film), 93

Northmen: nomadic, 2;
Komsans/Fosnans, 3

Norway, vii, 2, 6, 19, 20, 47,
68, 125, 140

Norway/Norwegian (events):
Period, 3;
Contribution, The, 4–5;
Diaspora, 5;
Jumpers Immigrate, 13–16;
Influence, The, 36

Norway/Norwegian (landmarks):
Christiania, 5, 12;
Drammen, 26;
Gudbrundsdal, 3;
Holmenkollen Hill, xi, 5, 8, 143;
Kongsberg, 50, 62;
Lillehammer, 3;
Melbo, 43;
Mjøndalen, ix, x, xi, 18;
Oddnes Hill, 39;
Stavanger, 9;
Telemark, 4–5, 9;
Tinn, 9;
Troms, 5;
Tromsoe, 5;
Trondheim, 14.
See also Oslo, Norway

Norway/Norwegian
(people/organizations):
Parliament, xi;
Olympic Ski-Jumping Team
(1928), xi;
Birkenbeiner soldiers, 3;
ski patrols, 3, 124;
emigrants, 5, 9, 13–16, 26;
Olympic Committee, 8;
Young Folks Society
(N.U.F. Sportslag), 26;
-American Athletic Club, 26;
community, 27;
at Dry Canyon, 28.
See also
Eriksen, Marius, Sr.;
Eriksen, Stein;

Kolstad, Johanna;
Prydz, Frithjof;
Ruud, Sigmund;
Snowshoe Thompson;
Tokle, Torger

Norway/Norwegian
(winter equipment):
skis, 1, 6, 7;
snowshoes, 9, 13;
"snow-skates," 11

Norwich [VT], 143

Nunn, Jimmie R., ii, vi

N.U.F. Sportslag, 26.
See also Utah Ski Club

O

Oberstdorf, Germany, 147

O'Connor, William J., 73

O'Neal, "Dub," 24

O'Neill, Mike, 82, 83, 106

Oddnes Hill, Norway, 39

Official American Ski Technique,
Bill Lash book, 118

Ogden [UT], 93, 105;
Becker Hill near, 20, 37, 103;
Canyon, 24–25, 32, 90;
Gus Becker's brewery in, 30;
Chamber of Commerce, 30, 104;
Winter Sports Committee, 30;
"festival of festivals" at, 32;
Standard-Examiner, on Bjørn-
gaard Hill dedication, 74;
Ski Club, 103;
River, 104;
Valley, 110;
Alan Miller of, 124;
Glenn Adams of, 142.
See also
Becker Hill,
Nordic Valley,
Powder Mountain,
Snowbasin

Ohio, 79

Oimoen, Caspar, 54

Oklahoma, 103

Old Country/Old World,
x, xi, 11

Oliver, Robert "Cornish Bob," 12

Olsen, C. J., 75

Olympia, Greece, 141

Olympic Award, Salt Lake City
[UT], 142

Olympic Committee.
See under
International;
U.S.

Olympic Games:
(1896), 7;
(1912), 139

Olympic Ski-Jumping Team,
(1928) Norwegian, xi

Olympic Winter Games:
(1924), 8, 141;
(1928), 8;
(1932), 8, 52, 141;
(1936), 8, 49, 58, 62;
(1940), 67, 100;
(1944), 67, 100;
(1948), x, 69, 75–80,
115, 117, 142;
(1952), 69, 79;
(1956), 69, 123, 124;
(1960), 69, 78, 86, 124,
125, 126;
(1964), 124, 126;
(1968), 126;
(1972), 141, 142;
(1976), 142;
(1992), 127;
(1998), 143;
(2002), vi, vii, viii, xi,
103, 104, 111–12, 141,
143, 144, 148, 150

Omaha (NE), 20, 61, 91

Omtvedt, Ragnar, 18

Onion Valley [CA], 13

Oquirrh Mountains [UT], 21

Oregon, 85, 127, 130

Orr, David, 40

Oslo, Norway,
xi, 8, 43, 79, 139, 143.
See also Christiania, Norway

Ostler Land and Livestock
Company, 104

Other Side of the Mountain, The
(film), and Jill Kinmont, 83

Otten, Les, 110–11

St. Moritz, Switzerland,
	x, 69, 75, 77, 90, 93, 115, 124
St. Paul [MN], 14, 56
Standard-Examiner (Ogden [UT]
	newspaper), on Bjørngaard Hill
	dedication, 74
Stanwyck, Barbara, 92
Stavanger, Norway, 9
Steamboat Springs [CO],
	16, 69, 71, 111, 123, 138
Steen, Charlie, 108
stem christie turn, 6, 7
Steorts, Lee, 82
Stern, Bill (sports commentator),
	on Suzy Harris Rytting and the
	1952 Olympic Games, 79
Stern, Edgar, 140
Steward, Frank, 14
Stewart, Ava, 108
Stewart, Hilda, 108
Stewart, Paul "Speed," 108
Stewart, Ray, 108
Stiles, Maxwell (writer),
	on Alf Engen win at
	Big Pines [CA], 39
Stillwell, Howard, 98
Stockholm, Sweden, 2, 139
Stone Age petroglyphs, 2
Stone, Nikki, 148
Stoney, Charles T., 24
Story of Ski-ing, The,
	Sir Arnold Lunn book, 3, 4
Stowe [VT], Mt. Mansfield, 81
Straley, Monte, 128
Strand, Martinius "Mark" A.:
	26, 27, 28, 30, 32, 36, 47,
	49, 60, 97, 141
Strømstad, Thoralf, 8
Stuben, Austria, 7
Sugar Bowl [CA], 117
Sugarhouse [UT], 25, 130;
	Park, 131, 133
Suicide Hill, Ishpeming [MI],
	14, 15
Summerhays, Preston,
	121, 120, 124
Summer Ski Jumping, 130–34
Summer Snow,
	65–66, 130, 131, 133–34

Summers, Mark
	(artist, *Alf Engen*), 151
Sumner, Sharf, 55
Sun Valley [ID]
	(competitions/exhibitions):
	1937 National Downhill and
		Slalom Championship, 58;
	triple jump at, 69;
	1948 Winter Olympics Alpine
		tryouts held at, 75;
	Harriman Cup, 77–78, 91,
		100, 124;
	Mary Cornelia Trophy, 100;
	1947 U.S. collegiate
		competition at, 119
Sun Valley [ID] (landmarks):
	Challenger Inn, 93;
	Dollar Mountain, 91, 92, 93;
	Proctor Mountain, 91;
	Ruud Mountain, 69, 93, 135;
	Sun Valley Lodge, 92, 93;
	Sun Valley Ski School, 139;
	Warm Springs Run, 93
Sun Valley [ID] (people/history):
	Felix Schaffgotsch, 28, 90, 91;
	first chairlifts opened, 62, 91;
	photos of 69, 91, 92;
	U of U Ski team at, 78, 119;
	history of, 90–93;
	Brass family land became, 91;
	Steve Hannagan at, 91;
	personalities attracted to, 91;
	World War II, during/after, 91.
	See also
		Engen, Alf;
		Eriksen, Stein;
		Lawson, Janet Quinney
Sun Valley Serenade (film), 91
Sundance, Provo Canyon [UT],
	63, 90, 108, 117, 129.
	See also Timp Haven
Sundown Lodge,
	Powder Mountain [UT], 110
Supreme Lift, Alta [UT], 101
Surdlie, Ole, 14
suski, 2
"swan dive," Stein Eriksen's, 139
Sweden, 1, 2, 3, 124, 125, 139, 140
Sweeney, Ed, 150

Swensen, Gilbert, 30
Switzerland/Swiss:
	Hans Klopfenstein of, 3;
	Crans-Montana, 7;
	Plaine Morte Glacier, 7;
	Engelberg, 61;
	Davos, 69, 76;
	1952 U.S. Winter Olympic
		team in, 79;
	Ed LaChapelle in, 85;
	"J" Laughlin in, 100;
	Zurs, 100;
	ski techniques, 118;
	Marvin Melville in, 124.
	See also St. Moritz
Syracuse [NY], 127

T

"talking" tombstones, 23
Tangren, W. E., 57, 84, 85
Tanner's Flat, Little Cottonwood
	Canyon [UT], 102
Taos [NM], 109
Tappen, Col. Jack, 67
T-bar lift, 61, 62, 95, 97,
	107, 108, 112
technologies, developing ski, 70, 89
Telemark, Norway, 4–5, 9
telemark turns, 4
Tellefsen, Carl, 14
Tenth Mountain Division,
	69, 85, 126
Teton Annual, on Mike O'Neill's
	altered skis, 106
Teton Pass [ID], 106
Tetrault, Tim, 143
Thatcher, A. M., 11
Thayne's Canyon, Park City
	[UT], 25, 97
Theobald, Art, 130
Thiokol lift, 110
Third California Volunteers, 21
Thomas, Brig. Gen. Edward H.:
	on winter warfare, 67;
	photos courtesy of, 68
Thomas Nygard Gallery, Bozeman
	[MT], photo courtesy of, 87
Thompson, Agnes, 11

Thompson, Conrad, 14, 90
Thompson, Deanne, 90
Thompson, Gregory, vi, 150
Thompson, Gro, 10
Thompson, Hall, 55
Thompson, John.
	See Snowshoe Thompson
Thompson, Olaf, 19
Thompson, Snowshoe.
	See Snowshoe Thompson
Timberline Lift/Lodge, Powder
	Mountain [UT], 110
Timp Haven, Provo Canyon
	[UT], 63, 108, 117.
	See also Sundance
Tinn, Telemark, Norway, 9
Todd, Tom, 55
Tokle, Torger, 68–69, 70
Tombstone, Misspelled (sidebar), 11
Torgersen, C. C., 19
Torsteinson-Rue, Jon, 9
Tostenson, Jon, 9
Tragedy on Ecker Hill, 45–46
Tragedy Strikes in Minnesota, 56
tram, first aerial, 61
Trappers Loop Highway [UT], 103
Treasure Mountain, Park City
	[UT], 97
Trøgstad, Steffan,
	19, 31, 32, 33, 74, 152
Troms, Norway, 5
Tromsoe, Norway, 5
Trond Engen Hill, Snowbasin
	[UT], 75
Trondheim, Norway, 14
Trua, Tom, 115
Truckee [CA], 32, 60
Tschaggeny, Judy, 109
Tuckerman's Ravine [NH], 58
Twentieth Century Fox, 98
Twin Falls [ID], 117

U

U of U.
	See University of Utah
Ulland, Olav, 54
Ulland, Sigurd,
	19, 31, 32, 33, 40, 50, 54, 152